Show & 5 Tell

WRITERS ON WRITING

FIFTH EDITION, REVISED & EXPANDED

THE PUBLISHING LABORATORY

UNIVERSITY OF NORTH CAROLINA **WILMINGTON**

The collection *Show & Tell: Writers on Writing* © 2001, 2002, 2003, 2004, 2006 University of North Carolina Wilmington
Individual pieces are copyrighted by the contributors. Acknowledgments at the back of the book constitute a continuation of this copyright notice.

Book design: Kerry Molessa
Cover design: James Dempsey

Produced by the Publishing Laboratory
Department of Creative Writing
University of North Carolina Wilmington
601 South College Road
Wilmington, North Carolina 28403-5938
www.uncw.edu/writers

Fifth edition, revised and expanded, published summer 2006
ISBN 0-9719308-9-9

CONTENTS

INTRODUCTION

THERE ARE THREE RULES FOR WRITING THE NOVEL," Somerset Maugham once remarked. "Unfortunately, no one knows what they are." Instead, *Show & Tell: Writers on Writing* provides a glimpse into the artistic method and working habits of writers whom apprentice writers in UNCW's classes will meet face to face in the course of this semester's study.

This book contains two types of writing: published creative works, and essays on how to create stories, poems, essays, and novels. The published works are offered not as models of perfect writing, only as examples of how particular writers have written. If you are using this book in UNCW's program, you will enjoy the rare opportunity to ask questions of each author about his or her work—that's why we have included their work and not the work of strangers. Feel free to analyze or critique their work as part of your own developing creative process. The essays reflect the authors' beliefs about their own creative processes, as well as sound observations based on long experience with the art and craft of writing.

Chances are, you will never be able to read a poem or a story the same way again. You'll read like a writer.

Good reading—and good writing.

THE EDITORS

FICTION
PROCESS

On Choosing a Subject

Wendy Brenner

I WOULD AMEND THE OLD DIRECTIVE TO "WRITE ABOUT WHAT you know" to: "Write about what you only half-remember," or "Write about the subject which—for some reason that's a mystery to all your friends, who are sick of hearing about it—obsesses you." In my view, the most important rule for student fiction writers is to not know the whole story before you try to write it. You should write fiction not only to show and tell what you know, what you've seen and experienced (and if you've lived seventeen years on earth, my creative writing professor in college used to say, you've already seen enough to provide you with material for a lifetime of fiction writing), but to discover what you don't know, what you long to know, about those subjects—people, places, events, images—which most intrigue and excite and trouble you.

These subjects need not involve complete plots (not when you start writing them, anyway) or even large ideas; they should probably not be ideas at all, but rather, tangible things: a sad old house you stayed in one summer as a child, an odd conversation you overheard in a doctor's waiting room, a girl you knew for years but never really understood, an inexplicable billboard you passed on a road trip. If you want to write about a concept (e.g., good versus evil, symbolized by two rival race-car drivers, eventually the good driver wins), you should probably consider writing an essay or philosophical treatise rather than a story. Fiction is not meant to moralize, to teach lessons, but to give the reader an experience which cannot be gotten in any other way, or easily paraphrased, summed up. A good story or novel leaves you with new questions about the mystery of life, our lives, what it is to be human—not with easy answers. The tangible, sensory details are necessary to the story because they are the story.

Most writers use some form of journal to collect and keep track of these details, possible subjects and material for their fiction. A writer's journal is often more of a scrapbook than a diary; rather than recording everything important that happens to you, in a writer's journal you are interested in saving items you suspect you can use in your fiction (or poetry), though you don't necessarily have the slightest idea yet how. For example, you might clip "Police Blotter" stories from the local newspaper that you find especially compelling, or national or international news shorts that make you ask, "What kind of person would . . . ?" A sampling from my journal: Woman Jailed for Feeding Pigeons (she put out a hundred loaves of bread in her yard each week). Boys Hold Up Drugstore for Valentines (an eight-year-old and a ten-year-old, who planned to give the valentines to their classmates). Cannonball Smashes into Side of House (no one saw it happen, and the cannonball was of the type used in World War II). The great thing about these stories is that, like good fiction, they inevitably raise many more questions than they answer about the human experience.

You might then use one of them as a starting place for a story you write by assuming the point of view of one of the people involved, or a character you invent yourself who has some relation to the story, such as a neighbor or family member. However, it is very important if you try this exercise to resist the urge to "solve" why the story happened. You don't want to explain everything away, sum it all up, because then there is no story. Rather, your job as a fiction writer is to spend some time with a person who has nothing and everything in common with the rest of us, take us somewhere we might otherwise never go.

Other items for your journal might include lines of overheard dialogue and descriptions of particularly vivid people, objects, and locations you observe in your day-to-day life, in your travels, or on television. I especially like talk shows and the local news, for people speaking candidly and uncoached about subjects of importance to them, and I like locally produced commercials, for their often Zen-like absurdity and artlessness. You might also use your journal as a place to keep track of ideas for plots, conflicts, and characters, and memories from your childhood that you hadn't thought about for years until you started taking creative writing classes.

I like the following exercise for generating subject material because it not only helps you access sensory experiences from your childhood but also helps you create or rekindle a sense of longing and inner conflict, something that's present in all successful fiction. Recall a toy or object you always wanted but never got, something you coveted for weeks or months or just momentarily. Perhaps a friend of yours had one, or perhaps you only saw the item on TV, or in a catalog. Perhaps it was something around the house. One student in my class wrote about his mother's flour sifter, which was kept on a high shelf away from him after he'd gotten his hands on it once when he was three and put dirt, soap, cookies, and water through it. He remembered and was devoted to the powerful, weapon-like feel of it in his hand, the sound it made—*schwit, schwit*. Write a page of fiction describing your toy or object in full sensory detail, focusing as much as possible on the object. (Don't worry about characterizing yourself or anyone in your family.) Make your readers see the toy or object as you did at the time. What did it look like, remind you of, feel like, smell like, sound like? What would you do with it if you got it? Avoid summarizing from the point of view of an adult looking back, from a distance: "Boy, was I a greedy kid." Instead, immerse yourself in the past, so your concrete description comes from that place of purest, most intense desire. This exercise can be developed into a scene or a complete story in itself. (As an example of a story that could have come from such an exercise, you might check out Andrew Alexander's "Little Bitty Pretty One" in Algonquin Books's *New Stories From the South*, 1999).

Finally, you will discover when you present your work in creative writing workshop that the material you thought the least about or consider boringly personal is often the stuff your classmates find most original and exciting; do not fail to trust that your own predilections, aversions, and loves will shine through on the page, illuminating and transforming what you fear is mundane. Poet Adrienne Rich says that "students learn to write by discovering the variety and validity of their own experience." ❖

On Writing Fiction

Clyde Edgerton

CAROLINE GORDON, A TEACHER AND FICTION WRITER, advised Flannery O'Connor through the mail. O'Connor, in her letters, collected by Sally Fitzgerald in *The Habit of Being* (1979) advised other young writers. Some of that advice, paraphrased or quoted here, may help young writers as they think about the creative process.

Ignore criticism that doesn't make sense.

Make the reader see the characters at every minute, but do this unobtrusively.

Never do writing exercises. Forget plot; start with a character or anything else you can make come alive. Discover, rather than impose meaning. You may discover a good deal more by not being too clear when you start. You sometimes find a story by messing around with this or that. Once you have finished a first draft, see how you can better bring out what it says.

Read *The Craft of Fiction* by Percy Lubbock and *Understanding Fiction* by Robert Penn Warren and Cleanth Brooks.

If there is no possibility for change in a character (i.e., a character is hopelessly insane) then there is little reader interest in that character. If heroes were stable, there wouldn't be any story—all good stories are about a character's changing. Sin is interesting;

evil is not. Sin grows out of free choice; evil is something else. Characters need to behave as themselves as people, not as abstract representations of some idea or principle which is dear to the writer. Be careful about a tendency to be too omniscient and not let things come through the characters.

Add a character to make another character "come out."

You can write convincingly about a homesick New Yorker if you have never been to New York but have been homesick. A character must behave out of his or her motivations, not the author's. Don't try to be subtle . . . or write for a subtle reader.

Write two hours a day, same time, sitting at the same place, without a view—either write or just sit. Follow your nose. To get a story you might have to approach a vague notion from one direction and then another, until you get an entrance. Sit at your machine.

In a short story, write for a single effect and end on what is most important. At the end of a story gain some altitude and get a larger view. You shouldn't appear to be making a point. The meaning of a story must be in its muscle.

Use dialect lightly—suggest. Get the person right.

"A word stands for something else and is used for a purpose and if you play around with them irrespective of what they are supposed to do, your writing will become literary in the worse sense."

A novel or short story says something that can be said in no other way. A summary or an abstraction will not give you the same thing.

"The less self-conscious you are about what you are about, the better in a way, that is to say technically. You have to get it in the blood, not in the head."

"My business is to write and not talk about it."

Writers seeking the secrets to good writing might keep in mind O'Connor's statement from *Mystery and Manners* (1969): "My own approach to literary problems is very like the one Dr.

Johnson's blind housekeeper used when she poured tea—she put her finger inside the cup."

One final—delicate-yet-crucial—requirement for writing fiction: "Perhaps you [a correspondent] are able to see things in these stories that I can't see because if I did see I would be too frightened to write them. I have always insisted that there is a fine grain of stupidity required in the fiction writer."

See also Sally Fitzgerald, ed., *Georgia Review*, vol. 32, no. 4, letter from Caroline Gordon to Flannery O'Connor (1979); E. M. Forster, *Aspects of the Novel* (1927); L. Rust Hills, *Writing in General and the Short Story in Particular* (1987); André Maurois, *The Art of Writing* (1962); Louis D. Rubin, Jr., *The Teller in the Tale* (1967); Eudora Welty, *The Eye of the Story* (1978). ❖

True Fiction and Fictitious History

Philip Gerard

A T THE INTERSECTION BETWEEN FACT AND FICTION, THE historical novelist makes crucial decisions about "truth" and "truthfulness."

A stranger comes to town—me.

The town is Wilmington, North Carolina.

Like any stranger, I hear stories about my new town. Every community is built on stories—they define who we are, why we live in a place. Stories are the collective memory of a community, the narrative of our past, the demonstration of what we value.

Between all the brave local histories—plucky Minutemen fighting off Cornwallis's Redcoats, Confederates with fire in their bellies beating back the first Yankee wave against Fort Fisher—I hear a rumor of another kind of story—a story of race riots, murder in the streets, the breakdown of civil order, a hundred years ago.

It sounds like a classic case of racist violence: a small cadre of rich white men manipulate a lot of poor white men with guns into attacking the black community. Nobody can agree on the details, but there's one thing they all agree on: the flashpoint for the violence was a young black writer, the editor of the *Daily Record*, which billed itself as the first "Afro-American" daily newspaper in the country, Alex Manly. He was banished from Wilmington under a death sentence and his newspaper burned to the ground for a colorful editorial he wrote against lynching. I seek out every book, article, dissertation, and newspaper story on the event, and the outline takes shape:

On November 10, 1898, in a thriving river town that was two-thirds black, a thousand armed white men and boys took to the streets and killed an untold number of blacks. Some they executed by firing squad. Scores of blacks and their white political allies were rounded up and put on trains out of town at bayonet point. For three days, Wilmington lay under martial law.

In the midst of the violence, after signing a "White Declaration of Independence," the vigilantes hauled the mayor and the board of alderman—which included a number of black men—into city hall at gunpoint and forced them all to resign. It is widely believed to be the only coup d'etat in American history.

I wanted to write about the coup. More accurately, once I knew what I knew, I couldn't not write about it. I lay awake at night thinking about it. Every daily event seemed to relate to it. The book *Cape Fear Rising*—as yet unformed—already had a life of its own. The subject gripped my imagination, ignited my passion.

Not just because it was a case of racism run amok, though it was. Not even because it hinged on freedom of expression—though like most writers I am passionate about the right to free expression. For me the real story was the failure of democracy—the faultlines running through a prosperous and seemingly tolerant community were deep and long, and when push came to shove, the community split apart.

The book would address that moment when the social contract breaks down, all bets are off, and a progressive community with good schools, telephones, an opera house, and a well-educated citizenry turns into a war zone.

So why not write the story as nonfiction?

Well, in a practical sense, the record was incomplete. Some archives had been deliberately purged of incriminating material. Others had been looted by researchers. And as with most historical events, most of what happened never got recorded at all. Or if it appeared in newspapers or memoirs, the accounts were usually self-serving, written by participants or their descendants trying to justify their actions. A nonfiction book would have had an unsatisfying, squishy center.

But I had a more important reason for turning the story into a novel—or more precisely, using the novel form to get at the truth of the event. I was concerned with motive—with the *why* of the violence. For that I needed access to the interior lives of the "characters." The nonfiction writer can't possibly know what goes on in the minds of his characters. He's stuck in the first person—his own point of view—even when the story seems to be told objectively. Unless, of course, he can interview his characters, put their voices on the page—and mine were all dead.

But fiction thrives on the interior life.

Through the imaginative act, the fiction writer can enter the consciousness of another human being.

When you're dealing with actual lives, with real people who were somebody's ancestors, you'd better get it right. No matter how certain you are that your version of their interior lives is true, it's always possible that you're dead wrong. The mystery of the human personality always humbles a good writer.

The only way to guard against being dead wrong is to do thorough and imaginative research—striving for "truthfulness" of event, just as though you were setting out to write nonfiction. And even that's no guarantee.

Before I wrote a word, I spent more than a year in archives, libraries, museums, courthouses. I walked the streets of Wilmington, measuring distances—how far the mob marched, how long it took to flee their guns. I walked under the city in the secret tunnels that honeycomb the Market Street district—tunnels possibly used by the conspirators. I pored over 1897 Sanborn-Perris insurance maps, learning which buildings were brick and which wooden, where the roads and streetcar lines ran, where the cotton mills stood. I searched out tombstones in the Oakdale Cemetery. I drove five hundred miles to the U.S. Army Ordnance Museum at Aberdeen, Maryland, so I could handle a Gatling gun like the one that was used by the white supremacists. I wanted to feel the story under my hands, to smell it, to feel its heft.

I read diaries, memoirs, recipe books, letters, newspaper accounts, business ledgers, marriage and death certificates. I wanted to learn definitively the truth of the events. My first aim was to write about the public actions of the men and women who struggled through those dark days as truthfully and accurately as I possibly could. So I wrote a long chronology of actual verifiable events and an equally long series of biographies of the principal players, detailing the things we know from the record that they actually did.

My second and more important aim—which depended on first writing truthfully—was to discover the why of such a civic failure: What were the conditions that made the city ripe for violent revolution? Was it inevitable, or could determined men and women of conscience have stopped it? What are the implications of the event for us, a hundred years later?

Who were these people? What did they hope to gain? What made them do what they did? They were not evil villains—that would make it easy to dismiss them as monsters, aberrations. We could tell ourselves: We're not like them. We'd never do that.

But we are like them. They were mostly decent family men, deacons in their churches, good fathers and husbands, civic philanthropists. At least one was an ordained minister. Yet for a brief moment in their lives, they shot down unarmed neighbors, beat and imprisoned others, drove many more from their community. So why did they do it?

Here the letters and memoirs provided clues. One of the ringleaders had written about his plans to solve the problem of "King Numbers"—the majority ratio of blacks to whites—by attracting white European immigrants. Another had recently lost his job as customs collector—the highest paying job in the state—to a black Republican. Another lectured on the Aryan theory of racial purity. And so on. From their business ledgers, their letters, their diaries, and their memoirs, their personalities emerged.

And sometimes the archives were most illuminating when they had nothing to do with race, no direct connection to the events. So the young wife of the sixtyish lawyer who led the mob writes in her "receipt" (recipe) book, along with the ingredients for a Lady Baltimore cake, a coy poem alluding to her husband's infidelity.

In a series of letters to the editor of the local newspaper, her husband duels with a Catholic priest over whether damnation for sinners is eternal, the soul truly immortal.

A letter yields the information that one ringleader and his brother blackmailed their sister's suitor to keep him from marrying her.

Another's later memoir reveals an admiration for Mussolini, the Italian dictator.

All these are clues to the interior lives of real characters.

When they speak in the novel, they are saying out loud the sorts of things they wrote in letters or journals or memoirs, often verbatim. The scene is concocted to make explicit what was only implicit, but the invention happens within a very narrow range.

One last important tactic: I created some fictional characters.

Some sixty real-life people played important roles in the events of 1898—far too many for the cast of a novel. I narrowed this down to a couple dozen—and invented a few key characters, either as composites of real people, or as narrative focal points. The novel oscillates among various points of view, but it always comes back to that of Sam Jenks, the fictional reporter newly arrived in town, and his schoolteacher wife, Gray Ellen. They have access to all the white and black communities and watch events unfold with the fresh eyes of outsiders.

This mixture of fictional and real characters upset lots of people, including some of the descendants of those portrayed in the novel. But the book is called a novel for a reason: the contract between a novelist and his reader is truth. The contract between the nonfiction writer and his reader is truthfulness.

That doesn't mean the novel isn't as truthful as I could make it—only that where a thing could not be proved, or where the abstract could be made concrete, I interpreted the moment dramatically.

As it turned out, *Cape Fear Rising* was not about a Southern city in 1898. It was about every city in the world in 1998, or, for that matter, 2098. The tension of a democracy to fray apart is always with us. Built into the very idea of democracy is danger—the temptation for the few and powerful to manipulate the many and powerless. The temptation not to trust the ballot when it goes against you. In the end, the novel is a cautionary tale.

That's my version—my truth—and I'm sticking to it.

That's one way of looking at what historical novelists do when we tackle large public subjects: we are entering the truest version we can in the marketplace of stories. The reader—and the community made up of all the readers—will choose which story to live by. ❖

How to Talk a Character into Your Story

Rebecca Lee

A FRIEND OF MINE ONCE HAD A DATE WITH A GUY NAMED Ross (this is true), and prior to going out to dinner, she showed him around her apartment. Right before they left, he asked to use her bathroom. Yes, of course, she said, gesturing, and then a few minutes later he emerged, with her makeup on his face. Some blush, a little eyeliner, glossy lipstick. It wasn't particularly garish, and he wasn't smiling as if it were a joke. It was just tastefully applied. And off they went.

I mention this only to make this distinction—this is not necessarily an especially good thing for a date to do, but it is an excellent move for a character in a short story. Which leads me to suspect that maybe all good stories resemble, in some ways, bad dates; that is, both are concerned with the rifts that open suddenly and subtly between people as they try to communicate, both involve people usually carefully scrutinizing faces and situations for small, but crucial clues, both teeter precariously always on the edge of disaster, comic or otherwise. Most significantly, and this is the point I really want to make, both involve surprise, psychological surprise, a surprise that springs out of the complicated, unpredictable nature of human emotion. My feeling is that the surprise of a story, the moment when it turns and reveals a different face than predicted, should be internally motivated, not externally. For instance, if a boulder suddenly falls on a character, that's not so interesting dramatically, but if a character suddenly turns to another and realizes the other is actually plotting against them, even as they're declaring their love, then that's a dramatic moment. Again—bad date, good story.

One of the real pleasures of writing (and thank god there are a few, since it is so difficult) is that a character, if you give it time, will always be larger, or wiser, or stranger, or more eccentric than you could ever dream at the outset of the story. The best thing you can do for your characters is release them slowly and carefully from your initial idea of who they are and let the deep and fertile powers of your concentration and imagination produce changing, and therefore living, characters. Graham Greene wrote, "The moment comes when a character does or says something you hadn't thought about. At that moment he's alive and you leave it to him."

How does the writer allow for this? This is the great mystery, but I believe it involves patience and intensity, simultaneously. I think that writing often feels less like construction, less like you are building characters, and more like you are finding them, waiting on them, taking care of them, being nice to them, giving them a home in your imagination for long enough that eventually they tell you who they are. "Be very patient," Katherine Mansfield wrote, "until she steps slowly into the light."

Once I asked Bob Reiss what to do when a character you are trying to write into a story continues to elude you, and he gave me this simple but extremely useful piece of advice, which was to ask the characters what they desire, and also what they are afraid of. A character's desire leads them to action, and their fear throws up boundaries, and suggests limits. And it is this tension that runs quietly under every story. It seems that to know a character's desire is the starting point of any story—it sets the machinery spinning. Somebody wants something, and from that flows plot as they set about to get it, failing or succeeding along the way. It's impossible to find a story that doesn't embrace this idea in some way. I suspect that if the writer spends a few days dreaming on paper about what the character truly wants from the world—love or money or another person or a second chance or forgiveness or to set foot on their native land—then this desire will ripen and spill over into action, and there will follow the whole beautiful skein of consequence and decision and heartbreak that we call fiction.

A footnote: My friend didn't again date that guy Ross, but they became friends, not fast friends really, but long-distance, dinner-once-every-few-months-friends, and years later, she found herself visiting with him around his tiny, kinda dingy kitchen table in his apartment in the East Village. He'd had a brief career as a comic, and had been in a few commercials, and then abruptly had fallen on some hard times; now he was unemployed, kind of alcoholic, generally a little depressed. But this night, he was in a nostalgic mood. "Remember that time," he said to her, "when we put on makeup together?"

"No," she said. "I don't remember it quite that way." But she smiled. It was a nice moment, the strung lights of the Village twinkling into the small dark room, and she saw suddenly how he had seen that occasion long ago, as if it had been really sweet and companionable, a lovely memory. He had surprised her again, and cast a somewhat different light on the past, made her think twice, which is sometimes what stories can do. ❖

FICTION
SELECTIONS

The Fourth Prussian Dynasty: An Era of Romance and Royalty

Karen Bender

Ella believed that she had begun the journey toward her husband, Lou, long before she met him, when she took a salesmanship class at George Washington High School. Seventeen girls and three boys were enrolled in the course. They were all immigrants or the children of immigrants, and they were all sixteen years old. On the first day of school, the teacher, Mr. Reilly, asked them to come back the following morning in their best clothes—or, rather, their best selling clothes—so that he could examine them. He was going to tell them if they had the skills to become salespeople; he was going to tell them who they were.

Ella had grown up in Dorchester, in a four-room tenement apartment, with five other people: her parents and her three older sisters. The ceiling was tin, and the air in the rooms seemed always to be the color of dusk. The hallway smelled of unclean breath and sour urine from the toilet they shared with their neighbors. The apartment itself couldn't contain the relentless sound of six personalities trying to assert themselves in a small space, and Ella was never sure how to make her own voice distinct.

Ella was the only one of the sisters who had been born in America. Her father had emigrated from Russia alone, and it had taken him six years to make enough money to bring the others over to Boston. She was the product of her parents' reunion. At the dinner table, she sometimes went hungry, because in Russia her sisters had learned early how to grab. Sometimes she suspected that they secretly wanted to starve her. They were big, anxious girls with thick accents, and they seemed less like sisters than a force of weather.

What had her parents been like before their lives here? The rest of the family knew this history, and thus inhabited a world of feelings that was forever denied to her. It was hard to believe that her parents could have been different from who they were now. Her mother was shy and tousled and smelled of boiled meat. She poured herself so completely into her tasks that, at times, she seemed to disappear. Ella's father was too tall for the apartment and was often restless, eager to get away. Sometimes she, came upon her parents in a kiss that looked stronger than love; in its rage it reached toward an innocence. It was only in such moments that they really seemed married.

From the time she was young, Ella had wanted to be loved, and she needed that love to be immense, ferocious. After her sisters married and moved away, she often sat alone in the bedroom she had shared with them, wondering whom she would love. And who would love her? The streets outside her window at night were empty, silvered by the moon. She longed to be able to walk down them joined wholly with someone else.

A job led you to the man you would marry, but in 1920 only a few jobs were available to unmarried girls in Boston. Ella watched her sisters to see what they chose. Their jobs shaped them in basic ways. Every day, Esther, the oldest, limped home after ten hours of shouldering huge plates of food at Bloom's Kosher Restaurant, barely able to make it up the stairs. She got married first, to one of her customers, a large, moonfaced man who frequently ordered omelettes; they met when he let her sit in his booth to rest her feet. Ruth worked the graveyard operator shift at New England Telephone and turned into a pale, ghostly person who rarely spoke. She married late, in part because she spent her time packed in a room with fifty other female operators, and few people bothered to flirt with a voice on the telephone.

Deborah had the best job. She worked at the women's hat counter in Filene's, where there were silver mirrors at the jewelry counters and the aisles were sweet with fragrance. Ella felt as though she knew a famous person—her sister, Filene's hat girl—and she enjoyed watching Deborah smoothly tell a well-dressed woman, someone who would not even nod to her on the street, "I know this hat would be perfect for you."

* * *

On the second day of Salesmanship, Mr. Reilly moved around the classroom, examining the students as they stood by their desks in their best clothes. He told them that not only had he been born in this country but his parents had been, too—and he, therefore, knew what was what. "Look at this jacket," he said to Jacob Katzman. "It's red. You look like a clown. From a circus. Do you want the world to laugh at you? Do you want a red nose to go with it?" Trish O'Donnell, a slight girl, stood shivering in a mealy black sweater. "You," he said, "are a scaredy-cat. Why would anyone want to buy anything from you?" To Rosie Delano, done up in wrinkly, baby-pink chiffon, he said, "You think you're a princess? You're coming out of the castle for us?"

Mr. Reilly complimented only three students, and not on what they were wearing. He praised John Delaney for his impressive height—six feet one—"like an oak tree." He approved of Pearl Johnson's melodious voice and told her to say "Pleasure to meet you" several times; and then he admired Ella's smile. "Look at this," he said, turning her head, like a doll's, for the other students to see. "Is this a smile you would buy a hat from? A dress? A vase?" He paused and answered, "Yes!"

He gave them rules, and Ella wrote down every one. When a woman walks into the store, watch her closely to see which piece of her clothing she wears most proudly, then compliment it. Make sure your hands are perfectly clean. Nod one full second after someone asks you a question, not before. When a customer walks in, count to ten before you say, "May I help you?"

The students practiced looking into each other's eyes with confidence. "Pretend you see a flower inside your customer's head," Mr. Reilly said. Face to face with her classmate Pearl, Ella tried to find roses, lilies, marigolds blooming behind her nervous eyes.

"This time, look interested," said Mr. Reilly. "The flower is shrinking. Keep watching it until it goes away." Rosie Delano was better at looking interested than anyone, but John Delaney had the most confident look. When the others asked him what flower he saw, he answered, "A very big, blue rose."

"There's no such flower as a blue rose!" they shouted, and he shrugged.

"That's what I saw," he said.

During the semester, they had to sell numerous absurd items that Mr. Reilly brought into class: an ugly rag doll, a satin shoe without a heel, a cracked marble, a banana peel. At first, almost everyone stuttered and spoke in a wispy voice. Mr. Reilly stood at the back of the room and yelled, "What? I can't hear you! Americans speak loud." He pounded his chest. "Loud! Are you an American? Or do you want to go back?"

Some of the items were impossible to sell. It took three students to get rid of the banana peel. (By that time, it had dried up.) Of course, no one actually bought anything, but Mr. Reilly knew when a customer was ready to buy. It was a specific moment, and Ella learned to detect a subtle change in the room, a longing that hadn't been there. When Anna Stragowski held up the black banana peel and said, "You need this. You must buy. Why? Because it is a duster!" and then whirled around the room, whisking the stiff peel against desks and windows, the students were quiet with amazement, breathing softly: there really was one more thing that they could want.

Mr. Reilly was hard on Ella for the whole term. She did not live up to the unintended promise of that first smile. So she wanted to do well when he handed her the final object to sell—a tiny, broken child's tooth. Ella cupped it in her hand. She could not think of what to say.

"Hello," she whispered. "I am Ella and I have something—"

"Louder!" Mr. Reilly yelled. "Who's talking? I can't hear you!"

"I am Ella—"

Mr. Reilly was shaking his head. She felt as though she were yelling, too.

"Do you have trouble chewing?" she asked. "This is what you need!"

The field of faces blinked and yawned. A few students laughed. "With this extra tooth you can have a better smile!"

"They already have teeth," Mr. Reilly said. Ella's panic was rising. She popped the tooth in her mouth and swallowed it. She and the other students stared at each other, stunned.

"Where'd it go?"

"She ate it!"

Ella put her hand on her stomach. She had swallowed a stranger's tooth. Whose mouth had it come from? Why had she swallowed it? Would it harm her insides? Would Mr. Reilly want it back?

Mr. Reilly stood up. The class was in an uproar. "Mr. Reilly! Now we can't buy the tooth!"

"Ella, where is the tooth?" asked Mr. Reilly. Ella gently patted her stomach.

"Tell me, class. Do you want that tooth?" Mr. Reilly said.

Nineteen pairs of eyes looked at her. "Yes!" the students shouted.

"Then I have to say that you pass," Mr. Reilly said.

Ella stood in front of the class for one more moment before she sat down, feeling those rapt, hungry eyes on her. She knew that the others wanted the tooth only because it could not be had.

Ella's tooth-swallowing trick so impressed Mr. Reilly that when she graduated from high school two years later he referred her to his friend Marvin, a floorwalker at Johnson Massey Treasure

Trove. It was a plum job, even more prestigious than being a hat girl at Filene's.

The Treasure Trove was situated on the fifth floor of the elegant department store. On the directory posted in each elevator, the shop was indicated by a scrolled gold plaque. The moment Ella walked into the Treasure Trove, she knew that she did not belong. It was full of the things she imagined finding only in rich people's homes—vases and lamps and china figurines. The door was flanked by two black Grecian columns, and inside were jade dogs and horses and rabbits and domed chests encrusted with purple stones. There were gentlemen customers with bowlers and ladies in silk dresses and feathered hats. Above, a teardrop chandelier sparkled like frozen raindrops. Ella kept her hands out of her pockets to show everyone that she was not a thief.

"Reilly sent you?" asked Marvin. He had a strange accent, almost English. His face was thin, with fine cheekbones that made him appear sophisticated. Ella nodded.

"Let's get a look at you," he said.

She turned around, arms held out, and tried to smile. He looked her over. "What do you think of all this?" he asked her, gesturing at the room.

"It's beautiful," she said. Her voice was thick with feeling.

"Fine," he said. His accent slid a little. "We'll fit you up in a uniform. Be here tomorrow at nine."

And, that quickly, Marvin had hired her. She came in every morning and dusted off the figures made of jade or ivory or gold. She wore a uniform, a forest-green cap-sleeved blouse with a calf-length skirt. On her collar, she had a sparkling rhinestone lapel pin with the initials "JM," for Johnson Massey. Ella did not think that the pin's jewels were real, but she also did not want anyone to tell her they weren't.

She memorized everything Marvin told her about the objects; the information seemed culled from an encyclopedia. "Jade is much prized in the Orient. Different methods for carving it are used in China and Japan." Sometimes, when she was tired, she made up her own facts. "This fine chest stored dishes in the castle of King Howard the Fourth," she said. She loved how the customers nodded as they listened, vulnerable with fragile objects in their careful hands.

* * *

Ella and Lou had met when Lou wandered into the Treasure Trove by chance. She came up behind him and asked, "May I help you?" Lou turned around and saw her. He lowered his hat.

"I'm just a salesgirl," she said. "You can put your hat—"

"You're Ella," he said, reading her name tag. "A pleasure to meet you. I'm Lou." He gazed at her. "I'm searching for a gift from"—he looked around—"the Fourth Prussian Dynasty," he announced.

"Yes," she said.

"From 1834 to 1857. A great era in history. A time of riches. Beautiful queens." His voice echoed strangely. She could not recall anything about the Fourth Prussian Dynasty.

"Ella," he said. "Show me what you have."

They strolled past the delicate, glimmering objects. There were no other customers or salesgirls in the store just then. He followed her, his shoulders hunched, assuming a protective posture.

"Prussia," she said, hoping for more help from him.

"I'd say the year 1852," he said.

She gazed around the room. A feeling of boldness came over her. "This!" she tried, pointing to a gold-filigree grandfather clock. "This is from that time."

He went up to the clock, rapped it with his knuckles. His face went soft with approval. "It is," he said.

Ella stepped back, surprised. The clock was certainly not from the Fourth Prussian Dynasty, whatever that was.

Each understood that the other was lying. The light in the room seemed to brighten.

"It chimed to call them to dinner," he said.

"I think so," she said, smiling. A puff of glee burst in her chest.

They walked around the room. Almost all the objects in it, they decided, must be from the Fourth Prussian Dynasty. "This," Lou said, gripping a vase dangerously by its neck, "held the bracelets that belonged to Edwina, the Prussian princess."

"No," she said. "That was for her earrings. Her bracelets"—she tapped a long, curved ivory tusk—"hung on this."

Ella began to feel a little dizzy. Lou walked close to her, so close that it was as if they were already intimate, and when she took her place behind the counter again he looked lost. He bought the least expensive item in the room—a tiny jade rabbit—and seemed stunned that he had purchased anything.

"Thank you very much, Ella," he said in a puzzled way, clutching the store bag. "Thank you for helping me today." And then, as though afraid of what he might say next, he dashed out of the store.

*   *   *

A few days later, as she came out through the glass doors of Johnson Massey, she saw Lou standing by the store windows. He was moving his hat restlessly from hand to hand; when he saw her, he quickly put it on. "Ella," he said, his face stern, "I'm Lou."

It was a fall day, and the sky was pale with cold. His hands seemed clumsy and large in brown mittens. His breath curled in the chill air. "What a lovely pin," he said, looking at the sparkling "JM" on her lapel.

"I think they're diamonds," she said, and then stopped, embarrassed.

He smiled, so that she knew that he knew the stones could not be diamonds. They began walking together, toward nowhere. The afternoon seemed to part before them.

"If you're still looking for presents," she said, knowing he wasn't, "Sophie can help—"

"I have something for you," he blurted. They stopped. He held out a package, badly wrapped. It was easy to accept the present; she was curious. She unwound the tissue. It was the rabbit she had sold him.

"There was no Fourth Prussian Dynasty," she said. She had looked it up in an encyclopedia.

"No?" He laughed. He knew. His face was as open as a child's. "But you were so . . . helpful. I wanted to give it to you."

She touched the rabbit's glossy ears. She had never owned anything from the Treasure Trove.

"Have dinner with me," he said. The words seemed to come from a tender place inside him. He stepped back a little. There was a brisk gust of wind, and his coat flapped around him.

*   *   *

Ella began to look forward to seeing Lou come through the Grecian columns of the Treasure Trove. Soon he was visiting her several times a week. She was cautious, but she liked him, partly because the other girls did. They hovered beside him, laughing at his jokes, the way he made fun of the gaudiest, most grotesque objects. "What fool would buy this?" he said, lifting a huge gilt ashtray with cupids balancing on the edges. The girls shrieked with laughter. Ella watched them change lipsticks, looking for the one color that would make him love them. They acted like men when they flirted, slapping him playfully, calling him "mister" or "kid," as though this gave them new rights to him. They smiled coldly at Ella. She did not understand her claim on Lou, but she tried to love him almost to appease them.

After work, Ella and Lou took walks together. He was full of opinions, and he seemed so happy to be with her that she wanted to listen. He told her about the classes he had taken in college; how he helped manage his mother's suit store; how he had read about California and wanted to live in a place that was always warm. Lou was full of jokes when he visited the store, but when they were alone he had an earnest quality that told her that he took her seriously. His admiration seemed to be part of him, like bone.

He had money. That gave him confidence; he entered restaurants, stores with none of her trepidation. She began to love the careful, greased slickness of his hair, which gleamed like black licorice, and the way he shook his coat on, commanding and sharp. He was educated; he read all the sections of a newspaper. He walked through the world knowing he belonged in it.

One night, she was eating dinner with Lou in a bright-red booth in a diner in Brookline. She sat, anxious, straightening the fork on her napkin. She had ordered brisket, but it wasn't a fancy place and when her meal arrived the meat was too tough to cut. Her knife skidded from her hand to the floor.

"They should take it back," Lou said. "It should be more tender." Ella felt embarrassed, responsible somehow.

"No, I like it this way," she said. He looked at her.

"Then let me try," he said.

Lou slid her plate over to his side, pressed his fork deeply into the meat, and carefully cut off a small piece. He held it up as though it were a jewel.

"How's this?" he asked.

She stared at him. "Fine," she said.He cut the meat into bite-sized pieces for her. Then he set the plate back in front of her. "That should be better," he said.

She could not look at him. It was wonderful, the way he cut her meat for her. Lou chewed his green beans. For a moment, Ella stopped eating her brisket. She was so certain of her future, she did not feel she needed to do anything—pick up her fork, drink her water. An odd happiness filled her. Life would carry her to the next good place.

* * *

The wedding was a rush of images: the rabbi's gray, acne-marked face, her boned, ivory-satin dress, paid for by Lou's family, and the juicy red roast beef they had also provided. At one point, she was held up in a slight wooden chair, dozens of hands reaching for her, as though she were floating on a wild sea. She barely saw Lou during the party, until, emerging from a flurry of rice, they disappeared into a taxi that took them to the Hotel Essex. Lou registered them as Mr. and Mrs. Lou Rose. It was that easy; this was who she was.

She had never been inside a hotel. Their room was creamy-walled, with a ruby-red carpet. There were dark-blue linen drapes, and a big, tidy bed. A bottle of champagne sat in a silver bucket. The room smelled clean, antiseptic. Ella wanted to touch every-thing. She moved around, examining the night table, opening and closing the drawers.

Lou followed her. "Let me introduce my wife to the dresser," he said. His voice was hoarse. "Let me introduce my wife to the lamp—"

The word "wife" startled her, as if an intruder had entered the room. In the bathroom she found fragrant squares of soap, and picked one up. "It's our first soap," she said to Lou. "Hold out your hands." He did; his palms were exquisite and pale pink. Gently she washed their hands together. He dried his with the plush hotel towel. They went back into the bedroom, and Lou leaned toward her face and kissed her.

It was all very fast. She wanted to be a good bride, to be still as Lou unzipped her dress and pushed it down her shoulders, but she also wanted to kiss back. She stepped out of her dress in one quick, determined motion. He unhooked her bra and took her breasts in his hands. It was an astounding sight, her breasts, pale and soft, in his hands. It seemed too easy, too calm.

Lou gently guided her down to the bed. The gold bands on their fingers gleamed, ghostly in the darkness, as though they belonged to the same club. His fingers had a rubbery quality, and she felt the edge of his fingernail inside her. There was a loneliness that she had not expected. "Ella," he whispered. Suddenly fright-ened, she wrapped her arms around him; she was aware of the cotton sheet and the clock ticking on the wall and his breath, so fast, doglike. She pressed her forehead into his shoulder, wanting to touch more than his body.

Then he stopped, and rolled off her, pushing his face into a pillow. His ear was so close to her lips she wanted to shout into it, but she did not know what she would say.

"Well, my love," Lou said. "We're married."

They blinked into the brackish, honeyed smell of each other's breath.

Lou fell asleep, and Ella watched him as he slept. Suddenly, she understood that no one completely owned anyone else in the world. Even together in their wedding bed, they would separate into two different people in their dreams. As her eyes adjusted to the darkness, she saw her wedding dress, stiff and opalescent in the deep-blue light. It looked as if it had fallen and were trying, very delicately, to stand up.

It took nothing to send them to California: a cramped attic apartment; a newspaper article that said homes in Los Angeles were cheap. It was 1924. They moved West, a new bride and groom, in a used Ford. Gripping hands, Ella and Lou watched as each state fell away behind them, revealing the vast country, alternately brown or verdant beneath the springtime sun. ❖

I Am the Bear

Wendy Brenner

I said: Oh, for God's sake, I'm not some pervert—you think I'm like that hockey puck in New Jersey, the mascot who got arrested for grabbing girls' breasts with his big leather mitt at home games? I'm a polar bear! I molest no one, I give out ice cream cones in the freezer aisle, I make six dollars an hour, I majored in Humanities, I'm a girl.

I was talking to the Winn-Dixie manager in his office. Like every grocery-store manager, he had a pudgy face, small mustache, and worried expression, and he was trying very hard, in his red vest and string tie, to appear open-minded. He had just showed me the model's letter of complaint, which sat, now, between us, on his desk. *The polar bear gave me a funny feeling,* the model had written; *I was under the mistaken impression that the bear was male but much to my surprise it turned out that I was wrong. The bear was silent the whole time and never bothered to correct me.*

It was part of my *job* not to talk, I explained to the manager. I read to him from my Xeroxed rules sheet: *Animal representatives must not speak in a human manner but should maintain animal behavior and gestures at all times while in costume. Neither encourage nor dispel assumptions made regarding gender.* I said, See? I was holding my heavy white head like a motorcycle helmet in the folds of my lap, my own head sticking out of the bureau-sized shoulders, my bangs stuck to my forehead, a small, cross-shaped imprint on the tip of my nose from the painted wire screen nostril of the bear. I can't help my large stature, I said. That's why they made me a bear and not one of those squirrels who gives away cereal. I was doing exactly what I was supposed to do. I was doing what I was *designed* to do.

She would like an apology, the manager said.

You say one becomes evil when one leaves the herd; I say that depends entirely on what the herd is doing, I told him.

Look, the manager said, his eyes shifting. Would you be willing to apologize, yes or no. He reminded me of a guy I knew in high school—there was one in every high school—who made his own chain mail. They were both pale and rigidly hunch-shouldered even as young men, as though they had constantly to guard the small territory they had been allotted in life.

Did you notice how in the letter she keeps referring to me as "the bear"? I said. No wonder she didn't know I was a girl, she doesn't even know I'm *human!* And incidentally, I added, when the manager said nothing, you would think she'd be more understanding of the requirements of my position—we are, after all, both performers.

The manager seemed offended that I would compare myself, a sweating, hulking bear, to a clean, famously fresh-faced girl, our local celebrity, and I was let go. This wasn't dinner theater, he said, and at headquarters, where he sent me, I was told I could continue to be a polar bear but not solo or in a contact setting. This meant I could work corporate shows, which in our area occurred never. I saw myself telling my story on *People's Court,* on *Hard Copy,* but I was a big, unphotogenic girl and I knew people would not feel sympathy for me. Plus, in the few years since college I had been fired from every job I'd had, for actual transgressions—rifling aimlessly through a boss's desk drawers when she was out of the office, sweeping piles of hair into the space behind a refrigerator in the back room of a salon, stopping in my school bus, after dropping off the last of the children, for a cold Mr. Pibb at Suwannee Swifty—and I believed absolutely in retribution, the accrual of cosmic debt, the granting and revoking of amnesty. I was, simply, no longer innocent. I was not innocent even as I protested my innocence.

No, I hadn't molested the girl, but even as I sat in the manager's office I could still smell the clean spice of her perfume, feel the light weight of her hands on either side of my head, a steady, intoxicating pressure even through plaster and fake fur. I could not fully believe myself, sitting there, to be an outraged, overeducated young woman in a bear suit. Beneath the heavy costume, I was the beast the manager suspected me of being, I was the bear.

The girl had been shopping with her mother, a bell-shaped generic older woman in a long lavender raincoat. The moment they rolled their cart around the corner into my aisle, still forty feet away, the model screamed. She was only eighteen, but still I was surprised—I would have thought Florida natives would be accustomed to seeing large animals in everyday life. She screamed: Oh my god, he's so cute! She ran for me, and I made some ambiguous bear gesture of acknowledgement and surprise. Hey there, sweetie, she said, pursing her lips and talking up into my face as though I were her pet kitten. I scooped a cone of chocolate chip for her but she didn't even notice. Mom, look, she yelled.

The lavender-coated mother approached without hurry or grace. Her face, up close, was like the Buddha's, and she took the ice cream from my paw automatically, as though we had an understanding. The model was rubbing my bicep with both her narrow tanned hands. He's so soft, she said. I faced her, making large simpering movements, and noticed the small dark shapes of her nipples, visible through her white lacy bodysuit. I blushed, then remembered I needn't blush, and that was when she reached for me, pulling my hot, oversized head down to her perfect, heart-shaped face. The kiss lasted only a moment, but in that moment

I could feel how much she loved me, feel it surging through my large and powerful limbs. I am the bear, I thought. And then it was over, and I remembered to make the silly gestures of a human in a bear suit pretending to be embarrassed. The model's mother had produced a small, expensive-looking camera from some hidden pocket of her raincoat and matter-of-factly snapped a photo of me, a bear pretending to be a friendly human, with my arm around the model's skinny shoulders, my paw entangled in her silky, stick-straight golden hair.

They left then, the mother never speaking a word, and they were all the way down the aisle, almost to the other end, when the produce manager stuck his head around the corner right in front of them and yelled my name, I had a phone call. The model looked back once before they disappeared, and though she never saw my face—I wasn't allowed to take off my head in public—it was obvious from her expression that she understood. It was an expression of disturbed concern, the way she might look if she were trying to remember someone's name or the words to a song she once knew well, but there was something else, too, a kind of abashed sadness that looked out of place on her young, milky face.

*   *   *

I could imagine how she must have felt, having once fallen in love with an animal myself in the same swift, irrevocable way I imagined she had. The Good-Night Horse, he'd been called—that heading had appeared beside his picture on the wallpaper in our cottage's bathroom at the Sleepy Hollow resort, and the words stayed in my head for years, like a prayer. The wallpaper featured reprints of antique circus posters and flyers, the same six or seven over and over, but the good-night horse was the only one I paid attention to: he was a powerful black shape that seemed to move and change form like a pile of iron shavings under a magnet, quivering slightly. He was muscular, a stallion. I was six. "Katie is masturbating," my mother said, in her weary, matter-of-fact voice.

I would lie on the floor on my side under the toilet-paper dispenser, my face a few inches from the wall. The good-night horse was shown in a series of four different postures. In the first two pictures he was wearing boots and trousers on his hind legs, but in the wild third picture, my favorite, he was tearing the trousers off dramatically. Clothes were flung on the ground all around him, his tail swished in the air, and the trousers waved wildly from his mouth. In the last picture he was, with his teeth, pulling back the covers of a single bed with a headboard, like my bed at home. "The World's Greatest Triumph of Animal Training," the poster said.

There was no problem with my masturbating, because my parents were intellectuals; they had given me a booklet called "A Doctor Talks to Five- to Eight-Year-Olds" that included, as an example of the male genitalia, a photograph of Michelangelo's statue of David. The photo was small and black-and-white, so you couldn't really get a good look at what was between his legs, but it appeared lumpy and strange, like mashed potatoes, and I found it unsettling. The book had already given me a clear picture of sexual intercourse: it was a complicated, vaguely medical procedure in which you were hooked up to an adult man and microscopic transactions then occurred. And though my parents had said, "You're probably too young to picture it, but someday you'll understand," I *could* picture it—I saw an aerial view of me, naked, and the statue of David lying side by side on a white-sheeted operating table, me in braids and of course only half his height. But this vision was the furthest thing from my mind when I looked at the good-night horse.

I wasn't stupid, I knew people didn't marry horses, or any other animal. I just wasn't convinced that the good-night horse was necessarily an animal—the more I looked at his picture, the more he seemed to be a man in some important sense. It was not his clothes, or the tricks he did, but something both more mysterious and more obvious than that. He reminded me a little of Batman—and, like Batman, he might have a way of getting out of certain things, I thought. He was sensitive, certainly—his forelock hung boyishly, appealingly, over his eyes, and his ears stood up straight, pointing forward in a receptive manner (except in the trouser-flinging picture, where they lay flat back against his head)—but you could tell that he was in no way vulnerable, at least not to the schemes and assaults of ordinary men. He was actually more a man than ordinary men, and something began to swell in my chest unbearably after a few days, weighing me down so that I could not possibly get up off the floor, and my father finally had to carry me, sobbing, from the bathroom. I was sobbing not only because the good-night horse and I could never meet, but because I understood with terrible certainty, terrible finality, that I would never be happy with anything else, anything less.

And it was true that no man had yet lived up. I had been engaged once to a social theorist who was my age but refused to own a TV and said things like "perused" in regular conversation and expected to be liberated by what he called my "joyous nature," but it ended when I discovered while he was writing his thesis that he had not gotten around to treating his three cats for tapeworm and had been living with them—the cats and the worms—contentedly for weeks. And now, at twenty-eight, I only dated, each man seeming a degree more aberrant than the last. The last had been a stockbroker who was hyperactive (rare in adults, he said) and deaf in one ear—he yelled and slurred and spit when he talked and shot grackles with an AK-47 from his apartment window but was wildly energetic even late at night, boyish and exuberant and dangerous all at once, a little like the horse. On our second and last date, however, he took me to an Irish pub to meet his old college roommate, and the roommate engaged me in an exchange of stomach-punching to show off how tightly he could clench his abs, only when it was his turn to punch mine he grabbed my breasts instead, causing the stockbroker to go crazy. He dragged the roommate out onto the sidewalk and pushed him around like a piece of furniture he could not find the right place for, and I kept yelling that it was only a joke, I didn't mind, but in the scuffle the stockbroker's visor—the kind with the flashing colored lights going across the forehead band—got torn off and flung into the gutter, its battery ripped out, and when the fight was over he sat on the curb trying in vain to get it to light up again and saying, "He broke my fucking visor, man," until I told him I was taking a cab home, at which point he spit, on purpose, in my face.

So I could understand how the model might feel. I could see how, from looking at me, the miserable, small-minded Winn-Dixie manager would believe I had no business comparing myself to her, but, not being a bear himself, he did not understand that appearances meant nothing. I was a beast, yes, but I also had something like x-ray vision; I was able, as a bear, to see through beauty and ugliness to the true, desperate and disillusioned hearts of all men.

* * *

It was not difficult to figure out where she lived. She had been profiled earlier that month on *Entertainment Tonight* along with her sister, who at twelve was also a model, and the two girls were shown rollerblading around their cul-de-sac, and I knew all the cul-de-sacs in town from having driven the bus. So, a few days after I was fired, I drove to her house. To be a bear was to be impulsive.

It had been a record-hot, record-dry July, and the joke topic of the radio call-in show I listened to as I drove was "What have we done to antagonize God?" Callers were citing recent sad and farcical events from around the world in excited, tentative voices, as though the DJ might really give them the answer, or as though they might win something. Only a few callers took the question personally, confessing small acts of betrayal and deception, but the DJ cut these people off. "Well, heh heh, we all do the best we can," he said, fading their voices out so it would not sound as though he were hanging up on them mid-sentence. Asshole, I thought, and I made a mental note to stop at the radio station sometime and do something about him.

The model's house was made of a special, straw-colored kind of brick, rare in the South, or so *ET* had said. As I drove up, I saw the model's mother step out onto the front steps, holding a canister of Love My Carpet, but when she saw my car she stepped quickly back inside. The model's sister answered the door. She was a double of the model, only reduced in size by a third and missing the model's poignance. Her face was beautiful but entirely devoid of expression or history; her small smooth features did not look capable of being shaped by loss or longing, not even the honest longing of children. This would be an asset for a model, I imagined, and I could see where the mother's Buddha-nature had been translated, in her younger daughter, into perfection: desire had not just been eliminated, but seemed never to have existed in the first place.

"I am a fan," I said, and, perhaps because I was a girl, showered and combed and smiling, I was let in. I had also brought, as props, a couple of magazines which I held in front of me like a shield, but I was not nervous at all. I understood that I had nothing to lose, that none of us, in fact, had as much to lose as we believed. I sensed other bears out there, too—my fierce brothers, stalking through woods and villages, puddles and parking lots, sometimes upright and sometimes on all fours, looking straight ahead and feeling the world pass beneath their heavy, sensitive paws.

The model's sister led me past ascending carpeted stairs and a wall of framed photos to the back of the house, where the model's bright bedroom overlooked a patio crowded by palmetto and bougainvillaea, visible through sliding glass doors. A tiny motion sensor stuck to the wall above the glass blinked its red light as I entered. The model was bent over her single bed, taking small towels of all colors and patterns from a laundry basket, folding them, and placing them in piles. "Fan," the little sister said, and the model straightened and smiled and came forward, her perfume surrounding me and sending a surge of bear power through me, a boiling sheet of red up before my eyes. For just a moment as we shook hands I was sure she would know, would remember the feel of my paw. But then she stepped back, and my face cooled back down.

"I'm a huge fan," I said.

"Well, thanks, that's so sweet," she said. She had taken the magazines from me automatically, just as her mother had taken the ice cream at the store, and was already scribbling across the shiny likeness of her face. "Should I make it out to anyone?" she said.

"My boyfriend," I said, and I told her the stockbroker's name.

"You're so lucky you're so tall," she said, handing the magazines back. "That's my biggest liability, I can't do runway. Well, thanks for coming by."

I looked around at the white dressers, the mirrored vanity, not ready to leave, and was shocked by a short row of stuffed bears set up on a shelf on the wall behind me. They were just regular brown teddy bears with ribbon bows at their necks, no pandas or polar bears, but they stared back at me with identical shocked expressions, another motion sensor glowing on the wall over their heads, unblinking. "Nice bears," I said. I had to force myself to turn away from them.

"Oh, I've had those forever," she said. "See that one in the middle, that looks so sad? I found him in the street when I was six years old! Doesn't he look sad?"

"Yeah, he really does," I said. The bear was smaller and more lumpish than the other bears, with black felt crescents glued on for eyebrows.

"I used to make them take turns sleeping in my bed with

me," the model said. "But even if it wasn't his turn I let him, just 'cause he looked so sad. Isn't that funny? I used to kiss him thirty-two times, every night, right after I said my prayers."

"Thirty-two," I said.

"My lucky number," she said brightly.

"But you don't kiss him anymore," I said.

She stared at me, frowning. "No," she said. She stared at me some more and I stood, my arms hanging, as a bear would stand, waiting. "Well, I better get back to work," she said.

"On your towels," I said.

She put her hands on her hips and gazed helplessly at the towels, as though they had betrayed her. "They're dish towels, isn't that queer?" she said. "I got them from a chain letter. My cousin started it, and I was second on the list, so I got like seventy-two of them sent from, like, everywhere. Isn't that pathetic—she's, like, twenty-two, and that's her hobby. You can have one, you want one?"

"Seriously?" I said.

"God, take your pick," she said. "I guess I have to remind myself sometimes that not everyone's as lucky as me, but, like, dishtowels, I'm sorry."

I had to brush past her to get to the bed, the snap on the hip pocket of my jeans rubbing her arm. I took the top towel from the nearest stack, a simple white terrycloth one with an applique of a pair of orange and yellow squash. "Thanks, I'll think of you every time I use it," I said. I held the towel, stroking it. It was not enough, I was thinking.

"Well, thanks for coming by," she said. She had moved to the doorway and stood looking at me in the same way she had looked at the towels. The row of bears watched from over her shoulder, the slumped, sad one seeming braced by its brethren. I imagined the model and her soulless sister laughing at me after I'd gone, at my terrible size, my obvious lie about a boyfriend.

"I really have to get back to what I was doing . . ." she said.

"I'm sorry, I was just so nervous about finally meeting you,"

I said, and I could see her relax slightly. "I almost forgot to ask, isn't that funny? I hate to ask, but do you by any chance give out photos?"

"No, you'd have to contact the fan club for that," she said. Her face was final, and I turned, finally, to go. "But actually, wait," she said. "I do have something, if you want it."

What happened next was certainly not believable in the real world, but in the just, super-real world of the bear it only confirmed what I had known. She slid an envelope out from beneath the blotter on her white desk, picked through it with her slim graceful fingers, and pulled out a photograph which she passed to me hurriedly, as though it were contaminated. "Here, isn't that cute?" she said.

There we were, her and me, her small, radiant face beside my large, furry, inscrutable one, my paw visible, squeezing her small shoulders together slightly, the flash reflected in the freezer cases behind us, making a white halo around both of our heads. Something seemed to pop, then, noiselessly, as though the flash had just gone off around us again in the bedroom. Like a witch or spirit who could be destroyed by having her photo taken, I felt I was no longer the bear. "He's so cute," I murmured.

She snorted, but it had no heart to it, it sounded like she was imitating someone. Then, for a moment she no longer saw me; she just stood there looking at nothing, her dark blue eyes narrowed, the faintest suggestion of creases visible around her mouth.

I had to take a step back, such was the power of her face at that moment. Then she too became herself again, and we were just two sad girls standing there, one of them beautiful and one of them something else. "Well, goodbye," I said, and she looked relieved that I was leaving—but also, I thought, that it was only me deserting her and not, as before, the heartbreaking, duplicitous bear.

On the way out I encountered her mother, who had materialized again beside the front door. It was the simple gravity, the solid, matter-of-fact weight of the woman, I decided, that made her silent appearances and disappearances so disconcerting, so breathtaking—wasn't it more impressive to see a magician produce from the depths of his bag a large, floppy rabbit, to see the ungraceful weight of the animal dragged up into the light, than to watch him release doves or canaries, already creatures of the air, flashy but in their element? "Goodbye," I said. "Sorry."

She smiled and did not step but rather shifted several inches so that I could get past her, and then stood in the open doorway, round and lavender, smiling and watching my retreat. Only when I was halfway down the walk to my car did she say goodbye, and then her voice was so deep and strange and serene that I was not sure if I had really heard it, or, if I had, if it had really come from her.

*   *   *

I did use the towel and sometimes thought of the model when I used it. The photo I didn't frame or hide or treat with any ceremony, but I did look at it often, trying to experience again that moment of transformation, that rush of power that had gone through me in the seconds before it was snapped.

But after a few months even the memory of it became weak. I was after all no longer the bear and could no longer remember well what it felt like to be the bear. The animal in the picture appeared only to be a big, awkwardly constructed sham, nothing you could call human. When I looked at it I felt only confusion and shame. How had I become that shaggy, oversized, hollow thing? Once I had been an honest little girl, a girl who had to be dragged away from the object of her love, but somehow, somewhere, everything had changed. How had it happened, I wondered. I studied the photo as though the bear could answer me, but it only stared back with its black fiberglass eyes, its grip on the real human beside it relentless. ❖

Lunch at the Picadilly

Clyde Edgerton

W E'RE IN THE NURSING HOME PARKING LOT. AUNT Lil and me. She's behind her walker. She pushes it way out in front of her. Arm's length. Humped way over and all fell in the way she is, and weighing less than ninety pounds, her arms look longer than a broom. To see where she's going she has to look up through her eyebrows.

"Is that my car?" she says.

"Yes ma'am. I washed it."

"Well, it looks good."

She's wearing a striped jacket, Hawaiian shirt, tan slacks, gold slippers, silver wig, and a couple of pounds of makeup.

"I'll let you try to drive it after we eat," I tell her, knowing damn well she ain't able to drive. I've been putting it off—letting her practice her driving, that is—by driving my truck when I take her to lunch instead of her car. She keeps asking me when she can practice her driving and I keep putting it off. Because for one thing, as far as when she's going to get out of this place, I don't think it's going to happen. And she won't be able to drive again in any case, and it's my job to tell her. I'm it. It's one of the most worrisome things in my life because I'm about all she's got left, as far as people. Everything is pretty much up to me.

But today we've got her car, and after I let her try to drive after lunch, in the mall parking lot there at Picadilly's, for just a minute or two, I'm going to tell her she can't drive anymore. It's past time to just break the news.

I get her walker fitted in the back seat, get her in the passenger seat—her head about as high as the button on the glove compartment. She drives—drove—an Oldsmobile, 1989, kind of a maroon color, with a luggage rack on the trunk lid. She drove it seven years before her problems and it ain't got but 21,000 miles on it. She's always had something kind of sporty in cars. Back in '72 she had a 1967 two-door Ford Galaxie with fender skirts. White with red interior, and she let me drive it to my prom.

We park on top of the two-deck parking lot at the mall. It's mostly clear of cars. I tell her that after lunch I'll let her drive around up there a little. Mainly, I'm simply going to let her prove to herself that she can't. Can't drive. That will make it lots easier for her to take the news, which I will probably deliver as soon as she makes her first mistake, which might even be before she cranks up.

We get inside Picadilly, and since it's only eleven-thirty there's not a real long line, but on the way past the food toward the trays and silverware where the line starts she wants to stop and take a look at what they're serving today. Right here I want to say, Aw, come on Aunt Lil, you'll get to see it in a minute. But I'm thinking, Be patient. Be good. She's in the hardest time of her life.

We get the trays, silverware. She gets a bowl of Chinese stuff without the rice. I get it with the rice. I'm trying not to help her. See, my mother, her sister, would be talking to her about what she might want, might not want, how much the special is, this that and the other, trying to push both their trays, and worrying the hell out of her, and so I'm telling myself not to worry her. Let her do what she can. It's going to be bad enough when she sees she can't drive. Aunt Sara, before she died, said stopping driving was the worse thing she ever went through, including Uncle Stark's death.

Down at the cash register a small black man, maybe sixty years old, takes Aunt Lil's tray and leads us to a table. She wants the smoking section. She smokes Pall Malls. He puts her tray down. She says thank you and starts getting all settled in. She can't figure out where to put her walker. I move it over against the wall.

All she's got on her tray is this bowl of Chinese stuff and a biscuit and iced tea and a little bowl of broccoli with cheese sauce. I got the Chinese stuff over rice, fried okra, string beans, fries, cucumber salad, pecan pie, and Diet Coke. She reaches for my little white ticket slip and puts it with her own. She'll get me to pay with her MasterCard.

She says, "That was Larry," talking about the man that brought her tray over. "Let me get him a little something," and she starts looking around for her pocketbook.

I'm thinking, Oh no, the quarter tip.

"You know," she says, "he's lost some weight." She finds her pocketbook, but can't get it open. I help her.

"He'll be back," I say.

"He's been working in here for twenty years at least," she says.

Here comes Larry, walks right by before I can say anything. I check his name tag. It says LEWIS CARLTON. "There he goes," I say. She raises her hand, misses him. "His name tag said Lewis," I say. "Lewis Carlton."

"No, it didn't."

"I think it did. 'Lewis Carlton.'"

"Then it's Larry Lewis Carlton," she says. She's sort of twisted around in her seat, like a buzzard in makeup looking over its shoulder. "There he comes back. Larry! Larry, come over here."

The man, Mr. Carlton, comes over.

"Here, I want you to have this." She hands him a quarter.

"Thank you, thank you." He steps back a couple of steps, starts to turn.

"You've lost some weight, ain't you?" says Aunt Lil.

He frowns. "Oh, no ma'am."

"You've lost at least twenty pounds."

"No ma'am, ah, I been at one-sixty for quite a few years now."

"Well, I remember when you weighed a lot more than that."

He looks at me, kind of smiles and backs off.

"He's been here a long time," she says. "I don't know if they want you to tip them or not, but I always do."

Yeah, I'll bet he's glad to see you coming. "Say he's lost some weight, huh," I say.

"Oh yes, he used to be a great big old thing."

So we eat along, and talk about the normal things.

Last time we were in here, a woman named Ann Rose wanted to carry Aunt Lil's tray from the cash register. Aunt Lil saw her coming and said to me, "Lord, she'll talk your head off." Aunt Lil shunned her, but Ann Rose took the tray anyway, said she'd saved Aunt Lil a table, but Aunt Lil don't want no part of it. Said she wanted to sit someplace else. So Ann Rose looks at me with this nod of understanding. I'm staying out of it. Later at the end of the meal, Aunt Lil says, "Go tell Ann Rose to come on over here. I don't want to make her feel bad." So Ann Rose comes over, sits down and starts right in about how she worked forty-four years at the cigarette factory—American Tobacco—and they'd all told her that whenever she finally left they'd have to close it down, and sure enough she left in June of '91, and then in July they sure enough announced they were closing it down, and then there was a woman had been working in there got cut loose, then joined an accountant firm that came right back and was doing a audit of the very people who'd just let her go, and "I want you to know they lost a hundred retirement checks and only one showed up and that was at somebody's P.O. box and nobody knows how in the world that happened, that all the one's with regular addresses got lost," and blah blah blah blah blah. Like to drove me crazy.

Just about every other time we come in here, somebody comes over. Because Aunt Lil made all these friends, coming up here all these years. I like it when they don't come over.

* * *

It's one of those giant two-decker parking lots, about the size of a football field, with a couple of ramps going down to the ground-level deck below it.

We drive to the far end of the lot, where it's away from the mall and empty. I stop, get out, get her out of the passenger side, the walker out of the back seat, and she plods around the back of the car in her walker. Remember, this is a two-decker parking lot, and we're on top.

This all started when Aunt Lil fell in her tub, twice on the same night, same bath, a couple of years ago. Then not long after those bathtub falls her back started breaking on its own—from gravity, you know, just broke and broke, then broke some more and the awful thing is that you could see so clear and fast the way it bent her right over. The worst thing was the pain it caused her. She cried a couple of times, and I'll tell you she is not the crying sort. The first few minutes in the nursing home after she got off the van she was following her walker—real slow, you know, with it ten feet out in front of her, and it hurt her just to walk. She sat down in her little room with her roommate—I helped her—and she said I don't know what I'm going to do and she started crying right there. It was almost like one month she was standing as straight as an arrow, walking as classy as a model, one foot in front of the other—eighty-seven years old I'm telling you—and then in a few months there she was with a walker and all bent over like that, crying.

I got my own business and can get off work when I need to, and this was say three o'clock in the afternoon and when she finished crying, she said to her roommate, "Don't you wish you had a nephew who'd do for you like this one?" and her roommate, name of Melveleen, says, "I got two nephews. They both work." Melveleen.

So, anyway, I help her in. I get in the passenger side, hand her the key, she puts it in the ignition, turns it, starts the car right up, and kind of looks around. I'm feeling a little sad about it all. This is it. This is the last time she'll ever do this. I'm about to break the news. She will not like what I have to tell her.

"Where's the exit?" she says.

"We're just going to drive around up here on top for a few minutes and let you get the feel of things."

"I got the feel of things."

Yeah, you got about one minute left in your driving history on earth, Aunt Lil. And I'm the one about to break the news.

She pulls it into drive and we're off—in a little circle.

"Where's the exit?" she says.

"We're going to stay up here on top, Aunt Lil. You can drive over toward those other cars if you want to. Maybe a little slower." We do.

All of a sudden, she says, "There's a exit!" and swings the car to the left, right down this down ramp. Because the sun was so bright up top, I can't see. I assume she can't either. I'm straining to see straight ahead, one hand on the dash board. Then I see the curbs on each side of the car—about two feet high, thank goodness. Aunt Lil is drifting left. I think about pulling the hand brake, but decide against it. She needs to see, to prove to herself what she can't do. We scrape the curb with the front left tire, or bumper, I can't tell which. She slows to a stop.

"We drifted left," I say. "Let's pull on straight ahead, on down there beside that column and I'll take her back over." This is all the proof I need. The proof I want her to know for herself: She is unable to drive anymore—the time has come. I will have to break the news to her—as soon as we stop.

The top of her head is about even with the top of the steering wheel. She starts out slowly, drifts left, and runs against the curb again.

"What's wrong?" she says.

"You keep running up against the curb."

"Oh," she says. She looks over at me, her hands up on the steering wheel. "Am I driving?"

"Yes, yes. You're driving. Pull straight ahead there and I'll take back over."

"I need a little more padding under me," she says. "I'm too low in this seat."

"I don't think that's the basic problem, Aunt Lil."

"And I need a little more practice. That's all." She pulls straight ahead and stops. We sit there. This is the time to tell her, I think, but I'll just wait until I'm back behind the steering wheel with everything under control.

"Okay," I say. "Put it in park."

She does.

I get out to go around and help her out. I'm sort of preparing my speech. I want to make it as easy as possible, to kind of set it up so she might make the suggestion herself, set it up in a way that if she doesn't take the bait, then I can say, Aunt Lil, I think you're just going to have to give up driving. And then I'll say something like, That way you won't have to pay car insurance and all that. That's costing you over a thousand dollars a year.

I open the back door, get out her walker. As I pass around the back of the car, I see her head leaning into the middle of the car, looking down at something. As I come around to her side I see both her feet hanging out the open door. I can't remember if she put it in park.

"Be sure it's in park," I say.

This is where she pulls the gear shift from park down into drive, and off she goes, them gold slippers hanging out the door. There she goes, very slowly at about two miles an hour, her door and the passenger door wide open. I'm standing there in the damn walker. I open my mouth. Nothing comes out. She's going in a big wide circle, missing one of those big columns, then another, circling around. I see her head now. I think she's steering. I decide to just stand and wait, because it looks like she might come on back around. All I have to do is wait. Something tells me if I holler at her she'll try to get out. She's not going fast. I must remain quiet.

She's now traveled one half of a large circle, missing everything. There are about five or ten cars in this area and many thick concrete columns. If I stand still I think she'll be back around. She must be holding the steering wheel in one position. I hope she doesn't straighten it out. But if she does, maybe she'll start up the ramp and the car will choke down—that thought crosses my mind. But then she'd roll backwards. Her foot is not on the gas because I can see those two little gold slippers. She misses another column, then another. I will wait.

Here she comes. I believe she's steering. I set the walker out of the way and move so that I will be on her side of the car when she comes by. Both doors are wide open. I see those gold slippers. I see her eyes above the steering wheel. Here she comes. I start walking beside her; fairly fast walk. "You need to put it in park," I say. I put my hand on the door. She's looking straight ahead, frozen. The passenger door hits a column and slams shut. "Put it in park, Aunt Lil."

There is a tremendous explosion and pain to my body and head. I've walked into a column. I stagger backwards, catch myself, and head out after the car. By God this proves she can't drive anymore. I run to the passenger door, open it, jump in, grab the hand brake between us, and pull it up slowly and firmly. We stop. I put the gear lever in park. Because her feet are out the door, she can't turn her head all the way around to see me, but she tries.

"Is that you, Robert?" she says.

"Yes ma'am. It kind of got away from you there, I believe."

"I was doing okay," she says.

God Almighty. "Let's get you out, and I'll drive us on back," I say, a little tenseness in my voice.

"I would have got out," she said. "But I couldn't reach that seatbelt thing."

"What would have happened to the car, Aunt Lil—if you'd got out?"

"You could have caught it. Just like you did."

I figure that as soon as we get back and sit down in her room and kind of recover and eat a couple of Tootsie Rolls, I'll break the news to her. She keeps Tootsie Rolls for everybody that comes in. I buy them for her, along with bananas and other stuff. It's not going to be easy, but I'm just going to have to tell her like it is. Her driving days are done and over. Ka-put. End of story. ❖

THE BURNING OF *THE RECORD*

FROM *CAPE FEAR RISING*

Philip Gerard

Thursday, November 10, 1898.

SAFFRON WAS STILL ASLEEP IN MIZ GABRIELLE'S SEWING room. The headless dressmaker's dummy stood in the corner, draped with folds of fine satin for Gray Ellen Jenks' evening gown. Bessie King busied herself in the kitchen.

David hadn't come back last night. Bessie didn't know exactly where he was. If there was trouble, that boy would find it, though he was a good boy at heart. Everybody said so. But he didn't think too clear. He was the kind of boy things happened to, never the right things.

Bessie served Colonel Waddell in the dining room, where he ate alone. He seemed all stirred up this morning, high color in his cheeks. Kept rubbing his legs and cursing softly. "Damned cavalry legs." Let him suffer, she thought. Pain was a boon to character.

She ducked into the pantry to fetch another jar of marmalade, and there she saw it: her spider, hanging on her web—upside down—an omen of death. "Lordy," she said out loud, and crossed herself. She grabbed the marmalade and went out quickly.

"Something spook you?" the Colonel asked her as she clattered down a plate of eggs, bacon and cheese grits in front of him.

She looked at him and saw a ghost. She saw him melting away like a haint, a bad dream of a bad man. "No, suh," she said, ducking her head.

"Do you know what today is, Aunt Bessie? What anniversary?"

"Suh?"

"Ninety-nine years ago Napoleon seized the throne of France."

"Yes, suh."

He sipped coffee. "Go see if Miz Gabby is up yet." Gabrielle deRosset Waddell, his young wife, who slept in her own room. "When you've served her breakfast, make yourself scarce."

"Yes, Colonel."

"And Aunt Bessie? Stay off the streets today."

"Colonel?"

He smiled. "Nothing you'd understand," he said, and forked into his eggs. "Just politics."

She left in a swish of skirts and he ate with gusto. He'd need a hearty meal today. Lately his appetite was enormous. His muscles were stretching, unbending, craving exercise, like the muscles of a young man. His brain was humming like an electric coil. His voice was tuned and strong. Only his legs gave him pain—cramps, poor circulation, knees that grated. Nothing a good brisk walk wouldn't cure.

In his mind, he counted off the men he would have to contend with. Hugh MacRae was the most formidable—but for the time being their interests coincided. And Hugh's brother Donald did as Hugh told him.

Next in order of prominence came the Taylor brothers. Colonel Walker Taylor, officially in charge of the State Guards, could be a problem. He seemed to want to run things. But he favored posture—intimidation and threat—over outright violence. Stand up straight, shoulder to shoulder, and you won't have to fire a shot. That was good. Walker Taylor had high-minded ideas about duty and honor. He would act with restraint. Still, if all hell broke loose, he was a brave man who would give orders to shoot to kill. Waddell must be careful when and how to use him.

J. Allan Taylor, who held no official claim to anything, was the brother to watch. He had close ties to Hugh MacRae and lacked Walker's patience and restraint. He would charge in and do the job, quick and dirty and mean. He wanted results. He didn't much care about the legal niceties—he was used to fixing them up later. He was still bitter about how much his father had lost in the war, and he aimed to get it back any way he could. If you crossed him, he was the kind of man who would pull a pistol and shoot you between the eyes in front of a hundred witnesses, then go take his supper.

George Rountree was the smartest of the bunch. Waddell liked him the least. In some ways, they thought alike—Rountree was scouting out the board three moves ahead of everybody else. And they both served the law. But Rountree was a fanatic on the subject: he wouldn't cross the street without the proper paper-work. He knew precedents and counter-precedents, ordinances and codes, right down to their subsections and footnotes.

For Waddell the law was a drama, the courtroom a theatre—exactly like the Courthouse meeting. The broad sweep of justice ranged from tragedy to farce. Each trial had its own set of play-ers, protagonist and antagonist, and a rising curve of suspense as they struggled toward the climax—that moment of decision after which nothing would ever be the same.

At the center of each trial was the nut: one actor wants some-thing, and the other will stop at nothing to keep him from having it. A stage-managed combat by proxy. The consequences might be staggering—fines, punitive damages, hard labor for years, life imprisonment, even death.

But for George Rountree, the drama was a nuisance. Human passions interfered with the law. The law lived in books. The law was the fiction everyone in the community had agreed upon so that their collective life might proceed with a semblance of order and decorum. The law was a kind of story that had already mostly been written, told over and over again. From time to time, one needed to revise it—as he was already revising the role of negroes and the ballot, Waddell knew.

In the courtroom, Rountree was formidable. He could not match Waddell for fiery eloquence, for inflaming hearts and winning over an audience of nervous jurors. Instead Rountree relied on the inexorable momentum of logic—fact following fact, figure proving figure, nothing overlooked, crushing his opponent by sheer weight of proof. Rountree won his cases in the law library.

Rountree thrived on information, Waddell reasoned, on knowing more than anybody else. The way to keep him off-balance, then, was to keep him in the dark. Already, at Waddell's urging, Hugh MacRae had cut him out of some key meetings. Time to cut him out of a few more.

Waddell pulled out his gold watch—already after seven. Before he had finished his plate, the committee men began to arrive. Within a few minutes, they filled up his parlor, dining room, and library, milling about, pouring coffee down their throats, all dressed up and talking in low tones, like a board of directors.

Aunt Bessie disappeared—she had not even removed the breakfast dishes. Miz Gabby had not come down yet. What ailed her lately? No matter—women had no part in this morning's business. And where was that reporter, Samuel Jenks? He had sent word for Jenks to meet him here bright and early. For what they were about to do, he wanted his biographer close at hand.

J. Allan Taylor stood in the entryway, thumbs hooked in the waistband of his trousers. He was nearly as tall as his brother Walker but lacked his bulk. He was a man with no room for extras. Every few minutes he yanked his watch out of his vest, snapped it open like he was knifing open an oyster, then dropped it back into the flannel pocket.

Hugh MacRae said, "Expecting somebody?"

"You don't think the niggers will send word?"

MacRae barely smiled. "As if that matters,"

"But if they give in to everything—"

MacRae clapped a hand on his shoulder. "Now listen, John. They can all sign over the deeds to their houses, it wouldn't change what we have to do."

Taylor took his thumbs out of his waistband. "I'm just thinking of George. He'll hold us to the paper. Like some goddamned contract or something."

MacRae had sent word to Rountree after yesterday's meeting that the thing was settled: no call for drastic measures. "You let me handle George." MacRae's eyes were flinty and bright, his face ruddy and smooth from good health and exercise. This morning he moved in a kind of aura. His heather tweeds were crisp. His riding boots—which he rarely wore on a business day—were spit-shined to a rich chocolate brown. His thinning blond hair was slicked in a side part, his ears as pink as if he'd been standing in the cold for an hour. He fairly glowed.

Beside him Waddell seemed spectral, a black-and-white figure cut from the fabric of an earlier century: pale gray eyes sunk in deep dark circles, silver hair and spiked goatee sheeny with oil, moustaches waxed to stiff points, high celluloid collar yellow against the white of his throat, his black clawhammer coat both ridiculous and somber at this hour of the morning.

With great ceremony, Waddell consulted his watch. Where was Jenks? No matter—he couldn't wait any longer. "Gentlemen," he said in a soft, deep voice, then snapped his watch case shut as if it were loaded to fire. "Time."

MacRae donned his brown slouch hat, precisely blocked into a campaign crown, and led the committee of twenty-five across the porch and down the middle of Fifth Street to Market, where his saddled horse stood waiting at the armory. To J. Allan Taylor, he said, "Never doubt me, John."

Striding hard on his sore legs, Colonel Waddell passed up the line of men and took his place at the head, beside MacRae and Taylor. In a few minutes, he would ride. He was walking so fast the breeze pushed at the broad front brim of his plumed chapeau, the same one he'd worn at Richmond and the Petersburg Pike. His hand reached reflexively to his left hip to pat the hilt of his cavalry saber—but in the rush he had forgotten to buckle it on.

Sam Jenks met him coming the other way, greeted Waddell and his cousin MacRae and fell into step with them. He could tell by the look on MacRae's face that these men were out to do serious business this morning. He could almost smell their nervous adrenaline, rank as sweat.

The Light Infantry had been mustering at the armory since before dawn. Everything had been arranged. All the right people had been told. Every man had his assignment. When Waddell's party arrived, Donald MacRae and Captain James were waiting. Several hundred men, armed with Winchesters and Colt pistols, were milling about in the yard by the steps. Some of them had spent the night guarding the First Baptist Church or patrolling the neighborhoods, reporting in at intervals to Colonel Roger Moore, grand marshal of the vigilantes. Moore had set up a command post a few blocks from Waddell's house in the other direction, at Fifth and Chestnut.

Moore had stopped by Waddell's house as a courtesy on the previous evening. During the War between the States, he had served with Waddell in the 41st Regiment of the Third North Carolina Cavalry. Moore had been commissioned a major on the same day Waddell had received his colonelcy. When Waddell had gone ill, Moore had taken over command of the regiment.

Waddell figured a command post was a good place for Colonel Moore this morning—one less chief to contend with. Let him wait there until they sent him his orders.

When the assembled mob caught sight of Waddell, MacRae, and the other committee men, they cheered and pressed closer toward the armory, waiting for the word. The mob parted to let the leaders ascend the marble steps and enter the armory.

Standing just inside the thick double doors, Hugh and his brother, Captain Donald MacRae, conferred briefly. Donald was still technically in command of the Light Infantry men who had volunteered for the Cuban campaign but never got there. "Form up your men," Hugh MacRae said without any inflection. His voice resounded in the high space. Waddell and J. Allan Taylor stood to either side.

Sam Jenks, loitering a step behind, said, "I don't get it—you're going to use force? But—"

"Keep quiet," MacRae said. "It's time to make a point."

Donald MacRae hesitated and rubbed his sharp chin. "I still hold my commission in the U.S. Army, Hugh," he said. "There may be ramifications."

J. Allan Taylor said, "He's right, Hugh—they could court-martial him for this. It would give them a pretext to send the Federals down—"

"Goddamnit!" He recovered his calm. "Why didn't you say something yesterday?"

"It didn't occur to me yesterday—"

"Get Colonel Moore on the telephone." On the wall in the meeting parlor just off the corridor hung the telephone. They clustered around it while MacRae rang Moore's house. He wasn't there—of course he wasn't there, Waddell reflected: MacRae must not know about the command post. Had Moore coordinated all that with Walker Taylor? MacRae didn't bother himself with particulars. He was the master of the big picture.

Next, they rang Moore's office, but of course he wasn't there, either. Waddell knew that Colonel Moore was barely two blocks away, waiting by a telephone for this very call, but he didn't say anything. MacRae hung up, looking baffled. His hair was mussed and there was soot on the sleeve of his tweed coat where he'd rubbed against the fireplace mantle.

"Get Walker on the telephone," J. Allan Taylor suggested. "Christ—why isn't he here already?"

MacRae rang him at home. "Walk? We've got a situation here. Come on over and straighten us out. We need a good officer out front." Then he listened, pressing the earpiece hard against his pink ear.

"What's he giving you?" J. Allan Taylor said. "Let's get on with this."

"Goddamnit, haul your fat ass over here!" MacRae shouted into the trumpet. The composure was gone from his voice. As he cursed into the trumpet, his tenor went shrill and broke. His face went scarlet. He listened some more. "We need some leadership on this thing."

"Let me talk to him," J. Allan Taylor said. He reached for the earpiece, but MacRae held onto it with a white fist.

Sam said, "I still don't see why—" Waddell grabbed him, hard.

"No, the city is not threatened, Walk, not directly. Christ Jesus—we've gone over all that! But this thing is necessary. The long-term threat is there. We've got to do this thing. We talked about that—" Walker Taylor must be shouting into the other end now, because they all could hear the shrill buzz of his voice rattling the earpiece.

"We may not need you later! Later may be too late—"

"Let me go get him," Donald MacRae offered. "He's only a block away."

MacRae ignored him and stared at the wall, still shouting. "We can't stop it now—it's too late, man!" He listened again, stamping his foot. "The Pinkertons' report? We talked to the Pinkertons!" Pause. "I don't give a good hoot in hell if you've changed your mind!"

Donald MacRae shook his head and stared at the Italian

marble floor. J. Allan Taylor stood by, wringing his hands, imagining what his namesake grandfather would do at this moment if he were standing right here beside them in the family house he had built. They were all letting Hugh down. It was all a matter of technicalities. Rountree must have been talking to Walker—it had his stamp all over it. Legalities—that's all it was. Paper laws.

Hugh MacRae clapped the earpiece into the cradle so hard he nearly tore the wooden telephone box off the wall. He didn't have to explain—they'd all caught the gist.

Sam had never seen MacRae so worked up—almost too angry to speak.

"Do it yourself," J. Allan said.

MacRae shook his head violently. "That's not my place. It's a military operation, That's how we planned the goddamned thing." He chopped the air with his hands. "We want action taken by the proper authorities." He swore again. "I thought I had some goddamned soldiers I could count on—"

His brother Donald said, "Tom James can do it. He's out on the steps."

MacRae flung open the big doors and marched out, boots clucking, onto the marble steps. The mob cheered. At the fringes, Red Shirts collected in knots and pumped their rifles over their heads. "Let's go get the niggers!" one of them cried, and the rest broke out in a chorus of cheering and hurrahs. They pressed in closer.

Sam was scared in his stomach: this mob had an air of premeditation—it was no spontaneous lynching party. These men had waited all night for this moment. Some had been waiting weeks. The inflammatory articles in the newspapers, the rousing hate speeches, the bogus election—everything had been moving toward this. And Sam's job was to write the story.

The infantrymen and several squads of naval reserves stood in loose formation in the side yard, checking their weapons.

Hugh MacRae said, "Captain James, if you please."

Captain James turned on his heel, looking puzzled.

"Captain MacRae requests you take command of this operation."

Captain James backed up a step, glanced sidelong at the mob, looked to Donald MacRae for some explanation. Donald MacRae stood with his brother and said nothing. "What—me lead that mob?" Captain James said.

The MacRaes nodded. The blood rose in Captain James's face. Automatically, he braced himself at attention. "I am a soldier," he said. "I won't lead a mob."

Sam scribbled James's reply in his notebook—he wanted to get it right. He understood it immediately to be a defining moment, a vivid declaration of character. He wished he himself were capable of such a moment.

Donald MacRae said, "Somebody has to do it—"

"Not me—never. I won't."

Hugh MacRae swore. Donald MacRae turned up his palms. "Be reasonable, Tom—"

Waddell stood beside them, beaming, then took one calculated step toward the crowd. "Waddell!" Solomon Fishblate shouted from the front of the crowd, and others took up the chant: "Waddell! Waddell! Waddell!" He stood at the edge of the top step and let them cheer. He waved. He bowed deeply from the waist, sweeping his plumed hat across his body in a graceful flourish.

Two of the Red Shirts grabbed him bodily and hauled him through the parting crowd, then hoisted him onto a horse. The stirrups were too long, but never mind that, he thought. He took the reins in one hand and, in a gesture he had not used in thirty-five years, lifted the other easily, naturally, palm open. He waited till the men had turned their attention from the armory steps to him. He sat above the crowd, feeding on their upturned faces, hand still raised. "We tried to reason with the niggers," he said, "but they have defied us. Alex Manly is still at large, free to slander the good name of our women. I say this nonsense has gone on long enough!"

The men hurrahed.

"Today we march on the nigger newspaper and seize Manly—are you with me?"

The din rattled the windows of the armory. With all eyes fastened on him, he casually let his arm drop forward as if he were tossing a baseball, and their cheers started his horse forward up Market Street.

Hugh MacRae stood momentarily paralyzed. It was too late to stop Waddell. He had picked his moment with perfection—outflanked him again. Colonel Moore, Walker Taylor, Tom James, even his own brother Donald, all had failed him at the moment of truth. He swore a string of oaths. J. Allan Taylor grabbed MacRae's arm and led him around back to their stabled horses. "Come on, Hugh—we can catch ahold of this thing yet."

Sam Jenks sprinted down the steps and followed the mob.

On the bone-white marble steps of the armory, Captain James watched them go. When the infantrymen formed up in ranks and started marching out of the yard, he leaped off the steps and stopped them. "If you follow that mob, leave your tunic here!" he shouted. The men milled about uncertainly.

Lieutenant White, the drillmaster, who wore wire-rimmed spectacles and styled himself after Colonel Roosevelt, said to Donald MacRae, "Captain—are we not to do our part?"

"I'm in command here," Captain James said. "If the city is threatened, we will move to keep the peace."

Donald MacRae swore, threw up a helpless hand, and retired inside the building.

The men remained standing in ranks, muttering. The tail of the mob was almost out of sight now, and a straggle of men and boys who had arrived late were sprinting through the pall of lime dust to catch up to it.

"At ease," Captain James said. "Stack your weapons. Go on

about your business. But don't leave the compound." The men shifted from foot to foot, talked briefly among themselves, swatted their gray, white- plumed hats against their thighs, and, with an exaggerated air of disappointment, began falling out. There were coffee and biscuits inside—they could smell the woodsmoke from the old iron cookstove in the basement club rooms.

*   *   *

Colonel Alfred Moore Waddell walked his horse so that the men behind him could keep up. Mounted Red Shirts took up positions as outriders, Winchesters cocked on thighs. By the time Waddell reached the turn onto Seventh, the mob stretched out two blocks behind him, all the way back to the Wilmington Light Infantry armory.

Waddell made the turn onto Seventh Street with five hundred men trailing him. MacRae rode somewhere behind him—he didn't look back to see. An army could have only one leader. Mike Dowling, captain of the Red Shirts, jogged along the flank on his skittish sorrel, his red tunic-front shirt freshly laundered for the occasion. Among the marchers on foot were ex-mayor Solomon Fishblate and the Reverend Peyton Hoge, both carrying Winchesters.

From out of nowhere appeared Father Dennen, the Catholic priest, waving his arms to stop them. "For the love of Jesus, boys, you can't do this!" he shouted. "You can't do this—"

Waddell's horse shouldered past him and the priest went sprawling onto the oystershell. He picked himself up and dusted himself off in a cloud of lime dust, grabbing men by the elbow, pleading for tolerance. But the sheer momentum of the mob carried him along and spit him out into the gutter, where he lay, stunned, and watched hundreds of wild-eyed men stream past.

Seventh was a quiet residential street. The mob flowed noisily along the narrow, tree-shaded corridor between modest frame houses, moving fast. They trampled flower beds, scattered stray dogs, sent whole wings of blackbirds exploding out of the twisted live oaks in black frenzied bursts.

A Red Shirt fired his rifle into the air. Pretty soon a dozen ragged shots cracked into the overhanging branches. A shotgun boomed twice, bringing down a rain of twigs and shredded leaves. Men hooted and yelled. A frightened horse kicked down a picket fence at the corner of Dock. At Orange Street, a team of matched grays pulling a landau reared up at the sudden appearance of the mob, and the carriage fetched up against a porch, its front wheel busted. Dr. Silas Wright, the mayor, peered out of the landau, clutching the useless reins in his white gloves, praying to go unrecognized.

The mob rushed through the neighborhood like a flash flood, carrying away everything in its path. White women stared out from behind curtains. Occasionally men ran outside to join the mob, buttoning their flies as they ran, pulling on coats, their pockets bulging with shotgun shells.

Past Orange Street, the faces turned darker. Negro workingmen, sleeping off the late shift at the mills, were roused abruptly. They fled out their back doors barefoot, wearing only flannel union suits. Many of the women were already at work in the better homes across town. Children dived under beds and into crawlspaces, stared through the broken boards of slat fences.

By the time it roared past the Williston School on Ann Street, the mob had swelled to almost a thousand men. Now Waddell could see a church and a white building just in front of it that must be Free Love Hall. The sign, THE RECORD PUBLISHING COMPANY, still hung from the second floor. A face appeared in the upstairs window, then disappeared. Waddell reined up at the front door, men milling so close around him that he could not moved his feet in the stirrups. All at once, he realized he was unarmed. The upraised barrel of a Winchester was bobbing out of the crowd on his right. He gripped the barrel, hauled it out of the owner's hands, and planted the butt on his thigh.

As the mob fetched up and surrounded the building, it went deathly silent, all at once, as if its angry roar had been caused by the constant movement. Waddell looked behind him onto a sea of hats. Rifle barrels poked up among the hats, here and there a brickbat.

Waddell held up his hand—an old cavalry habit. He drew himself up in the saddle and addressed the closed door. "Open up, in the name of the white citizens of Wilmington!" On cue, a dismounted Red Shirt hammered at the door with a brickbat. "We want Manly!" Waddell proclaimed.

Nobody answered.

Carefully, without turning, he backed his horse away from the door and gave a casual signal with his left hand. The mob spit out two men in overalls, each hefting a fire axe. Taking turns, they whacked at the door until it splintered off its hinges. Inside stood a lone negro, transfixed, wide-open mouth bubbling with saliva. A voice shouted, "Manly!" A little pistol cracked and the negro grabbed his neck, reeling as if he'd been punched. Then he vanished.

The mob rushed into Free Love Hall after him, but he was gone out the back. They slipped on his blood.

They smashed chairs and tables with nine-pound railroad mauls, gouged the walls with axes, shattered the windows with rifle butts and brickbats. They swarmed upstairs to the printing room and found the Hoe press. Four men heaved against it, but they could not budge it. So they overturned the drawers full of type, scattering the heavy leaden letters across the floor. They smashed more windows, busted every piece of furniture in sight, swept carefully filed stacks of back numbers of the *Record* off the shelves, then pulled down the shelves. Swinging axes and mauls, they pulverized two typewriters, a beer mug full of sharpened pencils, an old rolltop desk, and a glass paperweight.

Mike Dowling was so caught up in the melée that, by the time he had finished smashing things, the Winchester in his hand had a broken stock and a bent barrel. He flung it away, gave a blood-curdling rebel yell, and crawled out the window toward the Record Publishing Company sign. Hands gripped him by the belt as, swimming in thin air, he tore it loose from its chains and flung it down into the street. The mob axed it into kindling.

Downstairs, two Red Shirts discovered a storage closet. They smashed the padlock with a maul and raked cans of kerosene and turpentine off the shelves. Other men shouldered them aside, grabbed the tins of kerosene and turpentine, and doused the broken furniture. Somebody struck a match. The men upstairs barely got out as the flames flared into the rafters.

Outside Free Love Hall, Waddell was furious. The mob was out of control. They had come to get Manly, and Manly had fled. Somebody had already been shot—what had become of him? Was he Alex Manly? Other men were firing freely into the flames. "Call the fire brigade!" he yelled to one of Dowling's men, who merely grinned at him and popped off another round.

Solly Fishblate found Waddell. "I've put in a call to the negro fire brigade," he shouted.

"Can't you do something about these Red Shirts?"

"Should have thought of that before."

The flames were leaping out of the roof now, and the northerly breeze threatened to spread the fire to the church next door. That would never do—you could not burn down a church and expect the world to bless your cause. Hundreds of rifles were firing now. Men and boys were cheering. Horses reared and plunged, neighing in fear. To Waddell, the clamor had an old, familiar taste.

Sam Jenks, who had finally worked his way to Waddell's side, said, "I thought there wasn't supposed to be any violence." He hadn't been this scared since Cuba.

Waddell bent from his horse. "Welcome to the chaos of battle, son."

"Manly doesn't even seem to be here—"

"It's gone beyond that now. Men are going to die today."

A block north, at the intersection of Ann Street, a horde of

Red Shirts surrounded the horse-drawn fire engine of Phoenix Hose Reel Company No. 1 as it turned onto Seventh. The negro crew clutched the brass handrails as if they could not be harmed unless they let go. A dozen men grabbed the horses and held them. The others trained their rifles on the firemen and shouted obscenities. The firemen didn't reply—they hugged their machine.

Free Love Hall blazed so hot that the crowd fell back. The cool air rushed past their ears toward the suction of the fire, and the heat gusted back into their faces. Flames shot fifty feet above the roof. The pine clapboards, saturated with natural resin, burned blue and orange. Boards crackled and spit. Rafters buckled with claps like pistol shots. The flames sucked at the cool air with a sound like heavy surf. The shake roof erupted in half a dozen places, the shingles fluttering onto the heads of the mob. Some of the siding boards literally exploded, rocketing embers into the crowd. The embers arced out from the building and bloomed like fireworks. The crowd cheered each one and danced out of the way.

The fire spit out flaming splinters. Little white boys scrapped over them, ran in gleeful circles trailing plumes of smoke.

All at once a great tearing sound split the air—the joists were buckling. Waddell's horse heard it and reared up, almost tossing him off. He got the horse under control and listened: The upstairs floor was giving way.

A thousand men and boys stopped their spree and paid attention. Then they heard a great boom—as the Jonah Hoe press crashed through.

At the intersection of Seventh and Ann, the Red Shirts backed away from the fire brigade and let them through unmolested. For two hours the brigade fought the blaze, but they didn't have a chance—Free Love Hall was already a ruin by the time they arrived. They worked under the guns of the mob, concentrating on their apparatus.

Hugh MacRae watched the firemen work. "Such discipline," he observed.

One of the Red Shirts said, "You dress those monkeys up, they are crackerjack."

Sam could not turn away—his eyes were captured by the spectacle. When at last the heat made him look away, he spied the woman reporter in the crimson Eaton jacket, grinning toward the flames, scrawling onto her notebook pages with a blind hand.

* * *

Back at Colonel Waddell's house, Bessie King fretted. Her hands needed to be doing something. Those high and mighty men who had followed the Colonel out the door had murder in their eyes. She didn't want to know where they were going, or why. "Lord, bring my boy back to this house before the reckoning," she prayed out loud as she cleaned up the kitchen and rinsed the breakfast dishes at the sink. The cold water sloshed out of the pump and splashed her apron, but she didn't notice.

The parlor carpet was soiled from boots and men's heavy shoes. She fetched the vacuum sweeper, the newest gadget the Colonel had procured for the household. She could get the carpet much cleaner by hauling it out the back porch, folding it over the bannister, and whacking it with her broom, but her back was too tired today. She rolled the mechanical sweeper over the carpet back and forth, listening to the roller brush spin and the dirt rattle up into the metal canister. When she stopped, the house was silent. She rolled the gadget back into the kitchen closet and closed the door on it.

It was a powerful lonely morning. Her boy was out on the streets somewhere. Her little girl, too—slipped out during breakfast.

She sighed and held back tears. Humming softly to keep off the heebie-jeebies, she climbed the stairs to see about Miz Gabrielle. Surely she must crave some company, too. ❖

The Banks of the Vistula

Rebecca Lee

I T WAS DARK; THE CAMPUS HAD TURNED TO VELVET. I WALKED the brick path to Humanities, which loomed there and seemed to incline towards me, as God does the sinner in the Book of Psalms. It was late on a Friday afternoon, when the air is fertile, about to split and reveal its warm fruit, that gold nucleus of time, the weekend.

Inside, up the stairs, Professor Stasselova's door was open, and he lifted his head. "Oh," he said. "Yes." He coughed, deep in his lungs, which I found stirring, and motioned me in. He had requested this visit earlier in the day, following class. His course was titled Speaking in Tongues: Introductory Linguistics. Stasselova was about fifty-five, and a big man, his torso an almost perfect square. Behind his balding head the blonde architecture of St. Olaf College rose into the cobalt sky. It looked like a rendition of thought itself, rising out of the head in intricate, heartbreaking cornices that become more abstract and complicated as they rise.

I was in my third week of college. I loved every moment of it, every footfall. The students were the same students as in high school, Scandinavian midwesterners like myself, whose fathers were all pastors or some declension thereof—but it was the professors who thrilled me. Most had come from the East Coast, and those ones seemed so fragile and miserable to be in the Midwest.

Occasionally during class, you could see hope rising in them for us, and then they would look like great birds in a difficult landscape, pale and overextended, asking mysterious questions, trying to lead us someplace we could not yet go.

At any rate, I wanted to be noticed by them, to distinguish myself from the ordinary mass of students, and to this end, I had plagiarized my first paper for Stasselova's class. And this was why, I presumed, he had called me to his office.

The paper, which was titled "The Common Harvest," was on the desk between us. I had found it in the basement of the Kierkegaard Library. It was a chapter in an old green cloth book that so small I could palm it. The book had been written in 1945, by a man named Delores Tretsky, and not signed out since 1956. I began to leaf through it, and then crouched down to read. I read for a full hour; I thought it beautiful. I had not once in all my life stopped for even a moment to consider grammar, to wonder how it rose out of history like a wing unfurling.

I had intended to write my own paper, to synthesize, as Stasselova had suggested, my own ideas with the author's, but I simply had nothing to contribute. It seemed even rude to combine this work with my own pale, unemotional ideas. So, I lifted a chapter, only occasionally dimming some passages that were too fine, too blinding.

"This is an extraordinary paper," he said. He was holding his coffee cup over it, and I saw some had already spilled on the page in the form of a small, murky pond.

"Thank you," I said.

"It seemed quite sophisticated. You must not be straight out of high school."

"I am," I said.

"Oh. Well, good for you."

"Thanks."

"You seem fully immersed in a study of oppression. Any reason for this?"

"Well, I do live in the world."

"Yes, that's right. And you say here, a shocking line, that a language must sometimes be repressed, and replaced for the larger good. You believe this?"

"Yes."

"You think that the East Bloc countries should be forced to speak, as you say here, the Mother Tongue?"

Some parts of the paper I had just copied down verbatim, without really understanding, and now I was stuck with them. Now they were my opinions. "Yes," I said.

"You know I am from this region."

"Is that right?"

"From Poland."

"Whereabouts in Poland?" I asked, conversationally.

"The edge of it, the Black Forest, before Russia took it over completely. As a child, we were forced to speak Russian, even in our homes, even when we said goodnight to our mothers as we fell off to sleep."

"Oh my."

"When did you write this?" he asked.

"Last week."

"It reads like it was written fifty years ago. It reads like Soviet propaganda."

"Oh," I said. "I didn't mean it that way."

"Did somebody help you?"

"Actually, yes. Certainly that's all right?"

"Of course, if done properly. Who was it that helped you, a book or a person?"

"My roommate helped me," I said.

"Your roommate. What is her name?"

"Solveig."

"Solveig what?"

"Solveig Juliusson."

"Is she a linguistics scholar?"

"No, just very bright."

"Maybe I can talk to Solveig myself?"

"Unfortunately, you can't."

"Why not?"

"It's complicated."

"In what way?"

"Well, she's stopped eating. She's very thin; her parents were worried so they took her home."

"Where does she live?"

"I don't know."

We both sat silently. Luckily, I had experience lying to my pastor father, and knew it was possible to win even though both parties were aware of the lie. The whole exercise was not a search for truth at all, but rather a test of exterior reserve.

"I'm sure she'll be returning soon," I said. "I'll have her call you."

Stasselova smiled. "Tell her to eat up," he said, his sarcasm curled inside his concern.

"Okay," I said, and got up, hoisted my bag over my shoulder. As I stood I could see the upper edge of the sun, as it fell down off the hill on which St. Olaf was built. I'd never really seen the sun from this angle before, from above as it fell, as it so obviously lit up another part of the world, perhaps even flaming up the sights of Stasselova's precious, oppressed Poland, its black forests and onion-dome churches, its dreamy and violent borders.

*   *   *

My roomate Solveig was permanently tan. She went twice a week to the booth and bleached her hair frequently, so that it looked like radioactive foliage growing out of dark moody sands. Despite all of this, she was very sensible.

"Margaret," she said, when I came in that evening. "The library telephoned to recall a book. They said it was urgent."

I had thought he might check the library. "Okay," I said. As I rifled through the clothes on my closet floor, I decided it would have to be burned. I would finish the book and then I would burn it. But first there was tonight, and I had, that rare thing, a date.

My date was from Stasselova's class. His name was Rolf; he was a junior whose father was a diplomat. He had almost auburn hair that fell to his neckline. He wore, always, long white shirts whose sleeves were just slightly, almost imperceptively puffed at the shoulders, like a little elegant joke, and then very long so they hung over his hands. I thought he was articulate, kind. I had, in an astonished moment, asked him out.

The night was soft, warm. We walked through the tiny town, wandered its thin river. We ate burgers. He spoke of Moscow, where he had lived that summer. I had spent my childhood with a vision of Russia in the distance, an anti-America, a sort of fairytale, intellectual prison, but this was 1986, the beginning of perestroika, of glasnost, and all that was changing. The televisions were showing a country of rain and difficulty and great humility, and long shots of Gorbachev, who was always bowing to sign something or other, whose head bore the mysterious stain of a continent one could almost name, but not quite. I said to Rolf I wanted to go there myself, though it had never occurred to me before that moment. He said, you can if you want. We were in his small iridescent apartment by now. "Or perhaps to Poland," I said, thinking of Stasselova.

"Poland," Rolf said, "Yes. What is left of it, after men like Stasselova."

"What do you mean, men like Stasselova?"

"Soviet puppets."

"Yet he is clearly anti-Soviet," I said.

"Now, yes. Everybody is anti-Soviet now." The sign for the one Japanese restaurant in town cast an orange worldly light into the room, carving Rolf's body into geometric shapes. He took my hand, and it seemed then the whole world had entered his apartment. I found him intelligent, deliberate, high-hearted. "Now," he said, "Is the time to be anti-Soviet."

* * *

On Monday afternoon, in class, Rolf sat across from me. We were all sitting around a conference table, waiting for Stasselova. Rolf smiled. I gave him the peace sign across the table. When I looked back at him, moments later, Rolf's hands were casually laid out on the table, palms down. I saw then, for the first time, that his left hand tapered into only three fingers, which were all fused together to the top knuckle. It looked delicate, surprising. I had not noticed this on our date, and now I wondered if he had purposefully kept me from seeing it, or if I had just somehow missed it. I even, for a brief, confused moment, wondered if it had happened between then and now. Rolf looked me squarely in the eye. I smiled back.

Stasselova then entered the room. In light of my date with Rolf I had almost forgotten my visit with him on Friday afternoon. I'd meant to burn the book over the weekend in the darkness at the ravine, though I dreaded this. My own mother was a librarian, and I knew the vision of her daughter burning a book would have been like a sledgehammer to her kind and literate heart.

That class, it seemed to me that Stasselova was speaking directly to me, still chastising me. His eyes kept resting on me, disapprovingly. "The reason for the sentence is to express the verb—a change, a desire. But the verb cannot stand alone; it needs to be supported, to be realized by a body, and thus the noun. Just as the soul in its trajectory through life needs to be comforted by the body."

The sunrays slanted in on him, bisecting his own soulful body into clean shafts, as Stasselova veered into very interesting territory; "All things in revolution," he said, "in this way, need protection. For instance, when I was your age, my country Poland was annexed by the Soviet Union. We had the choice of joining what was called Berling's Army, or the Polish Wing of the

Russian Army. Many considered it anti-Polish to join the Russian Army, but I believed, as did my comrades, that more could be done through the system, within the support of the system, than without."

He looked at me. I nodded. I was one of those students who nod a lot. His eyes were like brown velvet, under glass. "This is the power of the sentence," he said. "It acts out this drama of control and subversion. The noun always stands for what is, the status quo, and the verb for what might be, the ideal."

Across the table Rolf's damaged hand, spindly and nervy, drummed impatiently on the table top. I could tell he wanted to speak up. Stasselova turned to him. "That was the decision I made," he said, "twenty years ago. Right or wrong, I thought it best at the time. I thought we could do more work for the Polish cause from within the Red Army than from outside it."

Rolf's face was impassive. He looked years older suddenly— austere, cold, priestly. Stasselova turned then to look at me. This was obviously an issue for him, I thought to myself, and I nodded as he continued to speak. I really did feel supportive. Whatever army he thought was best at the time, that was fine with me.

* * *

In the evening I went to the ravine in the elm forest, which lay curled around the hill on which the campus was built. This forest seemed deeply peaceful to me, almost conscious. I didn't know the reason for this at the time, that elms in a forest all spring from a single elm, unlike the wild, proliferating forests of my adolescence, which bred indiscriminately. Rather, this was in fact a single elm, which had divided herself into a forest. It was an individual, with a continuous DNA, in whose midst one could stand and be held.

The ravine cut through like an old emotional wound. I crouched on its banks, glanced through the book one last time. I flicked open my lighter. The book caught instantly. As the flame approached my hand, I arced the book into the murky water. It looked spectacular, a high wing of flame rising from it. Inside, in one of its luminous chapters, I had read that the ability to use language, and the ability to tame fire arose from the same warm, shimmering pool of genes, since in nature they did not appear, one without the other.

As I made my way out of the woods, into the long, silver ditch that lined the highway, I heard about a thousand birds cry, and I craned my neck to see them lighting from the tips of the elms. They looked like ideas would, if released suddenly from the page and given bodies, shocked at how blood actually felt as it ran through the veins, as it sent one wheeling into the west, wings raking, straining against the requirements of such a physical world.

* * *

I returned and found Solveig turning in the lamplight. Her hair was piled on her head, so unnaturally blond it looked ablaze and her face was bronze. She looked one thousand years old. "Some guy called," she said, "Stasselova or something."

He called again that night, at nearly midnight. I thought this unseemly.

"So," he said, "Solveig's back."

"Yes," I said, glancing at her. She was at her mirror, performing some ablution on her face. "She's much better."

"Perhaps the three of us can now meet."

"Oh," I said, "it's too early."

"Too early in what?"

"In her recovery." Solveig wheeled her head around to look at me. I smiled, shrugged.

"I think she'll be okay."

"I'm not so sure."

"Listen," he said, "I'll give you a choice; you can either rewrite the paper in my office, bringing in whatever materials you need, or the three of us can meet together, and clear this up."

"Fine, we'll meet you."

"You know my hours."

"I do," I hung up, and explained to Solveig what had happened—Stasselova's obsession with language and oppression, my plagiarism, the invocation of her name. Solveig nodded and said of course, whatever she could do she would.

When we arrived that Wednesday, the light had already left his office, but was still lingering outside the windows, like the light in fairy tales, rich and creepy.

Solveig was brilliant. Just her posture, as she sat in the spiny chair was enough to initially chasten Stasselova. In her presence, men were driven to politeness, to sincerity, to a kind of deep, internal apology. He thanked her, bowing a little in his desk. "Your work has interested me," he said.

"It is not my work, sir. It's Margaret's. We just discussed together some of the ideas."

"Such as?"

"Well, the necessity of a collective language, a mutual tongue."

"And why's that necessary?" Stasselova leaned back and folded his hands across his vast torso.

"To maintain order," she said. And then the sun fell completely, blowing one last blast of light across the Americas before it settled into what was left of the Soviet Union, and some of that light, a glittery, barely perceptible dust, settled around Solveig's head. She looked like a dominatrix, an intellectual dominatrix, delivering this brutal news.

"And your history in psycholinguistics?" he said.

"I have only my personal history," she said, "The things that have happened to me." I would not have been surprised, at that declaration, if the whole university had folded up, turned to liquid, and flowed away. "Besides," she said, "All the research and work was Margaret's. I saw her working on it, night after night."

"Then Margaret," he turned his gaze on me. "I see you are intimately connected with evolutionary history, as well as Soviet ideology. As well, it appears you've been steeped in a lifetime's study of linguistic psychosocial theory."

"Is it because she's female," Solveig asked, "that she's made to account for every scrap of knowledge?"

"Look," he said, after a long, brutal silence, "I simply want to know from what cesspool these ideas arose. If you got them from a book, I will be relieved, but if these ideas are still floating around in your bloodlines, in your wretched little towns, I want to know."

I was about to cave in. Better a plagiarizer than a fascist, from a tainted bloodline.

"I don't really think you should be talking about our bloodlines," Solveig said, "It's probably not appropriate." She enunciated the word appropriate in such a way that Stasselova flinched, just slightly. Both he and I stared at her. She really was extraordinarily thin. In a certain light she could look shockingly beautiful, but in another, such as the dying one in Stasselova's office, she could look rather threatening. Her contact lenses were the color of a night sky when it is split by lightning. Her genetic information was almost entirely hidden—the color of her hair and eyes and skin, the shape of her body, and this gave her a psychological advantage, of sorts.

Stasselova's lecture on Thursday afternoon was another strange little affair, given as long autumn rays of sun, embroidered by leaves, covered his face and body. He was onto his main obsession again, the verb, specifically the work of the verb in the sentence, and how it relates to the work of a man in the world.

"The revolution takes place from a position of stability, always. The true revolutionary will find his place within the status quo."

"And this is why you joined the Russian Army in attacking your own country?" This was Rolf, startling us all.

"I did not attack my own country," Stasselova said, "Never."

"But you watched as the Nazis attacked it in June of 1941, yes? And used that attack to your own purposes?"

"This night I was there, it's true," he said. "On the banks of the Vistula, and I saw Warsaw burn. And I was wearing the fur hat of Russia, yes. But when I attempted to cross the Vistula, in order to help across those of my countrymen who were escaping, I was brought down, clubbed with a rifle to the back of the head by my general, a Russian."

"That's interesting, because in accounts of the time, you are referred to as a general yourself, General Stasselova, of course."

"Yes, I was a Polish general, though. Certainly you can infer the hierarchy involved?"

"What I can infer," Rolf's voice rose, and then Stasselova's joined in, contrapuntally, "What you can infer," and for a moment it reminded me of those rounds of songs we sang at summer camp, "What you can infer," Stasselova drowned out Rolf, "is that this was an ambiguous time for those of us who were Polish. There is not a way to judge after the fact. Perhaps you think that I should be dead on those banks, making the willows to grow." Stasselova's eyes were shot with the fading light; he squinted at us and looked out the window momentarily. "You will stand there and think maybe certain men in certain times should not choose their own lives, should not want to live." And then he turned away from Rolf. I myself scowled at Rolf. So rude!

"And so I did live," Stasselova said finally, "mostly because I was wearing my Russian hat, made of the fur of ten foxes. It was always Russia that dealt us blows, and it was always Russia that saved us. You see?"

The next day I was with Rolf, in the woods. We were on our stomachs in a clearing, looking to the east, where the rain was stalking us through the trees.

"What I want to know," Rolf was saying, "is why's he always asking for you to see him?"

"Oh," I said. "He thinks I plagiarized that first paper."

"Did you?"

"Not really."

"Why does he think so?"

"Says it smacks of Soviet propaganda."

"Really? Well, he should know."

"I agree with him, that you're judging him from an irrelevant stance." "He was found guilty of treason by his own people, not me, by the Committee for Constitutional Responsibility. Why else would he be here, teaching at some Lutheran college in Minnesota? This is a guy who brought down martial law on his own people, and then we sit here in the afternoon and watch him stalk around in front of us, relating everything he speaks of, comma splices for chrissakes, to his own innocence."

"Yet all sorts of people were found guilty of all sorts of meaningless things by that committee."

"I bet he thinks you're a real dream, this woman willing to absolve the old exterminator of his sins."

"That's insulting," I said. But it was interesting to me, how fond I'd grown of him in his little office, drinking his bitter coffee, night descending into the musky heart of Humanities.

And then the rain was upon us. We could hear it on the tiny ledges of leaves above us, more than feel it. "Let's go," Rolf said, grabbing my hand with his left, damaged hand. The way his hand held mine was alluring; his hand had the nimbus of an idea about it, as if the gene that had sprung this hand had a different world in mind, a better world, where hands had more torque when they grasped each other and people held things differently, as hooks held things, a world where all objects were shaped something like lanterns, and passed on and on.

*　*　*

The next morning was gray, with long, silver streaks of rain. I dragged myself out of the warmth of bed, and put on my rain slicker. It was nine forty-five as I headed toward Stasselova's office.

"Hello," I said, knocking on the open door. "I'm sorry to disturb you outside your office hours." I was shivering; I felt pathetic.

"Margaret," he said, "Hello. Come in." As I sat down, he said, "You've brought with you the smell of rain."

He poured me a cup of coffee in a Styrofoam cup. During our last class I had been so moved by his description of that night on the Vistula that I'd decided to confess. But now I was hesitating. "Could I have some of this cream?" I asked, pointing to a little tin cup of it on his windowsill.

"There it is again," he said, as he reached for the cream.

"There is what again?"

"That little verbal tic of yours."

"I didn't know I had one," I said.

"Oh you do," he said. "Using definite articles where the indefinite would be more expected. It's quite moving."

I had no idea what he was talking about, so stayed silent.

"I noticed it first in class," he said. "You say 'this' instead of 'that'; 'this cream', not 'that cream'. The line a person draws between the things they consider this, and the things they consider that is the perimeter of their sphere of intimacy. You see. Everything inside is 'this', everything inside is close, is intimate. Since you pointed at the cream, and it is farther from you than I am, this suggests that I am inside the things you consider close to you. I'm flattered," he said and handed me the creamer, which was, like him, sweating. What an idea, that one could, by a few words, catch another person in a little grammatical clutch, arrange the objects of the world such that they border the two of you.

"At any rate," he said, "it's fortunate you showed up."

"It is?"

"Yes. I've wanted to ask you something."

"Yes?"

"This spring, the college will hold its annual symposium on language and politics. I thought you might present your paper. Usually one of the upperclassmen does this, but I thought your paper might be the more appropriate."

"I thought you hated my paper."

"I do."

"Oh."

"So you'll do it."

"I'll think about it," I said. He nodded and smiled, as if it were settled. The rain was suddenly coming down very hard. It was loud, and we were silent for a few moments, listening. I stared out the window beyond his head, which was blurry with water, so that the turrets of campus looked like a hallucination, like some shadow world looming back there, in his unconscious.

"This rain," he said then, in a quiet, astonished voice, and this word, this, entered me as it was meant to—quietly, with a sharp tip, but then, like an arrowhead, widening and widening, until it included the whole landscape around us.

*　　*　　*

The rain turned to snow, and winter settled on our campus. The face of nature turned away—beautiful and distracted. After Christmas at home (where I received my report card, a tiny slip of paper that seemed to have flown across the snows to deliver me my A in Stasselova's class), I hunkered down in my dorm for the month of January, and barely emerged. The dorm in which most of us freshman girls lived was the elaborate, dark Agnes Mellby Hall, named after the formidable virgin whose picture hung over the fireplace in our lounge.

As winter crept over us, the sun falling by three-thirty on the darkest afternoons, we retired earlier and earlier to Mellby. Every night in that winter, in which most of us were nineteen, was a slumber party in the main sitting room, amongst its ornate furnishings, which all had the paws of beasts where they touched the floor. There, nightly, we ate like Romans, but childish foods— popcorn and pizza and ice cream—most of us spiraling downstairs now and then to throw up in the one private bathroom.

On one of those nights, I was reading a book in the lounge when I received a phone call from Solveig, who was down at a house party in town, and wanted me to come help her home. She wasn't completely drunk, but calculated that she would be in about forty-five minutes. Her body was like a tract of nature that she understood perfectly—a constellation whose movement across the night sky she could predict, or a gathering storm, or maybe, more accurately, a sparkling stream of elements into which she introduced alcohol with such careful calibration that her blood flowed exactly as she desired, uphill and down, intersecting precisely, chemically, with time and fertility. Solveig did not stay at the dorm with us much, but rather ran with an older pack of girls, feminists mostly, who that winter happened to be involved in a series of protests, romantic insurrections, against the president of the college, who was clearly terrified of them.

About ten minutes before I was to leave, Stasselova appeared in the doorway of the sitting room. I had not seen him in over a month, since the last day of class, but he had called a few times. I had not returned his calls, in the hopes that he would forget me for the symposium. But here he was, wearing a long gray coat over his bulkiness. His head looked huge, the bones so widely spaced, like the architecture of some grand civic building.

The look in his eyes caused me to look out across the room and try to see what he was seeing—perhaps some debauched canvas of absolute female repose—girls lying everywhere in various modes of pajamas and sweats, surrounded by vast quantities of food and books. Some girls, and even I found this a bit creepy, had stuffed animals that they carried with them to the sitting room at night. I happened to be sitting above the fray, straddling a piano bench, with a book spread in front of me, but almost everybody else was lying about, on their backs with their feet propped on the couch, or stretched up in the air in weird hyper-extended angles, with extremities cast about. We were Lutherans, after all, and unlike the more promiscuous Catholic girls across the river, at Carleton College, we were losing our innocence right here, amongst ourselves. It was being taken from us physically, and we were just relaxing until it fell away completely.

Stasselova, in spite of all he'd seen in his life, which I'd gleaned from what he said in class—the corpulent Goerring marching through his forest, marking off Nazi territory, and later Stalin's horses, breaking through the same woods, heralding the swath that would now be Soviet—still managed to look a little scared as he peered into our sitting room, eventually lifting a hand to wave at me.

I got up, approached him. "Hey," I said.

"Hello, how are you, Margaret?"

"It's good to see you. Thanks for the A."

"You deserved it. Listen, I have something for you," he said, mildly gesturing for us to leave the doorway, since everybody was looking at us

"Great," I said, "But you know, right now, I need to walk downtown to pick up Solveig at a house party."

"Excellent," he said, "I'll walk you."

"Oh. Okay."

I got my jacket and the two of us stepped into the night. The snow had arranged itself in curling waves on the Mellby lawn, and stuck in it were hundreds of silver forks which the freshman boys had, in a flood of early evening testosterone, placed in the earth, a gesture appropriate to their sexual frustration, and also their faith in the future. As Stasselova and I stepped through them, they looked spooky and lovely, like tiny silver grave sights in the snow. As we tread across campus, Stasselova produced a golden brochure from his pocket and handed it to me. On the front it said, in emerald green letters, 9th Annual Symposium on Language and Politics. Inside, there was my name under keynote student speaker. It said, Margaret Weatherford, "The Common Harvest." I stopped walking. We paused there, at the top of the stairs which floated down, off the campus, into the town. I felt extremely, inordinately proud. Some winter lightning, a couple of great wings of it, flashed in the north. Stasselova looked paternal, grand.

* * *

The air at the party was beery and wildish and the house itself seemed the product of a drunken, adolescent mind—its many random rooms, and slanting floors. We could not spot Solvieg at first, so Stasselova and I waited quietly in the hallway until a guy in a baseball cap came lurching toward us, shouting in a friendly way, over the music, that we could buy a plastic glass for the keg for two dollars apiece. Stasselova paid him and then threaded through the crowd, gracefully for such a large man, to stand in the keg line. I watched him as he patiently stood there, the snowflakes melting on his dark shoulders.

And then Rolf was on my arm. "What on earth?" he said. "Why are you here? I thought you hated these parties." He'd been dancing, it seemed. He was soaked in sweat, his hair curling up at his neck.

I pointed to Stasselova.

"No kidding," Rolf said.

"He showed up at my dorm as I was leaving to get Solveig."

"He came to Mellby?"

"Yes."

"God, look at him. I bet they had a nickname for him, like the Circusman or something. All those old fascists had cheery nicknames."

Stasselova was now walking towards us. Behind him the picture window revealed a nearly black sky, with pretty crystalline stars around. He looked like a dream one might have in childhood. "He is not a fascist," I said, quietly.

"Professor!" Rolf raised his glass.

"Rolf, yes, how are you?"

"This is a wonderful party," Stasselova said, and it actually was. Sometimes these parties could seem deeply cozy, their wildness and noise a reeling affirmation against the formless, white midwestern winter surrounding us.

He handed me a beer. "So," he said, rather formally, lifting his glass. "To youth."

"To experience, " Rolf smiled, lifted his cup.

"To the party," Stasselova looked pleased, his eyes shining from the soft lamplight.

"The Party?" Rolf raised an eyebrow.

"This party," Stasselova said forcefully, cheerfully.

"And to the Committee," Rolf said.

"The Committee?"

"The Committee for Constitutional Responsibility."

In one of Stasselova's lectures he had taken great pains to explain to us that language did not describe events, it handled them, as a hand handles an object, and that in this way, language made the world happen under its supervision. And I could see Rolf had taken this to heart, and was making lurching attempts in this direction.

Mercifully, Solveig appeared. Her drunkeness and her dignity had synergized into something quite spectacular, an inner recklessness accompanied by great external restraint. Her hair looked the color of heat, bright white. She was wearing newly cut-off jeans and was holding the disassociated pant legs in her hand, absently.

"The professor," she said, when she saw Stasselova. "The professor of oppression."

"Hello, Solveig."

"So you came," she said, as if this had been the plan all along.

"Yes. It's nice to see you again."

"You as well," she said, "Why are you here?"

The whole scene looked deeply romantic to me. "To take you home," he said.

"Home?" she said, as if this were the most elegant and promising word in the language. "Yours or mine?"

"Yours, of course. Yours and Margaret's."

"Where is your home again?" she asked. Her eyes were glimmering with complexity, like something that is given the human after evolution, as a gift.

"I live downtown," he said.

"No, your real home. Your homeland."

He paused. "I am from Poland," he said finally.

"Then there. Let's go there. I have always wanted to go to Poland."

Stasselova smiled. "Perhaps you would like it there."

"I have always wanted to see Wenseslaus Square."

"Well, that is nearby."

"Excellent, let us go." And Solveig swung open the front door, walked into the snow, in her shorts and T-shirt. I kissed Rolf goodbye, and Stasselova and I followed her.

Once outside, Stasselova took off his coat and hung it around Solveig. Underneath his coat he was wearing a dark jacket and tie. It looked sweet, made me think you could keep undressing him, finding darker and darker suits underneath.

Solveig was walking before us on the narrow sidewalk. Above her on the hill hovered Humanities—great, intelligent, alight. She reached in her pocket and pulled out, to my astonishment, a fur hat. The hat! The kopek. The wind lifted, and the trees shook off a little of their silver snow, to get a better look. Humanities leaned over us, interested in its loving but secular way. I felt as sure as those archeologists who discover a single bone, and can then hypothesize the entire animal. Solveig placed it on her head, and turned to vamp for a moment, opening and closing the coat, then raising her arms in an exaggerated gesture of beauty above her head. She looked like some stirring, turning simulacrum of communist and capitalist ideas. As she was doing this, we passed by the president's house. It was an old-fashioned house, with high turrets, and then a bizarre modern wing hanging off one end of it. Solveig studied it for a moment as she walked, and then suddenly shouted into the cold night, "Motherfucker."

Stasselova looked as if he'd been clubbed again in the back of the head, but kept walking. He pretended nothing had happened, didn't even turn his head to look at the house, but when I turned to him I saw his eyes water, and his face stiffen with shock. I said, "Oh," quietly, and grabbed his hand for one moment to comfort him, to let him know everything was under control, that this was Minnesota and there would be no implications. Look, the president's house is still dark as death, the moon is still high, the snow sparkling everywhere.

His hand was extraordinarily big. After holding Rolf's hand for the last few months, Stasselova's more ordinary hand felt strange, almost mutant, its five splayed and independent fingers.

*   *   *

The next night in the cafeteria, over a grizzly and neon dish called Festival Rice, I told Rolf about the hat. "I saw the hat," I said.

A freshman across the cafeteria stood just then and shouted, in what was a St. Olaf tradition, "I want a standing ovation." The entire room stood and erupted into wild applause and hooting. Rolf and I stood as well, and as we clapped I leaned over to yell, "He's been telling the truth, about that night overlooking Warsaw; I saw the hat he was wearing."

"What does that mean? That means nothing. I have a fur hat."

"No," I said. "It was this big Russian hat. You should have seen it. This big beautiful Russian hat. Solveig put it on. It saved his life."

Rolf didn't even try to object, just kind of gasped, as if it hurt the great gears of logic in his brain to even pass this syllogism through. We were still standing, applauding. I couldn't help but think of something Stasselova had said in class, that in rallies for Stalin, when he spoke to crowds over loudspeakers, one could be shot for being the first to stop clapping.

*   *   *

I avoided my paper for the next month or so, until spring crashed in huge warm waves and I finally sought it out, sunk in its darkened drawer. It was a horrible surprise. I was not any more of a scholar, of course, than five months earlier, when I'd plagiarized it, but my eyes had now passed over Marx and a biography of Stalin (microphones lodged in eyeglasses, streams of censors on their way to work, the bloody corpses radiating out of Moscow) as well as the gentle Bonhoeffer. Almost miraculously, I had passed over that invisible line, beyond which people turn into actual readers, when they start to hear the voice of the writer as clearly as in a conversation. "Language," Tretsky had written, "is essentially a coercive act, and in the case of Eastern Europe must be used as a tool to garden collective hopes and aspirations."

As I read it, with Solveig napping at the other end of the couch, I felt a thick dread forming. Tretsky, with his suggestions of annexations and worse, of solutions, seemed to be reaching right off the page; his long, thin hand grasping me by the shirt. And I could almost hear the wild mazurka, as Stasselova had described it, fading, the cabarets closing down, the music turning into a chant, the boot heels falling, the language fortifying itself, becoming a stronghold—a fixed, unchanging system, as the paper said, a moral framework.

Almost immediately I was on my way to Stasselova's office, but not before my mother could call. The golden brochures had gotten out in the mail. "Sweetie!" she said, "what's this? Keynote speaker? Your father and I are beside ourselves. Good night!" She always exclaimed "good night" at times of great happiness, one of those lovely misfirings in the brain left over from childhood, a moment from deep in it when she had experienced great joy, perhaps, as somebody shouted good night from a far window, a sweet rag of long ago waving in the brain. I could not dissuade her from coming, and as I fled the dorm, into the rare, hybrid air of early April, I was wishing for those bad, indifferent parents who had no real interest in their children's lives.

The earth under my feet as I went to him was very sticky, almost lugubrious, like the earth one sometimes encounters in dreams. Stasselova was there, as always. He seemed pleased to see me. I sat down, and said, "You know, I was thinking that maybe somebody else could take my place at the symposium. As I reread my paper I realized it isn't really what I meant to say, at all."

"Oh," he said, "Of course you can deliver it. I would not abandon you at a moment like this."

"Really, I wouldn't take it as abandonment."

"I would not leave you in the lurch," he said, "I promise."

I felt myself being carried, mysteriously, into the doomed symposium, despite my resolve on the way over to back out at all costs. It is almost impossible to win an argument against somebody with an early training in propaganda. I had to resort finally to the truth, that rinky-dink little boat in the great sea of persuasion. "See, I didn't really write the paper myself."

"Well, every thinker builds an idea on the backs of those before him, or her, in your case," he smiled at this. His teeth were very square, and humble, with small gaps in between each one. I could see that Stasselova was no longer after a confession. I was more valuable if I contained these ideas. Probably he'd been looking, subconsciously, for me ever since he'd lain on the muddy banks of the Vistula, Warsaw flaming across the waters. He could see within me all of his failed ideals, the ugliness of his former beliefs contained in a benign vessel, a girl, high on a religious hill in the Midwest. Somebody he might oppose, and in this way absolve himself. He smiled. I could feel myself as indispensible in the organization of his psyche. Behind his head, in the winter sunset, the sun wasn't falling, only receding further and further.

The days before the symposium unfurled as the days before a wedding one dreads—both endless and accelerated, the sky filling with her springtime events—ravishing sun, great winds, and eccentric, green storms that lifted everybody's attention. And then the weekend of the symposium was upon us, the Saturday of my speech rising in the east. I awoke early, and fled the dorm to practice my paper on the red steps of Humanities, in whose auditorium my talk was to occur. Solveig was still sleeping, hungover from the night before. I'd been with her for the first part of it, watched her pursue a man she'd discovered—a graduate student, actually, in town for the symposium. I had thought him a bit of a bore, but I trusted Solveig's judgement on the affair. She approached men with stealth and insight, her vision driving into those truer, more isolated stretches of personality.

I had practiced the paper countless times, and revised it, attempting to excise the most offensive lines without gutting the paper entirely, and thus disappointing Stasselova. I was still, that morning, debating over the line, *If there could be a common language, a single human tongue, perhaps then a single flag may unfurl over the excellent earth, one nation of like and companion souls.* Reading it now I had a faint memory of my earlier enthusiasm for this paper, its surface promise, its murderous innocence. Remembering this, I looked out, over the excellent earth, at the town down the hill. And there, as in every view, was a tiny, gothic graveyard which looked so peaceful, everything still and settled finally under the gnarled, knotty, nearly human arms of apple trees. There were not apples yet, of course: they were making their way down the bough, still liquid or whatever they are before birth. At the sight of graves I couldn't help but think of Tretsky, my ghost writer, in his dark suit under the earth, delighted and preparing, thanks to me, for his one last gasp.

By noon, the auditorium had filled with a crowd of about two hundred, mostly graduate students and professors from around the midwest, as well as Rolf and Solveig, who sat together, and two rows behind them, my long-suffering parents, flushed with pride. I sat on a slight stage at the front of the room alone, staring out at the auditorium, which was named Luther. It had wooden walls and was extremely tall; it seemed humble and a little awkward in that way the tall can seem. The windows stretched its full height, so that one could see the swell of earth on which Humanities was built, and then above all manner of weather, which this afternoon was running to rain. In front of these windows stood the reformed genius of martial law himself, the master of ceremonies, Stasselova. Behind him were maple trees, with small green leaves waving. He had always insisted in class that language, as it rises in the mind, looks like a tree branching. From finity to infinity. *Let every voice cry out!* He'd once said this, kind of absently, and water had come to his eyes, not exactly tears, just a rising of the body's water into one's line of sight.

After he introduced me, I stood in front of the crowd, my larynx rising quite against my will, and delivered my paper. I tried to speak each word as a discrete item, in order to persuade the audience not to synthesize them into meaning. But when I lifted my head to look out at the audience, I could see they were doing just that. When I got to the part where I said the individual did not exist—*merely shafts of light lost, redemptively, in the greater light of the state*—I saw Rolf bow his head, and rake his otherwordly hand through his hair. . . . *And if force is required to forge a singular and mutual grammar, then it is our sacred duty to hasten the birthpangs.* I could hear, even from this distance, Stasselova breathing, and the sound of blood running through him, like a quiet but rushing stream.

And then my parents. As the speech wore on—harmony, force, flowering, blood—I could see that the very elegant parental machinery they had designed over the years, which sought always to translate my deeds into something lovely, light-bearing, full of promise—was spinning a little on its wheels. Only Solveig, that *apparatchik* of friendship, maintained her confidence in me. Even hungover, her posture suggested a perfect alignment between heaven and earth. She kept nodding, encouraging me.

I waited the entire speech for Stasselova to leap forward and confront me, to reassert his innocence in opposition to me, but he did not, even when I reached the end. He stood and watched as everybody clapped in bewilderment, and a flushed floral insignia rose on his cheeks. I had come to love his wide, excited face, the old Circusman. He smiled at me. He was my teacher, and he had wrapped himself, his elaborate historical self into this package, and stood in front of the high windows, to teach me my little lesson, which turned out not to be about Poland, or fascism, or war, borderlines, passion, or loyalty, but just about the sentence;

the importance of; the sweetness of. And I did long for it, to say one true sentence of my own, to leap into the subject, that sturdy vessel travelling upstream through the axonal predicate, into what is possible, into the object which is all possibility, into what little we know of the future, of eternity, the light of which, incidentally, was streaming in on us just then through the high windows. Above Stasselova's head the storm clouds were dispersing, as if frightened by some impending goodwill, and I could see the birds were out again, forming into that familiar pointy hieroglyph, as they're told to do from deep within. ❖

True Love in the Gilded Age

Robert Siegel

H E HAD LOVED HER IN SECRET FOR MORE THAN A decade, but there was no way to declare his feelings: too much was riding on their shared enterprise. Verena was the greatest spirit medium in the country, and Leopold Swann was her discoverer, the man who had made her famous.

He knew she was extraordinary from the moment he set eyes upon her at Mrs. Potter's spirit circle. She sat across the table from him in the dimly lit room, vibrant with grief over her lost husband. He could feel a strange charge pass through the circle of bodies and into the dry, twitchy hands he gripped in his. The power, whatever it was, originated in her eyes, those enormous magnetic orbs that seemed to carry a world of suffering inside them.

And then suddenly those eyes closed, her mouth went slack, her back arched, her chest began to heave, and a voice came out from the deepest part of her throat, rich and low as the notes of a cello. It was her spirit control, her husband, speaking from the other side. "My dearest little pussycat," it said, "my dearest little hummingbird. I am right here behind you, above you, inside you, though you cannot see."

It was the murmur of a man whispering in a woman's ear. The sitters leaned forward, faces twisted in exaltation at this purest music of loss. Leopold Swann sat very still, his heart slapping against the prison of his chest. He did not believe in spirits—he was a professional showman, after all—but he could not stop himself from believing in her.

He paid a call the next day and offered his guidance. She was worth money, of course, a great deal of money, but that was not really the point. He wanted to teach her, to make her into the splendid thing he could see so clearly in his mind. And so he showed her how to walk into a room as if she were a priestess, and how to keep one half of herself always out of sight, a mystery. Most importantly, he taught her to give the sitters just enough but not all: a brief taste of the loved one and then silence—for it was the silence, not the love, that made them return.

Only once did he reach out and place his hand on hers; she drew it away and then went over to a table to adjust some roses in a vase. Too soon, he told himself. Be patient. The husband, still. But he never tried again; there was too much to do, and once they were successful, too much at stake. If there were certain limits, he told himself, if he could not possess her completely, as a husband possesses a wife, he was nevertheless her most intimate companion, the one she could not live without. He saw her every day, chose her clothes and her perfume, dictated the way she wore her hair, read to her on those nights she was too frail to work.

And then one evening they were drinking coffee in her parlor when she told him that she had decided to quit. "No more weeping widows," she said. "No more crying mothers."

"No more money," he reminded her, and took a sip of his coffee. He was not alarmed; it was just one of her passing irritations, and soothing her nerves had become part of his job.

"I have enough," she said.

"And what about your husband?" Leopold and the dead man had become allies of late, their jealousies a thing of the past.

"Could you really abandon him like that? He would be alone without you."

A queer look passed over her face. "Of course, my feelings for him will not change." She stood up, turned to the mantle and made herself busy with a little porcelain figurine, a dancing bear. "Leopold, I have decided to marry again."

He felt something rushing inside him, filling him—the emptiness that the sitters brought to the spirit table, that turned them into such desperate and ridiculous fools. He rose slowly, unsteadily, as if in the dark. "Marry?" he asked. "Who?"

She did not turn around. "I'm sorry, Leopold, but I know you will get along fine without me."

* * *

A moment later, Leopold Swann was out on the street, walking downtown, block after block, oblivious to the changing scenery, until finally he noticed that they were lighting the streetlamps. He had made it all the way to Union Square, with its theaters, music halls, placards and billboards, electric lights and noise. Another block and the sidewalk grew crowded; the press of bodies made him realize how tired he was—exhausted, near toppling.

He stopped in front of one of the vaudeville houses, and without even glancing at the placard bought a ticket, climbing the stairs up to the balcony. He had arrived just at the change of acts: a troop of toy poodles was taking the stage—little dogs with their sleek woolen bodies and frothy heads. Leopold watched with a bitter sort of amusement. Had not Verena also seemed like a little poodle? Eager to please, quick to snap, in need of care. He watched as the dogs began their performance, leaping through hoops and over sticks, climbing ladders, diving off ledges, crossing paths in midair—a chain of acrobatic cause and effect. They seemed to know exactly what to do. Their trainer, a woman in dancer's tights and a gauzy tulle skirt, merely lifted her baton and off they went, like thoughts.

There had been moments just like that with Verena—moments of perfect accord, when a significant glance from him, or a press of the foot, or a squeeze of the hand, would launch her into the most thrilling acts of spirit ventriloquism he had ever witnessed. Someone would spring up from the table and yell, "Aunt Clara!" or "Cousin Jeb!" and the others would twist into postures of fear and awe and the deepest, truest satisfaction. At such times there was no Verena, no Leopold—only one perfect person in perfect command of the world.

Leopold sat forward in his seat now, interested in spite of himself. For their finale, the dogs wore human dress and sat at a table laid out with silver and crystal. Their trainer raised her baton, and they passed serving dishes to one another, ladled soup into bowls. Leopold followed one dog in particular, a little gray poodle in a frilly white gown. She bent her head to her tablemate on the left, then to her tablemate on the right, and then wagged her head up and down. All I wanted to do was help her achieve her true potential, thought Leopold. It would have saved us both. He stared at the dog trainer, who stood serenely to one side, and felt so deeply envious he could have murdered her.

* * *

He spent the next day burning anything he owned that was connected to Verena: letters, notebooks, photographs, posters and handbills, souvenirs of their travels spreading the spiritualist message. Maisie, his maid and sometime-assistant, hid in her room upstairs, coming out only to make him meals he did not eat. He finally fell asleep on the buffalo skin spread in front of the hearth, poker still in hand.

The next day, he dressed and went out, testing the world again, like a man with a hangover, sensitive to light and noise. He walked around Washington Square, and then the adjoining streets, pretending to window shop while thinking about the possibilities before him. If he wanted to stay in the spirit game, there was always Maisie. She knew a great deal already; it would not take much to train her to fill Verena's role. She would be pliant, easy to work with. There would be none of Verena's histrionics, her nervous difficulties. And he sensed a personal interest in him that would give him useful leverage, a means to control and shape her. Nevertheless, the idea did not appeal to him. Maisie did not have Verena's extraordinary talents, and would never be as good a medium. Leopold could not bear the idea that his life after Verena would be anything less brilliant than his life with her.

He stopped in at a bookseller's, more for the soothing darkness of the shop than for the books, and spent twenty minutes or so wandering up and down the narrow aisles, running a gloved finger over the spines, until one of the volumes happened to catch his attention. It was Pinchbeck's The Expositor: or Many Mysteries Unraveled—a classic treatise on the arts of magic and deception. He pulled it out and began leafing through it, browsing from magic tricks to mind reading acts to the training of "learned" animals—which reminded him of the toy poodles he had seen the week before, performing in such perfect unison, as in a lovely dream. Perhaps for that reason he bought it, thinking it might provide some distraction.

It did not work, of course. Each time he sat down with it, his thoughts drifted back to Verena. He remembered the exquisite frustration of sitting beside her on the couch, unable to reach over and take her hand, remembered the lovely pain of reading to her late into the night, when her nerves made it impossible for her to sleep. What a fool he had been—he, whose profession was the fooling of others!

It was in fact weeks till his mind quieted enough for him to look at Pinchbeck's treatise, but what he discovered was his liberation, and he read through the night. Far more than a manual on how to train animals, what Pinchbeck offered was a book of practical philosophy on the nature of love. It started from the principle that the hidden wish of all animals is a state of selfless devotion, and that it is by granting this wish that the animal trainer gains power over the animal. It went on to show how this power could then be used to make animals perform extraordinary feats—danc-ing, acrobatics, even arithmetic—to the point that they seemed almost to pass from the bestial realm to the human.

Selfless devotion! Verena had seemed selfless to him too. She had hung on his every word, asked only to become whatever he most wanted her to be—but then she had the natural duplicity of the human species.

He rose and looked out the window, now lit by dawn. He would never allow another woman to fool him like that.

* * *

There was no clear moment when Leopold decided to train a performing animal. He simply began visiting the various exot-ic animal dealers in the city, looking over pythons, cockatoos, hawks, vultures, ferrets and iguanas—even a seal with the face of a tragedienne. But when he came across the small brown she-bear cub he knew he had found the animal he would train. It was like a child transmogrified into something dangerous, with sharp little teeth and a blunt wet nose, and paws that were almost the wish for hands.

Leopold built a den for the bear cub in the cellar, and let it travel up the stairs and into the parlor as it chose. It slunk out on all fours that very first evening, head down, shoulder bones working one at a time beneath its loose coat of fur. The click of its toenails was light and strangely musical. It breathed with great concentration, its mouth open and loose black lips drooping like a band of India rubber, its babyish canines exposed to the air. It took the piece of meat Leopold offered and began to chew. Leo-pold stroked its back. "I am going to teach you some tricks," he told it. "Some very simple tricks. When you do them right you will be rewarded, and when you do them wrong you will be pun-ished."

Leopold had always known that his primary asset in life was his voice. Whether he was selling life after death or a cure for cancer, it had fired the desire of his audience. Verena too had felt its power. But he had never known anyone to listen like the bear listened, its nose in the air and black lips open, saliva falling in strings. It mattered not at all whether Swann read the paper or recited a nursery rhyme—it pulled the sound deep within itself like cigarette smoke. Leopold's voice was its religion and its music.

He began introducing the bear to the large alphabet cards that would be the learned animal act's most important stage properties. He arranged the cards in a semi-circle on the floor of the parlor, and led the bear to first one and then another, holding out a piece of sausage as a reward. Crawling on all fours, he demonstrated how to pick the cards up and hold them in the mouth without dropping them. The bear quickly mastered the technique. Soon, Leopold could simply point to the card he wanted it to lift, and eventually, he found that Pinchbeck had been right:

Intimacy will make speech and even gesture superfluous; you may relinquish them by degrees. Once that is done, the animal will appear to read your very thoughts. The way in which you stand will arise naturally from your anxiety and will determine the card to your pupil. Nothing else is needed.

* * *

Based on this wordless communion, Leopold taught the bear to spell—or rather, to simulate the act of spelling, picking up the alphabet cards he wanted it to pick up, yet with an air of independence and purpose. On the same principle, he taught it to do arithmetical calculations, using a set of numbered cards. He would read out the problem, the bear would pause as if calculating, and then pick up the card bearing the correct answer. From there it was a short step to factual questions of the sort that could be answered with a simple YES or NO—these two words imprinted on cards for that purpose. All these tricks depended on the same basic precept given by Pinchbeck: "Nothing can be done but her master must first know what he wants. Once her master knows, the animal will be ruled by his unspoken wishes."

Thinking it over, he decided to present the bear as a mind-reading act. It was a simple adjustment to make: Leopold already knew the basic techniques required of a mind reader—how to ask leading questions, how to read faces for hot and cold, true and false. As long as he himself could figure out the correct answer, the bear was assured of picking the right cards.

He began using Maisie in their practice sessions. Unflappable Maisie, who had rattled furniture, impersonated spirits, and otherwise helped at the séances, nevertheless had trouble with the bear. She stiffened as it approached and looked terrified. "Don't be ridiculous," Leopold scolded. "It's perfectly safe."

"It doesn't like me," said Maisie, her eyes fixed on the bear.

"That's because it knows you're afraid."

Maisie nodded at the logic of this. "I'm afraid because it wants to hurt me."

"Nonsense. This bear loves people." Leopold placed one hand atop Maisie's head, and the other on his own brow, and then called out, "Bear, tell us the woman's name!"

The bear sidled up close, clearly enjoying Maisie's discomfort. Hot meaty breath and a sharp nervous smell: the impression was not of an animal so much as a person gone terribly wrong. It held its wet nose just inches from her stomach, drawing short noisy sips of air, like an asthmatic. Its wet tongue lolled between its canines. Then, almost reluctantly, it moved off toward the semicircle of alphabet cards, its black nails clicking on the wooden floor. There was a preening feminine self-consciousness about its movements, as if it were aware of Leopold's gaze. It leaned over the oversized cards, staring nearsightedly with first one eye then the other. Finally it chose the M, lifting it in its mouth and carrying it over to Leopold's feet, to be followed in turn by the other letters, A, I, S, I, E.

"You see?" asked Leopold. "Just like Pinchbeck says. The bear has lived with us here like a normal human child. She knows nothing else. I am her master, I feed her, I am everything to her."

"It likes you too much," said Maisie.

Leopold laughed. "There's no such thing as too much! I am her father and her husband. She watches me like a farmer watches the sky. She cannot really spell, but she can read my face, my hands, the way I stand. I am her holy book, and—" he began to coo—"she is my sweet little girl." He popped a plug of sausage into her mouth, and then rubbed vigorously behind her ear. The bear's mouth snapped shut and she emitted a low obscene moan.

* * *

It was not hard getting a booking at one of the top houses on Union Square: traditionally, circus bears did nothing but the simplest of tricks, dancing and balancing on top of a medicine ball. They wore a muzzle and were led on a leash. But Leopold's bear was learned: it could communicate, display scholarship on most any subject, and most importantly, it could read minds. They were given the featured slot and top billing on the program.

Backstage in his dressing room, Leopold straightened his tie in the mirror and adjusted his top hat. He remembered how he had had to wrestle the sherry bottle away from Verena before séances, and how he had had to talk her through her deep-breathing exercises. Now he wondered if she had been doing him an inadvertent service. As long as she was frightened, he did not have to be. He could busy himself with taking care of her—with despising her, actually. But now that he was the only one around, he seemed to have inherited her role as the frightened one.

He found it odd that he was thinking about Verena, since he had all but forgotten her ever since he had bought the bear. There had been the late-night walks past her townhouse, of course, but those were something different, a kind of lash he used to intensify his dedication to the austerities of animal showmanship. There was no longer any need for that kind of motivational trickery. In just a few minutes he would be escorting the bear out on stage, and then everything in his life would change forever. He would be a public figure in his own right, free of any need for Verena or the spirits, or even the bear, for that matter. What he had achieved with this bear would be reproducible with any other bear—that was the beauty of the thing. The creature was just a tool. The skill, the knowledge, the vital force were all his own.

It was time; he led the bear from the dressing room to their place in the wings. There was a short wait for their cue, and then they were through the curtain. The footlights made it impossible to see the audience, but he could feel its presence just beyond the edge of visibility, as shapeless and powerful as the ocean at night, murmuring, rustling, whispering, breathing. He put the bear through her paces, forgetting for moments at a time that Verena might conceivably be out there in the audience, watching. The spelling earned polite applause; the mathematics and geography a little more. His request for a volunteer brought a little girl up from her seat to stand beside him. He whispered in her ear and bent down so she could whisper back in his. He placed one hand atop her head, pressed the other to his brow, and called out, "Madame Brunus, tell us the child's name!"

The bear wore a blue satin cape imprinted with star and crescent moon, eyeball and pyramid. Leopold had brushed silver dust into her thick brown coat, and it shone in the light, making her look like a creature from another planet. She circled the alphabet cards laid out on the floor of the stage till she came to the R, picked it up and carried it over to the little girl, who hung it on the board Leopold kept alongside. Next, in quick succession, she brought an O, S and E. "Is your name Rose, child?" asked Leopold. He held the little girl aloft in his arms so the audience could hear her shy assent.

Almost immediately, audience members were vying to ask questions about the future. The questions would come out of the darkness and Leopold would repeat them for the bear. "Will the gentleman get a promotion at work?" "Will the young lady marry her beau?" Madame Brunus would gaze into an enormous crystal ball—lit from within—and then choose one of the three cards laid out before her: YES, NO and BEWARE. Each answer met with great applause, and at the end of the show the audience pounded the floor with its feet, demanding more.

Leopold stood next to the bear, taking elaborate bows. "They love us!" he whispered into its ear, hoarse with excitement, and then broke off to bow again, grinning as if he had just won the entire world with a single roll of the dice. "The stupid fools! They see magic, a miracle, but what is a miracle? Anything where the mechanism is not explained. But there is always a mechanism. Always."

The clapping intensified. He began blowing kisses to the audience, the bear doing likewise beside him, as she had been taught—one ungainly paw rising to its snout and then out and away. Leopold's thoughts raced. He had been a fool to admire Verena, as gullible as the audience shouting its questions to the bear. Verena was an illusion, just like Madame Brunus. She was a set of attitudes and gestures, a way of wearing a dress, a perfume, a manner of talking—all of which, taken together, created a certain intoxicating effect he knew as Verena. That's all she was, an effect, just as the light from an incandescent lamp was an effect.

"The world is like a gigantic machine, with interlocking wheels and gears, one fitting inside the other," he told the bear, still blowing kisses this way and that. "You are forced by your very nature to love me, and I allow you to do so. I twitch the corners of my mouth, you pick a card, and the audience is amazed. Verena is just the same. Her choices are only the appearance of choices. She is a slave, and doesn't even know it."

It seemed like the applause would never end, but slowly it began to die away. They took one last bow together, and then the curtain closed. ❖

CREATIVE NONFICTION
PROCESS

CREATIVE RESEARCH

Philip Furia

S IR PHILIP SIDNEY ADVISED POETS, "LOOK IN THY HEART and write," but writers, including poets, also look in libraries, historical archives, and, nowadays, in the vast resources of information on the Internet. Pulitzer Prize–winning poet Philip Levine, who was visiting writer-in-residence at UNCW in 1997, wrote one of his greatest poems, "The Mercy," about his grandmother's childhood voyage to America and of a kind sailor who gave her the first orange she had ever tasted. Levine could have written the poem solely based on his grandmother's memory, but instead he spent days at the New York Public Library doing research on the *Mercy,* the ship that brought his grandmother to America:

> "The Mercy," I read on the yellowing pages of a book
> I located in a windowless room of the library
> on 42nd Street, sat thirty-one days
> offshore in quarantine before the passengers
> disembarked. There a story ends. Other ships
> arrived, "Tancred" out of Glasgow, "The Neptune"
> registered as Danish, "Umberto IV,"
> the list goes on for pages.

So not only had his grandmother had to endure an ocean crossing but then another month on the ship amid a cholera epidemic. That research enabled Levine to set his grandmother's story—and the kindness of the sailor—against the historical background of the ordeal of American immigration.

Sometimes research can be done in front of your computer. When Wendy Brenner saw the phrase, "Much is expected of the Merlot grape" in a magazine, it struck her that it could be the basis of a witty story about "great expectations." After a few hours of Internet research, she had enough information about Merlot grapes—and wine—to fill her story with telling detail.

At other times, a writer's research can be as demanding as a scholar's. Philip Gerard had to spend years researching *Cape Fear Rising,* his novel about the 1898 assault by white supremacists upon Wilmington's black population. Not only did he conduct "secondary research" by reading about the incident in books and essays, he had to do "primary research" by going to special historical archives and examining original documents—letters, journals, diaries, and contemporary newspaper accounts.

Then he had to conduct "lived research"—interviewing descendants of the participants, walking the streets of Wilmington with period maps to trace the course of the action, and even traveling to the Army Ordnance Museum in Maryland to see the kind of Gatling gun possessed by the leaders of the white supremacists:

> Not only did I look at it, I photographed it from many
> angles so I could describe it accurately later. Then I han-
> dled it, swiveling the four-hundred-pound drum with its
> ten rotating barrels, wrapping my fingers around the brass
> crank, sighting targets.

Research. Feeling the weight, smelling the gun oil, looking down the barrel.

If you are a poet or novelist, research usually comes after you have begun to write and find that a setting, a character, or an episode requires you to get more information before you can write about it accurately and vividly. For writers of creative nonfiction, however, writing often can't even begin until all the research has been completed. Your research, moreover, must be as "creative" as your writing. As you research, you are not just gathering information but looking for the lineaments of a dramatic story, the nature of your characters.

A student in my workshop on writing biography was researching the life of Wilmington architect Henry Bacon, who designed many famous buildings, most notably the Lincoln Memorial. Through his research in architectural history, he knew that Bacon was now regarded as a staunch upholder of classical building style at a time when pioneers like Frank Lloyd Wright were redefining architecture away from classicism and toward a new modernist style.

But what really brought Bacon to life was a contemporary newspaper story my student read about the dedication of the Lincoln Memorial in 1925. As President Harding and other dignitaries stood in front of the memorial, Henry Bacon was hauled on a barge, pulled by young architecture students, down the length of the reflecting pool that links the Washington Monument and the Lincoln Memorial. "Like a triumphant Roman emperor," thought my student, "at the very time when the course of modern architecture was leaving Bacon behind."

Another student was writing a biographical essay on Wilmington artist Claude Howell. Early in his research, he found a wonderful fact that gave him a superb "lead" (the opening of your essay where you must grab the reader's attention): Claude Howell was born in the same room he died in, in the Carolina Apartments building on Market Street in downtown Wilmington. Yet it took months of more research to reveal that this great lead also defined a pattern that ran throughout Howell's life. Here was a man and artist who needed tremendous stability—living for much of his adult life with his mother, seldom leaving his hometown of

Wilmington, and holding on to his "day job" in the offices of the local railroad company even after he became a successful painter. As that pattern emerged, my student interviewed an art historian about Howell's paintings. When the historian pointed out that the composition of almost every one of Howell's paintings was based upon the triangle, the most stable of geometric forms, the student saw a connection between Howell's life and his art.

Because my student had done his homework by learning all he could about his subject through library and archival research, when he interviewed the art historian he was primed for that illuminating insight. Don't waste travel or interview time on what you can learn in the library. You'll get the most out of your "lived research" if you use it to learn what you can't find in secondary or primary research.

When I was researching my biography of Irving Berlin, I had the opportunity to interview his oldest daughter. As she was showing me her father's book collection—his leather-bound sets of Shakespeare, Dickens, and other classic writers—I knew that Berlin had only a few years of school and never mentioned great literature in his many newspaper interviews. I needed to find out whether these beautiful books were just for show or whether Berlin actually read them.

To put such a question delicately, I talked to his daughter about what I had learned of Berlin's friendship with several poets in the 1920s, such as Dorothy Parker and Robert Benchley, then asked if there were any earlier poets he liked. I could see that his daughter, a writer herself, was intrigued by the question and was trying hard to remember. "There was one," she said, and I held my breath as she tried to recall the name. "Yes, I remember," she said, smiling. "He used to like to read Alexander Pope."

At first I was amazed, since Pope is one of the most difficult of English writers. As I thought about it, however, it was perfectly logical. Alexander Pope wrote all of his poetry, even book-length epic poems, in couplets—those tiny, two-line, ten-syllable units of poetry. Berlin also worked in a very constrictive form—the thirty-two bar song, which gave a lyricist about fifty or sixty words to say something fresh and moving. A songwriter who managed to turn out numbers like "White Christmas" and "Easter Parade" in that narrow format would naturally be drawn to a poet like Pope. If you've done your homework in the library and the archives, that's the kind of insight that can come from your "lived research." ❖

MEMORY AND MEANING IN NONFICTION

Philip Gerard

T HESE DAYS, IT SEEMS AS IF EVERYBODY IS WRITING A memoir—or at least some briefer version of a memoir, personal essays that recount autobiographical experience. In former times, we'd expect memoirs from retired generals, inventors, artists, explorers, revolutionaries, politicians, movie stars, and other celebrities, people who have strutted their hour on the world's stage in a very public way, whose policies and decisions and actions influenced millions, changed the course of history, altered the way we live, inspired us to new heights in our civic and cultural lives.

Unless you are such a public figure, a mover and shaker—a person whose life is demonstrably important—it takes real audacity to write about yourself, to claim that the world ought to listen up and take notice of the things that have happened to you personally in your life. Yet these days bookstores are so flooded with memoirs by twenty- and thirty-something unknowns that marketers have come to classify them into neat categories: survival memoirs, adventure memoirs, coming-of-age memoirs, travel memoirs, and just plain zany memoirs.

This irresistible urge to write about yourself is not necessarily a bad thing. In fact, the introspective literary essay has a long and noble history going back centuries: the tradition of the examined life. Small household truths can yield larger truths. Meditating on ordinary experience can yield insight, knowledge, and even beauty. A writer need not tell his or her whole life's story in order to find those parts that will resonate with an audience of strangers.

The key seems to be recognizing meaning in the memory. Just because something happened to you personally, just because you endured something or triumphed over a certain adversity, does not make you worthy of a reader's attention. The story itself has to mean something outside of your own personal claims to it.

So whenever I am tempted to write a personal essay, such as "Hardball," I'm always nagged by that question: Why will this matter to other people?

Almost from the moment I played on that baseball team in Vermont, I knew that the experience carried significance larger than just my own participation in a hard-played, hard-luck season. Yet it took many years to understand—years in which I abandoned certain dreams and embraced others, years in which my knee at last collapsed in right field and sent me three times under the surgeon's scalpel and out of baseball for good, years in which I watched Major League World Series games with increasing awareness of the cold-blooded professional skill required to play at that level of the game, years in which I watched some of the most promising individuals of my childhood fail miserably at their lives. Years in which I had the leisure to reflect on what that lost, long-ago season had meant.

At last the story I had participated in all those years ago seemed both more vivid than ever and also larger than myself. Not monumentally important, not a memoir by Sir Winston Churchill or Amelia Earhart, but a story worth telling to others. A story that might resonate with the ambitious young and the disillusioned old and all the ones in between who had made their peace with their lives, daring as much as they dared, learning how to handle success and come back stronger from defeat, and savoring the hard experience that chiseled their lives into the shapes they now recognized, the defining moments in which they created the character they would live with for a lifetime.

It was my memory, but the meaning now belongs to every reader—sharing at least what it means to me, overlaying my small memory with their own larger comprehension. If I have done my job, the reader may share what I alone experienced, and in my effort to make it possible for the reader to share it, the story grows larger than the author, and in this way the world grows larger for everybody. ❖

Why I Write

Terry Tempest Williams

D EAREST DEB, IT IS JUST AFTER 4:00 A.M. I WAS DREAM-
ing about Moab, Brooke and I walking around the
block just before dawn. I threw a red silk scarf around
my shoulders and then I began reciting in my sleep why I write:
I write to make peace with the things I cannot control. I write
to create fabric in a world that often appears black and white. I
write to discover. I write to uncover. I write to meet my ghosts.
I write to begin a dialogue. I write to imagine things differently and in imagining things differently perhaps the world will
change. I write to honor beauty. I write to correspond with my
friends. I write as a daily act of improvisation. I write because
it creates my composure. I write against power and for democracy. I write myself out of my nightmares and into my dreams.
I write in a solitude born out of community. I write to the questions that shatter my sleep. I write to the answers that keep me
complacent. I write to remember. I write to forget. I write to the
music that opens my heart. I write to quell the pain. I write to
migrating birds with the hubris of language. I write as a form of
translation. I write with the patience of melancholy in winter. I
write because it allows me to confront that which I do not know.
I write as an act of faith. I write as an act of slowness. I write to

record what I love in the face of loss. I write because it makes me less fearful of death. I write as an exercise in pure joy. I write as one who walks on the surface of a frozen river beginning to melt. I write out of my anger and into my passion. I write from the stillness of night anticipating—always anticipating. I write to listen. I write out of silence. I write to soothe the voices shouting inside me, outside me, all around. I write because of the humor of our condition as humans. I write because I believe in words. I write because I do not believe words. I write because it is a dance with paradox. I write because you can play on the page like a child left alone in sand. I write because it belongs to the force of the moon: high tide, low tide. I write because it is the way I take long walks. I write as a bow to wilderness. I write because I believe it can create a path in darkness; I write because as a child I spoke a different language. I write with a knife carving each word through the generosity of trees. I write as ritual. I write because I am not employable. I write out of my inconsistencies. I write because then I do not have to speak. I write with the colors of memory. I write as a witness to what I have seen. I write as a witness to what I imagine. I write by grace and grit. I write out of indigestion. I write when I am starving. I write when I am full. I write to the dead. I write out of the body. I write to put food on the table. I write on the other side of procrastination. I write for the children we never had. I write for the love of ideas. I write for the surprise of a sentence. I write with the belief of alchemists. I write knowing I will always fail. I write knowing words always fall short. I write knowing I can be killed by my own words, stabbed by syntax, crucified by both understanding and misunderstanding. I write out of ignorance. I write by accident. I write past the embarrassment of exposure. I keep writing and suddenly, I am overcome by the sheer indulgence, (the madness) the meaninglessness, the ridiculousness of this list. I trust nothing, especially myself, and slide head first into the familiar abyss of doubt and humiliation and threaten to push the delete button on my way down, or madly erase each line, pick up the paper and rip it into shreds—and then I realize, it doesn't matter, words are always a gamble, words are splinters from cut glass. I write because it is dangerous, a bloody risk, like love, to form the words, to say the words, to touch the source, to be touched, to reveal how vulnerable we are, how transient. I write as though I am whispering in the ear of the one I love.

> Back to sleep,
> I love you,
> Terry

CREATIVE NONFICTION

SELECTIONS

A Refrigerator, Odd and Wonderful

Tim Bass

F OR A MINUTE, THERE WERE ONLY TWO OCCUPANTS IN THE
new house: a refrigerator and me.

The refrigerator looked like a bulky brown cabinet—
an overgrown vertical box with a dark wood-grain face and two
long, skinny, rounded handles. I looked like an eight-year-old
boy, which I was at the time, back in the mid-Sixties—an under-
grown vertical figure with dark brown hair and a mouth full of
crooked teeth. And at that moment—when I pulled on those
woody handles and that refrigerator opened in the middle and
I saw its interior sparkling in white, blue, and stainless steel—at
that moment, I felt a sense of awe and wonder that I had never
imagined could be generated by an ordinary household appliance.
Then again, there was nothing ordinary about this appliance.

The refrigerator stood as a softly humming contradiction to
everything I had learned about refrigerators in my short life. The
front had the warm look of pecan-stained wood, not cold white
metal like all the other refrigerators I had encountered. This one
looked like an armoire, dark and stately, commanding respect for
itself and the precious treasures it preserved within. Beyond those
doors, surely there awaited chilled tubs of bright yellow butter

fresh from the farm, gigantic boxes of thick ice cream in whites and pinks and browns, and gallon upon gallon of the most luscious liquid on the planet—chocolate milk.

Another peculiarity was that this refrigerator had a freezer on the bottom, not the top, which seemed upside down to me. Even more peculiar was what sat down in the freezer—an icemaker that growled every once in a while and punched quarter-moon cubes over into a deep blue bucket. Until that moment, all the refrigerator ice I had ever seen had come from slender aluminum trays; my mother yanked on their frostbitten handles to break out the boxy cubes, which always left a trail of crystal slivers in the trays and on the counter tops. This bottom-mounted, automatic icemaker cranked out cubes every bit as cold as that (probably colder), and its ice required no muscle.

But the oddest oddity about the woody-looking, ice-bearing refrigerator was that it was new—my parents' single splurge as we moved to this street from our old neighborhood all of two blocks away.

Well, the house was a splurge, too. All my life, we had lived in a little brick place at the edge of the playground to my elementary school. To this day, I do not know if we rented that little house or owned it, and I don't remember how many bedrooms it had. All I know now is what I knew then: With four kids, two adults, and one red chow chow, we had outgrown the place, so now we were moving onto this street and into this house with the strange, exceptional, and unbelievably new refrigerator.

The new house was built by a feed-mill owner who bought a big field of weeds, cut a street through it, and went to work putting up brown-brick ranch houses with four bedrooms and wide carports for wide cars. Ours had two-and-a-half bathrooms (one-and-a-half more than the old place), a gigantic den covered in white linoleum with brown specks, and a slatted wooden door that swung into the hall. The ceiling had a pebbly Sheetrock finish that made it look like the surface of the moon, which I would see three years later when my parents woke me up one July night and told me to look at the TV, and I watched Neil Armstrong step onto another world (and then, on that historic moment in black and white, I fell back to sleep in our big brown recliner). The new house also had a fireplace we did not use and a hidden attic stairway with hinges that creaked when we pulled on a rope and lowered the folding steps. Within a few years, we had that attic packed with all the stuff we no longer needed—the out-grown clothes, the battery-powered plastic Model-T we drove as children, our aluminum Christmas tree with its spotlighted color wheel that turned everything red, then blue, then gold.

Our yard was a tree-less swath of thick, almost-impossible-to-mow centipede with a chain-link fence that rimmed the back like a property marker. The house had three doors, but we always came and went through the one on the side, under the carport; if the front doorbell rang, we knew it was either a salesman or somebody handing out church literature.

Our town had only about 5,000 people and the new house was two miles, tops, from the town square, but these were the Sixties and our new neighborhood was part of suburbia, as far as I knew.

Other families moved in around us, including our best friends from the old neighborhood. As kids, we played tackle football and Kick the Can, and we dug tunnels in a field that the feed-mill owner left vacant when he had sold all the houses he needed to sell and quit building. We kept six-ounce glass bottles of Coca-Cola in the refrigerator, next to the pitcher of sugar-sweetened tea and the quart cartons of chocolate milk.

Time passed.

My parents pulled up the stiff clover-green carpet in the bed-rooms and put down soft royal blue. They covered the broad den floor in beige. I got braces. Sofas came and went. We hung a bench swing under the carport, facing the sunset over the carport across the street. The formal drapes came down, country ruffles went up. We graduated from high school.

The woody new refrigerator got some age on it. The icemaker was always temperamental, and since we left it running all the time the motor burned out every now and then. When that happened we called our friend Jay Cannady, a master of appliance repair, and he always rescued us. Whenever I went home and saw Jay's white pickup truck in our driveway, I knew the icemaker had knocked off again. I knew, too, that I would go inside and find him sprawled on his back on the kitchen floor, his head and hands up in the guts of the freezer, and he would get us ice in time for supper.

Time passed, and more time.

In the Eighties, we modernized with a microwave oven, gas logs for the fireplace, pulsating shower heads, and a TV with a remote control. The brown recliner frayed at the seams, so we brought in new ones covered in green and gold velour. We got rid of the blue carpet and marveled at the oak floors preserved underneath, the honey finish glimmering against the sun. Grandchildren came, and my parents ripped up the back yard and put in a swimming pool and a deck. My father had a stroke one Tuesday morning and never worked again. Our chow chow died, then the basset hounds we got after her, then the Eskimo Spitz we got after them. My mother grew tired of the old kitchen and had it remodeled. The carpenters cut out a tall spot for the refrigerator, and its wood grain fit against the new birch cabinets like trees in a forest, only with plumbing.

The Nineties brought us a cordless telephone and a self-propelled lawn mower. In the bedrooms, den, and kitchen, the overhead lights came down and ceiling fans went up. The young neighborhood children grew up and families moved out, and new neighbors with new young children moved in.

Time. Thirty-one years have gone, and the house is—and isn't—what it used to be. It is still big enough for six, but only two live there now. It isn't new anymore. The place needs work:

The windows are drafty, the trim needs paint, and who knows how much longer the water heater will last up in the attic.

My parents considered selling the house a few times, but their hearts were not in it. They always set the price too high and after a few weeks, when no one showed up in a Brinks truck, the FOR SALE came down and my parents stayed put, content in knowing this was the place they were meant to be.

Then a couple came along a few weeks ago and said they wanted to see the house. The place was not even on the market, but they had heard that it once had been, and they asked to take a look around. They liked it. They said it looked like a good place to raise their children. So, yesterday, my parents sold the house. They went to the lawyer's office and signed the papers, then waited there while a courthouse clerk recorded the deed in a new name. It took just a few minutes.

Now they are going to build a new house. It will be smaller than the old one—a house for two, not six. They will build it on our same street, down a few doors from the old place, on a lot in the weeded field where my friends and I dug tunnels and laid out battlefields and pummeled each other with clods of dirt in the wars of children. The new house will be economical, easier to care for. The windows will be new, along with the paint and the water heater and everything else.

Except the refrigerator. My parents will take that with them. The icemaker still breaks down, so they will give the new address to the new guy who works on it. They found out about him a few years ago, after Jay Cannady got sick with cancer and was gone in just a few months.

That new house will be finished soon. I want to imagine that I will walk into the kitchen one day and all I will see is that old refrigerator standing tall and broad before me. I want to imagine it will be new again and I'll be a boy again, and I will gaze up at its odd and wonderful wood-grain doors, and I will open them and squint under the bright light and run my fingers across the frosty shelves, feeling manufactured cold for the first time. I want to imagine reaching in and pulling down a white and brown carton and pouring myself a giant glass of chocolate milk. I want to imagine drinking long and deep, letting the chill of the liquid run through me as I raise my eyes over the rim and look out ahead and see stretched out before me the years, all the many years. ❖

My Mother, 90210

Stanley L. Colbert

A RECENT ITEM SUGGESTS THAT AARON SPELLING, THE ubiquitous Hollywood producer, is writing his autobiography, and I hope he remembers my mother. If she had written her autobiography there certainly would be a chapter on Aaron, who nearly made my mother a star.

As in any Aaron Spelling story, there would be an assortment of ambitious and attractive supporting players living in the same Hollywood zip code, and a glamorous media enterprise to bring them together, in this case CBS Television's flagship live dramatic show, *Playhouse 90*. As in so many Spelling productions, an older and wiser and tougher woman would be dropped into the mix, to stir it up. Except this time the new cast member wouldn't be Heather Locklear, it would be my mother, Marcia, who, typically for her, breezed in and became the special guest star in this ensemble cast.

In the late 1950s, my mother was still in Washington, D.C., an irrepressible force in the Pentagon who had started as a two-finger typist in a temporary clerk's job and would eventually become one of the highest ranking women in the Department of Defense.

I was a recent import, a New York literary agent and later an editor at Henry Holt, tapped to head the literary department of the all-powerful William Morris Agency's Hollywood office.

Aaron Spelling was a client, but I had little contact with him. Long before the house with a bowling alley, decades before the Spelling name made Wall Street swoon, Aaron was the anonymous writer of pithy intros for actor Dick Powell's anthology series, the Zane Grey Theatre.

The show was a cash cow for William Morris. It served as an inexpensive spawning ground for a spate of other western series, all neatly packaged and commissioned by the agency, like Chuck Connors's *The Rifleman* and Steve McQueen's *Wanted: Dead or Alive*. For Aaron, the few hundred dollars he was being paid for each intro, after several years in the business, was hardly the zenith of a career. Yet, if anyone needed a clue to his ambitions even then, they had only to know he was probably the only intro writer in the business who had already secured the services of a business manager.

As far as his television agents were concerned, he told me one day, after introducing himself and settling his slight frame into a chair, puffing nervously on his pipe, their plans for him, however shortsighted they may seem today, consisted of more intros, for as long as Dick Powell wanted and whenever Dick Powell wanted.

"Don't get me wrong, I love what I'm doing and I love all the television guys, they've all been great to me, and I love keeping Powell happy but I gotta break into other shows. Will you help?" he asked.

The Morris office reputation for dealing with what it viewed as disloyalty, defined as anything not in the clear and narrow interest of the William Morris bottom line, was well known and far-reaching, as a number of former clients and former employees could attest. Tampering with the equilibrium of a money machine like Powell's show would certainly fit the definition.

Yet I already had discovered the other Morris agents were reluctant to engage the literary department in territorial disputes.

Perhaps their animal instincts told them we weren't worth the hunt, or we exuded a kind of dusty, protective scent that came from actually reading, from beginning to end, books, whole books, not synopses or reader's reports. It added to our mystique that a few top clients, like Frank Sinatra or Orson Welles, carrying a novel they discovered at Marian Hunter's Book Shop, visited with us to chat about whether we had read the book and to hear our opinions about its film possibilities.

Our special aura left some room for cautious maneuvering.

"Maybe we can find something you can write while you still do the Zane Grey intros," I said. "A one-shot. Something that won't upset the boys downstairs. Maybe a *Playhouse 90*," I suggested, idly.

Aaron jumped up. "God, I'd love to do a *Playhouse 90*," he said. "But most of my ideas are for Westerns. They're always done on film. Could you sell them on doing one live?"

Even then he knew how to manipulate an audience. In that moment I became his brash and fearless champion.

"Let's find out," I said.

I called Martin Manulis, the show's natty, energetic producer, and suggested I had a writer with a different kind of project that might excite his young and talented director, John Frankenheimer. I knew first-hand John was desperately looking for something big, or a feature film that would finally allow him to break out of television. When could we come over and pitch it?

"Keeping Frankenheimer happy is driving me crazy," Martin said. "C'mon over now."

In the car, story ideas tumbled out of Aaron, a skill he was to refine even further in the years ahead. One of them sounded more promising than the others, and we began to bounce it back and forth on the drive from El Camino to Fairfax Avenue, developing it until it had a beginning, a middle and an end, and Aaron felt confident he could not only tell his story, he could sell it. At CBS, Aaron pitched and Martin listened. From time to time he looked at Aaron and then at me. Horses? Cattle? Indoors? Here on the stages? So many characters? In and out on the dot of ninety minutes? I nodded. "It's a first and a challenge. Trust me. Frankenheimer'll love you for it."

Manulis agreed, and so did John. Aaron would write the script for *Playhouse 90* and still find time for his Dick Powell intros, and everyone would be happy. He bubbled as we drove back to my office, where he reported the deal, first to his business manager, and next to his then-wife and actress, the late Carolyn Jones, to whom he briefly described the story and the sole woman's part. Both were equally ecstatic. Carolyn called her agent. I called home.

"That's nice," my wife Nancy said. "Does it mean we can move back to New York?"

Days went by, the pages came in, and Carolyn got the part. Ethel Winant, the show's deadly efficient casting director, a wiry woman to whom everyone seemed to turn whatever the problem, was fretfully looking around for the rest of the cast. John, whose eyes were dancing at the prospect of doing an entire Western indoors, began working on overseeing the building of a western street on the ample but not cavernous *Playhouse 90* stage. Aaron continued writing furiously.

And about then, my mother Marcia decided to pay us a visit.

"Maybe you could get me a ticket to a quiz show," she said over the phone when she called to announce her plans. "I'd love to see how television works." She paused, then added, almost wistfully, "Maybe then I'll understand a little more about what you do for a living."

My mother's coming visit was the main topic of conversation at dinner that evening. At the time we had two writers-in-transit living with us full time and an actress living with us on occasion. Our home had become a halfway house for writers since, in those days, producers would not even consider hiring a writer unless they could meet face to face. So we were providing room and board while the meetings, prior to an assignment, took place.

Vanessa, the actress, was in the midst of a divorce from her surgeon husband and shrewdly felt an agent might be more useful in the thorny negotiations than a lawyer. When the discussions became complicated and the evening phone calls to the surgeon more heated, she would pace for hours in the courtyard of our house and then come in, exhausted, and collapse on the sofa to spend the night.

Everyone volunteered to move and make room for my mother, but it wasn't necessary. There was a bed in the nursery, alongside our first daughter, Jan, who was the real reason my mother was visiting. It was Nancy, the den mother of this unlikely brood, whose disdain of quiz shows had been thoroughly aired and subscribed to between the roast chicken and the salad, who came up with the suggestion that perhaps I could sneak my mother into the guest booth at *Playhouse 90*, where she could watch Aaron's show being shot.

Jim, one of the writers and still in awe of William Morris and the various fortunes it was about to deliver to him, believed his agent could do anything. "Why don't you get her on the show?" he blandly asked. "After all, it's your mother."

"Because there's only one woman's role and they've already cast Carolyn Jones," I answered, as if otherwise it were a possibility. Carolyn had already made her mark in a number of television dramas and in a memorable role in the film version of Paddy Chayefsky's *The Bachelor Party,* which brought her an Academy Award nomination.

Nancy looked up. "Talk to Ethel," she said.

The next day I attended the first reading of Aaron's script, where I happened to mention the previous evening's conversation to Lee Philips, an old friend who had one of the leads in the show. Lee barely listened, concentrating instead on learning to twirl a six-shooter on his finger, a task not yet established as part of the standard repertoire of young men who grew up in New York.

"Talk to Ethel," he said.

Ethel Winant, whose short tolerance for talent agents was well known but who rarely had been accosted by a literary agent, listened and said, "Have her call me when she gets here." That was six words more than she had said a few moments earlier to a talent agent from a minor agency, and I savored every one of them.

A few evenings later, my mother arrived. At the end of dinner, she had managed to become surrogate parent to our odd, makeshift family. She told Jim, "Don't be such a churchmouse. Talk more at the table." She advised Tiff, the other writer, to "sit in the sunshine, you're as pale as a lemon." For Vanessa it was simple. "Get rid of the bum and find somebody else. This time, not a doctor." To Nancy, her advice was short and sweet. She looked at our infant daughter, smiled, and said, "Have more."

With me, she was all business. "So what's with the quiz show ticket?" she asked.

"I'm arranging for someone to take care of you," I said. "You have to call her tomorrow."

"Not the show where you have to run up and down the aisles and wear funny hats," she cautioned.

"No funny hats," I said. I hoped Ethel would remember our brief conversation.

She did. An appointment was set for that day, and Nancy arranged for transportation to CBS while I went off to powerbroker a deal or two at the office. When I came home that evening and settled in for a drink before dinner, my mother braced me in the living room.

"I need a ride tomorrow morning," she said.

"Where?"

"To the studio. Where else?" Her tone suggested she had spawned an idiot. "You can drop me off on your way to work."

Nancy joined us. "Ethel came through," she said.

"What a lovely lady," my mother said. "She cast me as an extra in the Western show. I go in tomorrow for costume fittings."

I took a stiff sip.

"That's great," I said.

"There's more," Nancy said, "have another." I did. My mother sat. Nancy reached for my drink, took a sip, and handed it back.

"Ethel talked to Aaron the writer and he talked to Carolyn. . . ." My mother paused.

"Carolyn the actress, Aaron's wife," Nancy murmured.

"Right," my mother said. "And Carolyn insists I share her dressing room with her. Isn't that nice?"

I looked at Nancy. She was nodding. "Carolyn gave her some advice," Nancy said. My mother's nose told her the roast was about ready, and she pulled herself up and headed for the kitchen, but only to inspect. She stopped at the doorway and turned to me.

"Carolyn said all I get for this job is scale, I don't have to pay you any commission," she said. "It's in the agreement." And she was off to the roast.

I thought, and hoped, that was the end of it, but it wasn't.

The next morning, in a loose top and slacks and open-toe shoes, an outfit she dubbed her "rehearsal clothes," my mother joined the cast and extras on the floor, where the shots were being blocked, and somewhat apprehensively I went into the director's booth to see John.

"Aaron tells me that's your mother down there," he said, never taking his eyes off the monitors.

"She's visiting," I said. "First grandchild." I was about to assure him I'd see to it she wasn't any trouble on the set.

"Great lady," he said. "I've arranged a little piece of business for her." I looked at the monitor. The assistant director was huddled with my mother, who nodded, smiled, and began a slow, matronly walk across what had now become a western street, complete with a dry goods store, saloon, tethered mounts, and a covered wagon drawn by two horses plodding along the dirt-covered stage floor.

John hit the intercom button. "Camera three, tighten on the lady crossing the street behind the wagon and entering the dry goods store!" My mother's image filled the monitor. John turned to me. "I've given her a closeup," he said. "Something for her friends back at the Pentagon."

"Thanks," I said. "A star is born." I backed out of the booth and John waved.

I had nonchalantly survived more than a dozen *Playhouse 90* shows involving my clients, but the day of the show I was a nervous wreck. Not Marcia. My mother was cool as ice.

Nancy and I had elected to sit out the show in the dressing room, where Carolyn and my mother were deep in showbiz talk. As we waited, I recalled that the night before, I dreamed I had an important meeting with Martin Manulis and was shown into his office. Sitting behind his desk, on the phone with Abe Lastfogel, the head of William Morris, closing a deal for Tracy and Hepburn to co-star in an upcoming show, was my mother. The dream ended with Abe begging her to give him a break and find two parking spaces at the studio for his clients.

A few minutes before the players had to take their places on the floor, Aaron appeared at the door, his arms full of flowers. He presented one large bouquet to Carolyn and the other to my mother.

"To my two leading ladies," he said, graciously. Nancy almost gagged. My mother, however, unhesitatingly placed a kiss on Aaron's cheek. "You're a well-brought-up boy," she said. "You'll go far, mark my words."

The show went without a hitch. Aaron's script crackled, John's direction of a complex choreography of horses, cattle, gunfights, and, yes, actors, was masterful, and it all ended exactly ninety minutes later. There were fast congratulations, and we went home to watch the show an hour or so later when the kinescope was re-aired to the West Coast. The household cheered as the camera tightened on my mother crossing the street, and when the show was over she was on the phone to friends and relatives back East. Aaron had given me a lovely Dunhill pipe to mark the occasion. I broke in the pipe that night in relief and wonderment.

A few days later I had good news for Aaron and even better news for his business manager. A day or so before airing, I had alerted various studio story editors to catch the show, and Twentieth Century Fox now wanted to buy the script and turn it into a feature film. I made the deal quickly and reported it to the assembled group at dinner. My mother looked up from her plate.

"Interesting," she said, then she was silent for the rest of the meal. Nancy and I looked at each other. Jim rolled his eyes. Tiff snickered. Vanessa, the actress, smiled knowingly.

Later that evening, while the rest of us dissected the latest film on the art circuit, something from France, Vanessa and my mother strolled and chatted in the courtyard.

When they returned, my mother came over to the sofa and sat next to me.

"It's an interesting business you're in," she said. I nodded. "One day nobody knows your name, and the next day people are stumbling all over you."

"Crazy, huh?" I said.

"Too crazy for me," she said. "I was going to stay and try for my part in the movie, but Vanessa said they'll probably want a name like Thelma Ritter, so the hell with it." She leaned over and planted a kiss on my cheek. "Besides, you all spend too much time sitting around doing nothing. I'd go crazy." She left for Washington the next day with tears and kisses.

The rest of the ensemble went on to the next big show, which, for Aaron, just got bigger and glitzier as time went on. John Frankenheimer escaped weekly television for feature films, as all the Best Director lists confirm. Martin Manulis became head of a new television division at Twentieth Century Fox. Ethel Winant became a producer, and most recently faced the prospect of casting thousands in her drama, *Andersonville*. But my mother's career, as an actress at least, was over. When she got home she was happy just to buy the biggest television set she could find. And for as long as she lived my mother made it a point to watch every Aaron Spelling production that made it to the airwaves. ❖

In the following two excerpts, Philip Furia and Mary Ellin Barrett recount the same story—how Irving Berlin met his second wife, Ellin Mackay. The first excerpt is from a biography of Berlin, and the second is from a memoir about him by his oldest daughter. Compare and contrast the two excerpts to discern differences between the genres of biography and memoir.

Blue Skies

from *Irving Berlin: A Life in Song*

Philip Furia

ONE EVENING IN MAY OF 1924, IRVING BERLIN WANdered down to Jimmy Kelly's. Throughout his life he had a habit of returning to his old haunts in Union Square, Chinatown, and the Bowery, a habit easily indulged in a city where no matter how far up—or down—the ladder of success you had climbed, you could reach your antipodes by walking a few blocks. On this particular night, Berlin may have been more than usually reflective about the course of his career. While he was undoubtedly the premier American songwriter, his hold upon that position was tenuous. It may have already been clear that he could not maintain it by writing scores for revues at the Music Box Theatre, and he was not ready to plunge into the newly emerging genre of the integrated musical comedy. Already, younger songwriters were vying for his mantle. On February 24, 1924, Paul Whiteman presented a concert at Aeolian Hall that purported to fuse jazz with the classics. Much of that program, however, including a "Semi-Symphonic Arrangement" of Irving

Berlin's songs, proved drearily monotonous; only when young George Gershwin strode to the piano, nodded to Whiteman, then plunged into *Rhapsody in Blue,* did it become clear that jazz had found a new spokesman.

If Berlin could not clearly foresee his future in American song, a look backward at his past seemed to suggest that his stunning career had reached a plateau. His friend Alexander Woollcott was writing a biography of the songwriter—an enormous tribute, yet one that suggested a sense of closure. Woollcott traced Berlin's rise from the immigrant Lower East Side to the heights of American success, romanticizing his subject as an untutored genius who drew upon his melancholy heritage as a Russian Jew. Woollcott predicted that his music would endure only after a trained composer had transmuted it, as Liszt and Chopin had taken anonymous folk melodies and lifted them into the realm of classic art. While Woollcott acknowledged that it was unusual to write the biography of a man in his mid-thirties, his book implied that Berlin had come as far, creatively, as someone like him possibly could.

What may have made Irving Berlin especially reflective on this particular night, however, was that he had not come to Jimmy Kelly's alone. With him was a lovely and sophisticated young lady named Ellin Mackay. Earlier that evening, they had met at a fashionable dinner party. She had charmed him by saying, "Oh, Mr. Berlin, I do so like your song, 'What Shall I Do?' And he, after correcting her about the title of his latest hit, graciously acknowledged the propriety of her distinction between *shall* and *will:* "Where grammar is concerned," he joked, "I can always use a little help." After dinner, he invited her to accompany him to Jimmy Kelly's, which had become, in the parlance of the Prohibition era, a "speakeasy." Kelly had also moved from his old Union Square location to Sullivan Street in Greenwich Village, the heart of artistic experiment, social protest, and Bohemian lifestyles in the Jazz Age.

The transformation of Jimmy Kelly's was indicative of the vast changes in American social mores that had taken place since Berlin worked there as a singing waiter. The coming of the cabaret around 1910 had threatened to break down the barriers between the social classes, to place young girls from the highest echelons of society next to men from the lower and even immigrant classes. Dancing, dining, and the intimate floor show invited the expression and exploration of private experience, once confined to the homes of a closely knit society, into the open, public domain. The redefinition of the American girl that had started out with Irene Castle as the healthy, active, fox-trotting playmate of 1914 had, ten years later, transmogrified into the Jazz Age flapper, kicking up her stockingless legs in the Charleston.

The encounter between Irving Berlin and Ellin Mackay was the most dramatic upshot of these changes in American society. Barely twenty-one, the lithe, blonde Ellin came from the highest reaches of society. Her father, Clarence Mackay, on the strength of his father's fortune, spawned by the fabled Nevada Comstock silver mines and invested in the telegraph system, was one of the wealthiest and most prominent men in New York. Ellin had grown up at his estate on Long Island, gone to the finest private schools, and in 1922 made her debut into society at a ball at the Ritz-Carlton. In the fall of 1924, she would dance with the Prince of Wales, who was destined to become King Edward VIII of England until he, in an even more scandalous crossing of class barriers, gave up the throne to marry a divorced commoner.

Ellin, however, had literary aspirations, and she found herself drawn to Greenwich Village and to her mother's cousin, Alice Duer Miller, a member of the Algonquin Round Table. The Round Table itself exemplified social mixing among people like Woollcott and Franklin Pierce Adams, who came from solid gentility, George S. Kaufman and Dorothy Parker, who stemmed from wealthy Jewish families, and Jews like Berlin and Herbert

Swope, who had struggled up from poverty. For a flower of New York society like Ellin Mackay to mingle with such a mongrel group, however literate, testified to the breakdown of class distinctions. Ellin knew it and capitalized upon it. In 1925, she would write an essay, "Why We Go to Cabarets: A Post-Debutante Explains," for the *New Yorker,* the new magazine founded by Round Tabler Herbert Ross to set a standard of wit, insouciance, and urbanity.

Ellin's essay gleefully satirized the dreaded influence of cabarets on American society:

> Our Elders criticize many things about us, but usually they attribute sins too gaudy to be true. The trouble is that our Elders are a trifle gullible; they have swallowed too much of F. Scott Fitzgerald... They believe all the backstage gossip that is written about us... Cabaret has its place in the elderly mind beside Bohemia and bolshevik, and other vague words that have a sinister significance and no precise definition... We have privacy in a cabaret... What does it matter if an unsavory Irish politician is carrying on a dull and noisy flirtation with the little blonde at the table behind us? We don't have to listen; we are with people we find amusing.

In just such a cabaret Ellin Mackay had fulfilled the worst of those fears by finding companionship with an immigrant Jewish songwriter. In Ellin, Berlin found the high spirit of his first wife, Dorothy, together with the literate sophistication of his current friends from the Algonquin Round Table.

When he learned that his daughter was involved with Berlin, Clarence Mackay was incensed. The fact that his family was Catholic made him vigilant in guarding his social standing. While Mackay could be friendly with wealthy Jews who moved in his own social circle, such as Otto Kahn and Bernard Berenson, it was unthinkable that his daughter would be courted by an immigrant Jew from Tin Pan Alley. His vigilance was heightened by the fact that his own wife, Katherine Duer Mackay, had earlier become entangled in an affair with a prominent society surgeon, Dr. Joseph Blake. When Clarence Mackay refused, on Catholic tenets, to grant her a divorce, Katherine traveled to Paris, where Dr. Blake headed an American Red Cross hospital during World War I. There she married her lover and left Mackay to Harbor Hill, his magnificent Long Island estate, and to his bitterness.

That bitterness flared anew over his daughter's association with Irving Berlin. Although he himself had taken a mistress, Anna Case, she was from the upper echelon of the musical world, a concert singer who had been a star at the Metropolitan Opera, where Mackay was a member of the board of directors. When he learned that Ellin and Berlin were seen together at parties, he hired private detectives to investigate the songwriter and keep him away from Harbor Hill. When he could turn up nothing damaging, he whisked his daughter off to Europe in the hope that other suitors would expunge the memory of Berlin.

What Mackay did not realize was that removing his daughter from New York would only intensify Berlin's feelings, which do not seem to have been as committed to the relationship, until that point, as Ellin's were. Later, she admitted that in those early days she had been the pursuer. However, in her absence, Berlin seems to have felt his midlife emptiness all the more keenly. A newer, youthful era was emerging as epitomized by the success of the Gershwins' *Lady, Be Good!*, while Berlin, along with the revues to which he had committed himself and his theater, seemed to be ebbing into the past. In his first marriage he had hoped to find an escape from the demons that drove him to maintain the success he had achieved with "Alexander's Ragtime Band." As he contemplated this new commitment, it may have seemed a bulwark against the vicissitudes of time and fortune. ❖

Irving Berlin:
A Daughter's Memoir

Mary Ellin Barrett

B Y THE TIME I FIRST REMEMBER MY MOTHER, SHE WAS THIN and exquisitely pretty. Old friends describe the 1930s Ellin Berlin as "pale and etheral." The Ellin Mackay my father fell in love with was not ethereal, though she had a certain whimsy about her, an unexpected sharp wit—too sharp sometimes—that she called her "Irish sense of humor."

It is all history now, ancient history, the celebrated romance of the Catholic golden girl, born to millions, and the immigrant cantor's son from the Lower East Side who became America's greatest songwriter—the story that caught the world's imagination, *Abie's Irish Rose* in diamonds and waltz time, and canopied my childhood, matching any fairy tale or novel I might read. But in this haunted place, so soon after my father's death, that ancient story—our family's beginning—-seems close enough to touch.

It is through my mother that I and my younger sisters know the beginning, before any of us came onto the scene; she was generous with those memories; she delighted, after all, in that beginning. Our father told wonderful stories, too, but not on demand, only when the spirit struck him; and you had better listen hard, for with a few notable exceptions he did not repeat himself; mostly he preferred listening to you, asking you questions. But our mother loved to reminisce. And time and again, as I pieced the story together, I found her memories confirmed, in family documents, in letters, in the written or spoken recollections of relatives and friends, though not always in the newspapers, which, she would say, was obvious: Newspapers inevitably got things wrong.

They met on the evening of May 23, 1924, at a New York dinner party, by the merest chance, my mother always liked to note, for my father was a last-minute replacement.

The hostess was Frances Wellman, Mrs. Allen G. Wellman (later Mrs. Harold Brooks), a society woman with ties to the Long Island crowd—the crowd of my grandfather Clarence Mackay—and a taste for the newer, livelier company of theater people. My mother, the post-debutante, was a friend, a charming younger addition to any evening—and my father, the songwriter, such a good friend that Mrs. Wellman could call him the very day of a party and ask if he could fill in for someone who had unexpectedly dropped out. He could and would. As anyone who knew him knew, he liked nothing more than a last-minute plan—or less than a commitment made weeks ahead.

So except for some unknown fellow's indisposition or whim, those two might never have met, though there were other links: Alice Duer Miller, the novelist, an Algonquin Round Table regular and first cousin to my mother's mother; Cole Porter, a well-liked colleague of my father's whose wife, Linda, in earlier days, had been a Mackay family friend. There were other houses where they might have sat next to each other, a stylish young woman, a handsome older man. It was a time in New York for smart, intimate dinners that crossed lines.

But the meeting almost took place too late.

For my mother, in the spring of 1924, was engaged, though still unofficially, to a Washington diplomat. Engaged, not because she was really in love but because it was time—twenty-one was old for a girl who had made her debut, as her father wanted, instead of going to college—because she was bored and too bright for the idle life she was leading. An honor student at a difficult boarding school, St. Timothy's, she had tried for a while taking classes at Barnard, alma mater of Cousin Alice, sister college to Columbia, where her great-great-grandfather William Duer had been president. (The Duers and Traverses, her mother's side of the family, were a brainy as well as an aristocratic lot.) But Barnard in the twenties was a hotbed of reverse snobbery, she'd say. No matter that she wore her plainest clothes and had the family car deposit her blocks away, unlike her friend Consuelo Vanderbilt, who wore furs and jewelry to class and had the chauffeur drop her off in front of Millbank Hall. "They hated me not one bit less," my mother would say, and tell of naïvely inviting her class in Renaissance art to lunch at Harbor Hill, the fifty-room Mackay mansion in Roslyn, to view her father's famous collection: the Botticelli, the Mantegna, the Verrocchios, the Sassettas, the tapestries and armor. No one accepted. The professor was said to have mounted the snub. After a term she quit. So much for higher learning.

Four months on a grand tour of Europe, in the summer and fall of 1923, had killed more time. In Paris, Ian Campbell, the future duke of Argyll, was her escort. "Robbing the cradle," she called it (he was six months younger), but he was fun to be with, and more accessible than most upper-class British men. Then, back in New York, there was the diplomat (she never would tell his name), attractive, slightly older, solid, someone she was fond of, someone her father approved of. She had accepted a ring, though wasn't ready, not quite yet, to make a formal announcement.

As for my thirty-six-year-old father, who knows what the composer-in-residence and part owner of the Music Box Theatre was up to in May 1924 as he put on his dinner jacket, brushed down his hair to slick perfection, and walked out with that brisk, jaunty stride. He certainly was not engaged to anyone, "except Sam Harris," as he liked to say, the man who produced the Music Box Revues. On his mind, if anything, this springtime night, would have been the fourth in the annual series, coming up soon. The third edition, though it had run eight months and made a star of the unknown Grace Moore, had been a letdown, so the critics said, nothing in a pleasant score that compared to "Everybody Step," "Say It with Music," "Pack Up Your Sins and Go to the Devil," "Lady of the Evening," and "Crinoline Days." The charmed show in its fresh, beautiful theater, the show that ushered in the Jazz Age musical, Follies razzle-dazzle gone smart and small-scale, had lost some of its drive. And the composer was fretting, for the Music Box was something he cared about deeply, more deeply, certainly, than any lady in his life.

There was, to be sure, his friend Elsie Janis, the "Doughboy's Sweetheart" of the First World War, a singer and songwriter both; the Janis house near Tarrytown, presided over by Elsie's ever-present mother, was a favorite weekend destination; but there was no indication that this friendship was finally changing into something more. There was Neysa McMein the artist, recently wed to the dashing mining engineer Jack Baragwanath, the woman all the talented young men of New York fell for, my father's type, spirited, witty, with a certain hauteur; but there was no hint that he was carrying a torch for Neysa. He was a man with women friends: Anita Loos, Dorothy Parker, Alice Miller. If he had an occasional "girl"—one of those lush young women in a Ziegfeld Follies or Music Box Revue lineup—this was the best-kept secret in New York.

All people knew for certain was that he had been in love with Constance Talmadge, sparkling, seductive Constance, the movie queen, leading lady of Douglas Fairbanks and Ronald Colman. But Constance married a Greek millionaire. People also vaguely remembered that there was something tragic in his background: that he had married as a very young man, and his bride had caught typhoid fever on their Cuban honeymoon and died a few months later. He had poured out his grief in a ballad, his first to make a mark and one of his best, "When I Lost You," and tried to forget himself in work. That had been long ago, 1912, but something clung to him, made him elusive, different from the average attractive man about town.

But then there was something from the past that clung to her, too, the girl with the blonde madonna hair arriving at the party. Something she never talked about, would have liked to bury, but that gave her an edge, an elusiveness of her own. The miserable old business of her mother: Katherine Duer Mackay, mistress of Harbor Hill, style setter, loving maternal presence, who, when my mother was ten years old, had gone off with her husband's good friend, given up her three children as the price of her divorce. Loss was compounded by scandal, the kind of headline scandal that causes a ten-year-old child to pause before ringing the doorbell of a friend's house, in a cold sweat, knowing that when she enters there will be a sudden silence. People will stop talking because they have been talking about her, her family—poor Clarie, shameless Katherine. But she doesn't turn and run away; she walks into the house, holding her head high, smiling and daring them to feel sorry for her.

So there he was, eligible but elusive, and there she was, semi-engaged but still at liberty. And she faced him—during cocktails, over the soup, between the roast and the salad when the hostess turned the table—and said in the soft, clear, fluting, slightly affected accents of old New York, "Oh, Mr. Berlin, I do so like your song 'What Shall I Do?'"

Mr. Berlin gave her a look, told her the title—"What'll I Do?"—as it appeared on the sheet music, already having sold into the hundreds of thousands, and accepted her correction. "Where grammar is concerned, I can always use a little help," he said. His voice was also soft, clear, and of New York, a newer, blunter New York with a bit of the street about it, a bit of show business and totally unaffected. She was embarrassed but not too. He was amused. A spark was struck. She was a great heiress, a spoiled, stuck-up darling; he was a world-famous composer with the pride and assurance of a self-made man. But both had lifesaving senses of humor, and their humors matched—fast, playful, sometimes a little rough on others.

The rest of the conversation is lost, but it continued briskly, no doubt, interrupted by an occasional lighting by him of her Turkish cigarette, fitted into a long quill holder, the badge of a young sophisticate.

What my mother wore on this memorable night is not recorded, but you can assume the dress was soft in fabric and color—rose or dusty blue or cloth of silver, most likely French, and flattering to a slightly plump figure, showing off the pretty arms and neck and throat, bringing out the creamy coloring—and that it caught a gentleman's eye, pointed a gentleman's eye to the girl within, her skin, her eyes, her hair. A dress that was becoming first, fashionable second. Once, when my mother was quite old, I told her in my father's presence that she looked wonderful, and he said, "Haven't you noticed, your mother has the prettiest clothes around. She always did." On another occasion, in the middle years, I remember my father putting his hand on her shoulder, smooth, ivory-colored, barely tanned (she was wearing a bathing suit), and saying, "Have you ever noticed that your mother has the loveliest shoulders," and she bending her face toward his hand. When I recalled the episode as unusual, for they were rarely demonstrative in public, she said, "Oh, you know, he liked me."

The liking and the admiration were mutual and probably immediate, though she never said it was love at first sight, only that it had happened before they realized it.

When the dinner broke up, Mr. Berlin invited Miss Mackay to accompany him to Jimmy Kelly's in Greenwich Village, a cabaret where, in its earlier Union Square quarters, he'd once worked as a singing waiter. She accepted gladly; she hated to turn in early, didn't he? Another look: one night owl taking in another. Later, Kelly would tell people they'd met at his place, and my parents, with typical forbearance, didn't correct the story, which gave him such pleasure. After all, it was the same evening. And being alone in a nightclub surely constituted more of an introduction than being table partners at an uptown dinner party. ❖

Hardball

Philip Gerard

After college, when I lived in Burlington, Vermont, and tended bar at the Last Chance Saloon, on Main Street, only a few rough blocks above Lake Champlain and the tank farms and barge docks that are gone now, replaced by a tourist pavilion and a yacht basin, I got recruited to join a baseball team in one of the small outlying towns. We played other town teams, usually on weekends. Our home field was built on the edge of a granite quarry—beyond the outfield fence lay oblivion. The first practice, as I trotted out to my position in left field, the center fielder warned me: "Don't go diving over that fence after a ball—it's a long way down."

I leaned over the chain link fence and stared down a hundred vertical feet onto solid rock, flat and smooth where the gray stone had been carved away in great square slabs. "No prob," I said.

The infield was dangerous and fast, hardpan basepaths and close-cropped grass. The pitcher's mound was high and the batter's box was a ditch. It was as if whoever had designed this baseball diamond had tried to make it as hard on everybody as possible.

It was a country of hardscrabble farms and bone-cracking winters, sunk deep in recession. Half the men on the team were out of work; the others scrambled between two or three different jobs, trying to make ends meet. They stacked groceries or repaired cars all day and then spent their evenings splitting firewood for sale. In the winter they drove snowplows and repaired chainsaws. Their lives held little that was frivolous, and they loved the game with a fierce and serious intensity.

Our player-manager and catcher was a muscle-bound plumber who shaved his head and sharpened his cleats with a file before each game. He had a habit of firing the ball back sidearm to the pitcher after each pitch, daring him to catch it. That first day, as we loosened up, throwing and catching, he burned one into my glove so hard my palm stung. He grinned at me through missing front teeth. "We play hardball, son," he said. "Got it?"

"Right." I loped out to shag flies, wary of the low fence and the long drop.

Our outfield captain had come up through the Yankee farm system with Mickey Rivers. When Rivers went north to star in the Big Show, however, the Yankees gave him his release. After that, he roamed semi-pro outfields with an attitude and eventually found his way onto our team. He was a rangy, strong guy with remarkable instincts, good for at least one home run per game, and he could chase down any fly ball in the same county.

He played mad. He swung at pitches like a man murdering his wife's lover with an ax. When he chased the ball into left field, I cleared out of his way. I always had the uneasy feeling that one day he was going to leap over that fence after a fly ball. That he wanted to do it. That one day he would just take a running leap and catch the ball on the way down.

The Pirates had drafted our pitching ace and his eighty-five-mile-an-hour fastball straight out of high school—then released him after a single season, claiming he was psychologically unstable and a menace. So we'd heard. He'd get that light in his eye, and he wouldn't take signals from the catcher. He wouldn't take signals from anybody.

He always pitched with a manic grin on his face. His control was erratic—or so he pretended. I think now he always knew exactly what he was doing, and the crazy act was just a way to psyche out the hitters. He'd wing pitches over the backstop just to keep the batters guessing. The more furious the batter became, the bigger he grinned. He seemed to like keeping everything—his fastball, the batter, the fielders, the game—just on the verge of going out of control. If the other team got a rally going, he would knock down the next hitter, and no umpire ever called him on it.

In our league, you had to actually injure another player to get thrown out of the game, and then it was even money.

Our pitcher's brother was our second baseman, a spray hitter whose trademark was the headfirst slide—a dangerous play, since on a close throw your face winds up dueling with the baseman's knees, fists, and spikes. This was during Pete Rose's heyday, years before he disgraced himself gambling and wound up banned from the game for life. Rose had a way of never being satisfied—if he had a clean single, he hungered after a double, and he'd batter down anybody in his way to get it. Our second baseman showed that same hunger—tried to stretch every hit into a triple, and more often than he had any right to, he succeeded. His face and arms were always cut and bruised, as if he spent his time brawling in taverns and not hitting to the opposite field.

The other players were equally eccentric—aging jocks who had once had a shot at the big time and blown it, holding on, doing it the hard way, playing for keeps.

In that league, we slid high and threw low. No game was complete without a knock-down collision at home plate or a free-for-all at second base. More than once I came home with blood on my jersey.

I'd never been better than a mediocre player. I had no dreams of glory, but I've always enjoyed the game. When it is right, there is no better game, no better feeling than the smooth swing that connects with a fastball, no sound more thrilling than the crack of a line drive coming off the sweet spot of a wooden bat and already leaving the infield by the time you hear the sound. I could pound out doubles, hit a long ball once in awhile, and catch anything in the outfield that landed in front of me. But I couldn't hit a really slick curveball, and I couldn't make the over-the-shoulder catch going away.

In that league, though, pitchers preferred to smoke the ball right down the middle of the plate—mano a mano— and I could hit a fastball all day long. Defensively, I played with my back to the fence, out of pure terror. I charged in on everything. So I had the season of my life. That summer, I was power-lifting, and I handled a thirty-five-ounce Louisville Slugger easily. I rapped out vicious grounders that sent shortstops sprawling. I ricocheted frozen ropes off the center-field fence. That troubled crew made me believe I was better than I was, and I played harder than I ever had.

We played under summer skies choked with thunderheads that scraped open their black bellies on the craggy rims of the mountains and doused us with hard rain, in golden afternoon light cooled by the deep verdure of swaying evergreen trees, into the sudden chilly twilight that carries voices for miles and years and calls children home to their suppers. We played forever, that summer.

We slugged our way to the playoffs, in which I doubled in the winning run, and now it came down to a final game.

Like every contest in which winning carries virtually no reward, we fought the championship game out hard and for keeps. At long last, the classic moment arrived—how could it not, that season? Two out, bottom of the ninth, down by a run, two men on base. I stepped up to the plate. The pitcher winged a fastball down the alley, and I nicked it up over the backstop. He came right back at me with another fastball on the corner, and I slammed it down the third base line, just foul. The thin crowd in the bleachers was going nuts. I stepped out of the box to whack the mud off my cleats, took a breath, then stepped in.

I remember even now the quality of the light—that clear Vermont light, crisp as green apples, the field of vision opening beyond the scowling pitcher and the crouching infielders and the outfielders kicking at the grass like horses, beyond the silver toprail of the fence into absolute blue sky.

My wrists were loose and the bat felt weightless. Everybody was shouting—my teammates, the other players, the wives and girlfriends and younger brothers in the stands—and their voices blended into a kind of surfy incomprehensible murmur, and I had a clear vision of what was about to happen. The pitcher was rattled. His next fastball would sail in a little too high. I would get around on it quick and sock it into left center field.

Watch it arc over the fence.

Not start my home-run trot toward first base until the white ball disappeared into the quarry.

The pitcher wound up. His arm whipped past his ear in a blur. The ball came in high and fast, just as I had predicted. I dug in my back foot, took a short step with the front one, and swung from the heels. The power came out of my thighs and up my back and down from my shoulders into my thick arms and the wrists snapped around quick and the bat sang through a perfect arc.

But it was a curveball. It tailed magnificently toward my knees. I missed it by a country mile. I swung so hard, I cracked the thin handle of the barrel-heavy bat. When I swatted it against the ground in disgust, it busted clean in two.

*   *   *

A few months later, I left Vermont. I played one last season with a town team in Delaware—a young, careless bunch who played not hardball, but baseball. I never again played under such low skies, never again played with such desperate men, never again hit so hard or wanted to win so badly that, the night before a game, my stomach hurt.

Whenever I watch a big-league game on TV now, I can't help but think of all the guys who didn't make it. Who almost made it. Who couldn't hit the slick curveball. Whose defensive game was one step too slow, or whose character had some hairline fracture that revealed itself under the public stress of pro competition as under an x-ray. Whose timing was flawed, who guessed wrong just once too often, whose luck came up just one swing short of stardom. Whose imagined future never came true, leaving them baffled, bereft of any idea of how to live out their adult lives.

Who had been the boys with the high expectations, the heroes of their high schools, the older brothers whom their parents always bragged about, the boys all the other boys wanted to be like, who ached for glory, who never learned properly how to be men—how to take from disappointment hope, and from failure the dignity of their secret character.

That was the point of the game, of playing hard, of winning in that golden crisp light when you felt you could hit and run and throw forever—and also of striking out so wildly your neck stung with shame and losing a game that stuck like a pill in the throat: It was only a game, but it was a game that could teach you all you ever needed to learn about heartbreak and glory—provided you paid attention, and provided you let it go.

I imagine them out there still, roaming ugly hardscrabble fields in far-flung country places, throwing low and sliding high, inflicting as much pain on each other and themselves as they possibly can, season after season, waiting to take that last great flying leap over the fence and into oblivion. ❖

A POLYGAMIST OF PLACE

David Gessner

I BEGIN WITH A CONFESSION. WHILE IT'S TRUE I HAVE ONLY
one wife and no hidden mistresses, I am a polygamist of
place. The writers I've always admired most, from Thoreau
to Colorado's Reg Saner, have made it their habit to wedge into
one place, to know that place well through long association with
the land and people. In this way, they learn things that will only
reveal themselves after a relationship of good, hard duration.

I'm more fickle. My first book was a paean to the beauties and
wonders of Cape Cod. The book ended with my father's death,
and concluded with these words: "Like my father, I know where
I'll finally settle. He has committed to Cape Cod. I will follow
him." I wrote those sentences while typing in a study that stared
out at the Front Range of Colorado, two thousand miles from
the Atlantic. Not long after, I completed a book about my love of
Colorado. I penned its last line in an attic room overlooking the
white breakers and deep blue waters of Cape Cod Bay.

This division of devotion has caused me no small amount
of anxiety, not just for moral but for practical reasons. In these
competitive and crowded days, writers, like everyone else, tend to
specialize. Nature writers in particular carve out their little fief-
doms, niches to claim as their own, and, as a rule, these niches

keep getting smaller and smaller. Years ago Edward Abbey wrote
of how every place now has its own Thoreau, critics calling one
nature writer the "Thoreau of the Rockies" or the "Thoreau
of New Jersey" or the "Thoreau of Arizona." In the time since
Abbey's death it's only gotten worse: now we have the "Thoreau
of East Providence" and the "Thoreau of Mexican Hat." But as
others industriously settle their territories, I find myself charging
from coast to coast like an adulterous husband in a madcap Sixties movie, passionately declaring my love for one place before
hurriedly packing my suitcase to rush back and proclaim my
love for the other. This is not a stable position for an essayist to
work from, particularly one who is prone to lecture, at the slightest provocation, about how good writing should grow from local
ground.

Even more unsettling is the fact that two of my literary heroes,
Wendell Berry and John Hay, have made "marriage" to their chosen places a primary metaphor in their work. Hay has lived in the
same house on top of Dry Hill on Cape Cod for over half a century, while as a young man Berry returned to settle the land he
had loved as a child. In contrast I am a typical rootless American,
of no place and of many places, nervous if I stay still for too long.
On the one hand I am what I once heard John Hay call another
Cape Cod writer: "a flibbertigibbet." On the other hand, still not
having recovered from a high school encounter with Thoreau, I
can't quite give up on the idea of having my own Walden. So far
the closest I've come to a base camp is this house on Sesuit Neck
in which I now type, a house that I do not own. This isn't marriage of the sort that Hay and Berry exemplify; my affair with the
Cape has not been wholehearted and exclusive. And if that fact
causes me guilt, what about the fact that I have other lovers—
Colorado only most prominently—to whom I am almost equally
committed? Is there something wrong with me?

The truth is that all this talk of settling and geographical marriage makes me uneasy. I'm not ready yet to say a forever "I do"
to one town or county, and, despite the pressure of my nature-

writing forefathers, I'm not sure I have to. For all Berry's agrarian bullying, his is only one way to be in the world. "Firm ground is not available ground," wrote A. R. Ammons, and so it is for me. I won't go as far as to say that I am more comfortable with chaos, just that chaos is what life has dealt me. It would be nice if my world centered on one local place, but it does not. So I need to find another way.

But if marriage to a place is something of a strange metaphor, it's also a fairly natural one. Having spent more time on this small neck of land on Cape Cod than anywhere else in the world, I can see how the idea that I will be here forever appeals. Practically speaking, a long-term commitment to place means you are more likely to undertake a long-term study of place, of its woodchucks or terns, say. And even if you don't undertake anything systematic, you will begin to notice things over time—they will come to you. But of course you can know a place over time without being monogamous to that place, which the marriage metaphor implies. Marriage, as a cultural institution, seems too limiting a metaphor for our love of place, particularly since we are the ancestors of creatures who roamed the world over.

*   *   *

But, as always, I am nervous going to it alone. And so in hopes of support for my own polygamy I turn away from those literary settlers and toward other heroes. Specifically I turn to those two monumental westerners (and closet easterners), Wallace Stegner and Bernard DeVoto. Though both were raised in the West, they moved to Massachusetts as young adults, and took an almost giddy delight in their new homes. DeVoto called himself "an apprentice New Englander," but if he was an apprentice, then it was of the most passionate sort. He threw himself into the East, specifically into "the hallowed ground" of Harvard and Cambridge, with the passion of a convert. Stegner was no less effusive. "Cambridge was our Athens and our Rome," he'd say later. While both would work long and hard to debunk stereotypes of the westerner as rube, and the East, specifically the Northeast, as the country's center, their own attitudes and actions at least mildly mimicked the same stereotype. They wrote and acted as if they'd emerged from the dry western desert and could now gulp down a cold glass of eastern culture and sophistication.

DeVoto was particularly guilty of this. For all his bristling toughness, he never stopped angling for a full professorship at Harvard and, had it been granted him, one imagines he might have reacted like Sally Field getting her Oscar: "You like me . . . you really like me." While his words often traveled west, after his childhood he spent surprisingly little time there, much of his field work the result of hurried road trips before rushing back to "civilization." Stegner, on the other hand, would ultimately return to live in the west, but, like a man sipping a bottle behind the barn, could never stay away from the East for too long. Perhaps, after he had been ensconced as the dean of western writing, there was even an element of guilty pleasure in summering in New England.

Unsettled by my current crisis, I'm heartened to see signs of inconstancy in these two icons. As I sift through their lives for clues to put to use in my own, I keep coming back to the fact that both Stegner and DeVoto first wrote powerfully of the West after settling East. It makes me feel less guilty about having written about the wonders of Cape Cod while staring out at Boulder's flatirons. Of course, my own journey was in the opposite direction. Raised in Massachusetts, I worked hard to make sure I attended Harvard myself, at least in part to please my powerful father. Living in New England for seven years after graduation, I experienced feelings of claustrophobia, of clutter, of judgmental puritan eyes upon me. I could never put words to these vague feelings until I finally moved west at the age of thirty.

In heading west I lived out an American cliché. I moved to Colorado to get healthy and start anew. I don't remember if I ever said it out loud, but I knew that in my own small way I was living out our national myth—tossing off old burdens and moving westward to experience renewal and regeneration. The strange thing was, it worked. If DeVoto was inebriated stepping onto the hallowed ground of Cambridge, I was no less so hiking the mountains of the Front Range. Feeling ever stronger and healthier, I interwove these associations with my new place, a place that I believed was helping heal me. I became an apprentice westerner. Fittingly, my new western friends gave me a nickname that all but replaced the name my father gave me (a name that I also shared with him). Though Cape Cod was my first love, the West became the object of my affection and, as with any loved one, I reveled in it both physically and symbolically.

And then, when my love was strongest, something even stranger happened. I started writing well about the East. Like Stegner and DeVoto, I suddenly had the advantage of looking at a place from somewhere else, defining, as we always do, by differences. It's common to speak of "needing distance" to write about something important to us, and that distance can be literal as well as emotional or chronological. The thing that people who remain stuck in one place perhaps can't see is that America, for all our malls and McDonald's, is still a remarkably regional country with remarkably regional differences. Stegner himself might have remained what he most feared being—a "regional writer"—had it not been for his mental and physical straddling of the country. Perhaps to know and love a new region is to see the old region more clearly.

It may be true that transplanted trees don't always take, but one thing that I've found does transplant fairly well is the capacity to love a place. The tools you develop in one place—the bird books you skim through, the questions you ask and the people you find to ask them to—work well, with some slight adjustments, in other places. I've always been partial to Erich Fromm's take on love: love as the exercise and development of certain muscles. If the ability to love is a skill, that skill also allows us to love new places.

And here, trumpets blaring, I could tie things up neatly were it not for the facts. I'm back East again, here to promote the book I wrote in the West about the East (though, fortunately, it looks like the Western book I finished in the East may be published so I can move back west.) Hopefully, I'll soon settle in one place, or, at least, determine that one place play the role of steady wife, the other as mistress. I can see my two options in my two heroes. Stegner took West as wife and New England as summer fling; DeVoto made the opposite choice. Undecided still, I squat on Cape Cod while my books and belongings remain in a storage locker back in Colorado, a promise to myself that I'll make it back. I remind myself that Thoreau's time in the cabin was a passionate affair and not a lifelong marriage (though he certainly loved the place his whole life). In the meantime, like any good polygamist, I'll take Steven Stills' advice and love the one I'm with. If the model of polygamy may no longer be a practical one for physical love, for love of place I embrace it. As Stegner and DeVoto remind us, we often see what we love most clearly from a distance. ❖

Their First Patient

Virginia Holman

The gross anatomy laboratory at Duke University Medical Center is a surprisingly cheery place. It's in a sub-basement room with clean, white cinderblock walls. Lush fume-eating ferns and vines thrive in the high glazed windows to the east. The fluorescent lights overhead are bright and alarmingly clear—an effort perhaps to banish the possibility of shadow?—and the empty metal tables gleam. There are four bathtub-size sinks, each lined with three spigots operated by foot pedals not unlike those found on a church organ. Boxes filled with latex gloves and disposable plastic aprons are stacked in the cabinets. A large pegboard mounted on the wall is hung with common hardware: handsaws; bright blue, yellow, and red plastic mallets; chisels. All carry the scars of use, but each tool is clean and well maintained. This place—before the cadavers, students, and teachers arrive—could almost be mistaken for a commercial kitchen or the fanatically pristine woodworking shop of an elderly neighbor.

Gross Anatomy is the essential and incomparable crucible of all first-year medical students at Duke and every medical school. I'm here not as a student but as an approved witness, writer, and perhaps, potential body donor.

Though I have never had the slightest qualm about giving up my eyes or kidneys to some living soul who could use and benefit from them, the idea of giving the rest of my body to Science, as the saying goes, seems a much murkier proposition. What, exactly, would Science *do* with me? And would a gift of my entire mortal self be appreciated and valued enough to offset my trepidation and that of my surviving family? If I were dissected, what might become of my parts once they had outlived their use to Science? For instance, would my hand be dissected and studied by earnest future surgeons, or would it merely wind up as part of a student's Halloween prank? Could my body be buried or cremated after Science finished with it? Or would my remains be unceremoniously tossed out in the orange biohazard trash container?

In the eighteenth century, body donors and "anatomical gifts programs" were unheard of. Medical students dissected the corpses of executed criminals, stolen from fresh graves by "resurrection men" who also trafficked in unclaimed corpses, left by family in hospitals or mental institutions. At Duke, students learn *only* from donated bodies.

On the first day of Gross Anatomy, students assemble in a sleek modern amphitheater replete with Internet portals and an individual microphone for each of the 120 students in attendance. A group of anatomists and residents are also here to prepare the students for the emotionally grueling task ahead.

The first lecture is delivered by Dr. Matt Cartmill, a professor with unkempt hair and silvered muttonchop whiskers and bifocals. He reminds the students that the bodies are now quite dead.

"D E A D," he writes on the board. The room is silent.

"Nothing will happen when you cut these bodies. They will not cry out in pain. You will not be hurting these people." I find his blunt reassurance comforting. He talks about the use of humor to relieve the stress and tension during dissection and tells us that we will all feel tempted at times to make jokes in lab about the bodies and the experience we're about to enter into. Then he pauses, takes off his bifocals, and looks hard into the eyes of the students. "It's tremendously disrespectful. So *don't* do it," he says. "Just don't do it."

Several former anatomy students talk about the strong emotions they felt when they dissected a fellow human. A psychologist is on hand. The administrators of the anatomical gifts program at Duke are there. Excerpts from family members' letters are read aloud.

Before we go to the lab, Dr. Daniel Schmitt, a youthful anatomy professor, clips a small portable microphone on his tie and energetically walks about the room as he lectures. "The bodies here wanted to be here—on your dissecting table. Why? So you could learn. This is an amazing gift. The donors knew that you would take them apart, that you would cut into them. So be respectful of them, but do not be shy. You do not honor these people unless you learn well. Don't blow this chance."

*   *   *

The first day in the gross anatomy lab is hands-on. The drowsy, antiseptic odor of human preservative fills each breath I take. The room thrums with the pulse of the ventilator fans. Several of the students don paper masks in an effort to block out the chemical smell, and I reach for one myself. Dr. Bill Hylander, a Biological Anthropology professor and anatomist, notices and laughs. "You get used to the smells here pretty fast. And the plants love the formaldehyde." Clearly, the seven-foot ficus adjacent to the teaching skeleton is hyper-fueled by such salubrious vapors.

"You might want to dress for the occasion," he observes as I shuck the clear plastic apron over my wool trousers and turtleneck. I notice that many of the students have changed into scrubs or sweats. "You're fine today, but things can get, well, messy." He offers up a wry smile and an unapologetic shrug. His lab coat, like all the formal white cloth jackets of the anatomy professors, has stains on the cuffs and instrument pockets—an indication of the involvement level that is expected.

The students at my table convene. We turn back the thick,

crackling plastic sheet wound round the human shape laid out on our dissecting table. We begin familiarizing ourselves with the body we will spend the next two months dismantling and memorizing.

At our table, and at every table, there is an involuntary pause. Many students miss a breath. A lambent expression of shock plays upon the faces of the living. Nothing could ever prepare us for this moment: the cadaver before us is a person, a person dead. The cadavers are naked, and I am awed by the sturdy plain of skin that sweeps across each body. There's so *much* of it.

It startles me to see death and nakedness together, to see old age and nakedness together. I walk about the room to look at each table. Some bodies are only in their fifties, others are near-ancient at ninety-plus years. Age provides little indication of why one body appears robust or another frail. Occasionally there is sad evidence of infirmity, a bedsore or a feeding tube, but during this first intimate look, the bodies refuse to yield much more information than they would clothed and alive. I'm relieved there's no donor under fifty. Already I feel as mortal as the day I gave birth. The students here are over a decade younger than I am, and for some, this is their first exposure to a dead body. I can't imagine what this is like for them.

Tacked to the bulletin board, along with the lab schedule and exam dates, is the cadaver list. There are twenty donors, and for privacy's sake, the only information given is age and cause of death. That doesn't stop the students' desire to know more about the donors.

"I wish I knew her name." "I wonder what he did for a living." "Is there any way to get more information about the donor?"

Daniel Schmitt explains that the students will not receive more information about the cadavers, but that it is quite natural to wonder who these people were. He also reminds the students that there will be a memorial service held in Duke Chapel at the conclusion of the semester.

"Can we name the cadaver?" one student asks.

"Sure, if you find that helps. My personal view is that these people already have names, but if you find it eases your, mind, go ahead." Our table decides against selecting a name.

The first task of the medical students is not to begin to dissect the bodies but rather to protect them. We are instructed to wrap the hands, feet, and face. These are dissected late in the course and must be kept supple with a solution of formalin, glycerin, and pine oil.

This moment between the living and the dead is remarkably gentle. We wrap the donor's feet, one at a time, and ease them back down on the table. The same with the hands. One student holds the well manicured hand of the ninety-six-year-old woman at our table while another winds the gauze around it. Then it is time to wrap the head. The students study the faces of their cadavers.

One young man lets out a slight involuntary "Oh!"

"What?" I ask.

"Well, the cadaver is so real. Was so real," he corrects and pauses again to regard the woman who lies before us. Indeed, evidence of the individual before us is undeniable. Yet it is clear that the spark of life is long gone. What remains is a mere fraction of a much larger picture. The face of the woman on our table is quite elegant, and I find its deep lines and furrows from a long life a comfort. Her eyelids are open, but when I look into them I cannot find her eyes.

"Was she an eye donor?" I ask Dr. Christine Wall, the anatomist who supervises our group and four other tables. Eyes are the only organs that body donors can give without compromising the integrity of the dissection process.

Chris comes over and leans her face uncomfortably near to the cadaver's. None of us at the table has dared get that close. "No. Her eyes are right here. Look."

I take a breath, bend over, and peer into the cadaver's face. Our donor's eyes are sunk deep within their sockets and are clouded gray like a seal's. Daniel Schmitt comes over. "We'll bring up her eyes and dissect them when we do the skull."

"Bring up the eyes?" I ask.

"When you fill them with water, the eyes rise up."

"Oh." I am finding this whole experience unsettling, and I also see fear on the faces of the students.

I raise the woman's head from the table while a student winds damp gauze around the woman's face. Her skull is heftier than I expected. I look to the other tables. One student absently pats his cadaver's hand. It's O.K., the gesture seems to say. I imagine this really serves to soothe him for the task ahead—the first cut.

Since the first dissection will be of the back, the seven of us struggle to turn the body from supine to prone. I notice around the room that some students try to protect the dignity of the cadavers. One table spreads paper towels across the buttocks of a man, while another arranges the plastic sheet to cover all but the dissection site. A student tucks the plastic under the exposed leg of a woman on his table, as if putting a child to bed.

We open *Grant's Dissector* and place it on the bookstand at the end of the table. The first incision is long, from the neck straight down the spine. The students at my table look at each other to decide who will brave it. The student who volunteers makes several attempts to fit a blade into her scalpel handle without much luck. Chris Wall comes over to help. "Like this." In two adept movements she secures the blade in the handle and then abruptly walks away.

"Students are often terrified to start cutting," she tells me later. "If I stay too long at a table before the students are acclimated to their cadaver, I'll start doing all their work—I never tire of dissecting. But it's important that they get comfortable touching the donors. Anatomy is best learned when it's applied."

The student takes a delicate hold on her scalpel, her fingers grasp midway down the shaft. Gingerly, she draws the scalpel down a length of spine. The blade is keen but the student must repeat the cut again, pressing harder, to cut all the way through the skin and fat. Once the incision is made, another is drawn across the shoulder blades and yet another across the hips. The cuts look like the perforated doors on an Advent calendar.

On living tissue, blood would spring forth from an incision, but with these embalmed bodies, the flesh parted by the cuts merely affords us a clearer view into the small fissures. Now the students take turns at the tedious task of pulling and cutting the skin and fat away from the muscle underneath. The fat on our donor is bright yellow, cheesy-looking, and slick. We patiently "clear a field," as Chris Wall says, so that we will be able to see and identify the musculature of the back. It takes almost three hours to fully remove the skin and fat from the deep fascia—the thin pearlescent connective tissue shrink wrapped around the internal body structures. Once these winglike flaps of skin are pulled away from the body, I can see the superficial muscles below. The cadaver finally resembles the pictures in our dissector, and we begin the process of identifying the structures we've exposed.

After the first lab, I go home and bathe. My clothes and hair smell like ham and formaldehyde. I pack overalls and a T-shirt for the next lab. Before I go to bed, I worry what I might dream that night. How will this experience affect me? Suddenly I am a bit unsteady. Can I really do this for the next two months?

*   *   *

In the following weeks I decide to try out A.D.A.M., the Animated Dissection of Anatomy for Medicine, a computer software grogram that will take me through a human dissection by clicks of a mouse. There are a number of such programs available—Netter's and Digital Anatomist are two other popular packages—and many students use them as tutorials.

Everything on A.D.A.M. is lucid. I can identify structures readily, but when I go to the lab and try to identify the same structures, I find the cadaver labyrinthine and confusing. Organs and veins are displaced by fat and look only vaguely like those in my dissector and in A.D.A.M.

One student holds up what seems like a white elastic band in our cadaver's leg.

"I can't find this ligament in our dissector."

Chris Wall comes over and takes a look. "That's the sciatic nerve," she says. "We tend not to think of nerves as being large and dissectable, but they can be."

"It's enormous," the students murmur and admire the thin bundle in its slippery myelin sheath.

Nothing in the body looks the way it does in A.D.A.M. or the dissector. The placement of the ovaries varies remarkably in each female donor. Occasionally nerves and veins take maverick pathways and show up in unexpected places.

The students who take Gross Anatomy quickly learn that the bodies of the donors, and those of their future patients, aren't fungible. A rosy, dense lung removed from one cadaver may be mottled and diseased in another. Hysterectomies leave some tables without reproductive organs. Tumors unknown to the donor are found. At one table, students cut and peel back the patellar tendon of the knee only to unexpectedly reveal a shiny titanium knee replacement. Students come over from other tables and we marvel at the surgeon's work and the presence of something manmade so deep inside a man. One student whistles—"That looks like something straight out of *The Terminator*."

Daniel Schmitt and Matt Cartmill both extol the importance of the kinesthetic or tactile learning that dissection imparts: knowledge that can only be gained by the students' hands working on the bodies. After all, palpation is very much a part of a doctor's repertoire of skills.

Richard Brooks, one of the first-year medical students, says that though the software programs are adequate tutors, they can never give a full sense of a person or his parts. "For instance," he comments, "I could look at fat all day on A.D.A.M. but never understand without having had dissected a body that fat is heavy, that it's oily."

After we are through with the dissections, after we have removed and held the brain and lungs, bisected the skull and dissected the orbit of the eye, we replace the organs and wrap the bodies again so that they may be cremated whole. Some donors have requested that their remains be returned to family, others will have their ashes scattered at a special site in Duke Forest.

*   *   *

The memorial service, held in Duke Chapel, honors our most powerful teachers: the donors. There are over forty people seated in the section reserved for family. I cannot help but look at the first few pews and wonder if the family of the woman I helped dissect is present. In a way, we've already met.

Several students deliver short speeches and read poems of appreciation to the family members and teachers. They speak of their emotion upon first entering the anatomy lab and meeting the donors. Dr. Alison Weidner, Chief of the Division of Gynecological Services, thanks the family members. "We take this heavy responsibility very seriously. . . . It would be impossible to have these opportunities to learn without this marvelous and enormous sacrifice you and your loved ones have made."

Matt Cartmill delivers an eloquent speech on why dissection is an essential part of each medical student's training. He succinctly explains that "dissection teaches our hands" in ways books and software programs cannot. "We are all built to a common plan, but the details are always different. . . . This appreciation of human uniqueness is also of crucial importance to the student physician; and it, too, grows out of the practice of dissection."

It is Richard Brooks, however, who reminds me of the ultimate importance of this experience. "I know," he confides to me, "that I'll always think of the man we dissected as my first patient." ❖

RESTORATION

FROM *RED HOUSE*

Sarah Messer

IN HIS MID-SEVENTIES, RESTORATION CARPENTER EDGAR Wentworth had the air of someone who had seen houses like this before—New England homes that had been badly burned, some of them salvageable and some not, depending on how deeply the smoke had sunk into the walls, how much the fire had destroyed. He knew how the house would look: the walls melted and blistered, wood braided, charred table backs, a pantry of exploded bottles—jam, syrup, flour, vinegar—run over surfaces onto the floor, plastic melted over bread, lumps of copper and liquefied electronics. There would be puddles of candles in rooms the fire did not reach, frozen in cascades over the edges of things. Knots of melted wires, scorched hinges. Light switches with arched backs. The blackened faces of clocks. Iron latches would be turned red from the heat, the impurities rising to the surface of the metal; solder in the seams of lanterns flowed to liquid, the pieces strewn where they had fallen clanking to the floor.

The window glass would be almost gone—melted or blackened—the panes that remained run with cracks—blond hairs on a chalkboard. And light would come through faintly in these places, glowing amber. Fire made even an old house age lifetimes, made it seem desperate and abandoned. Smoke pulled across walls, across ceilings, and through rooms, tracing the lathing, every crossbeam and nail head visible. Sometimes the smoke-crossed lathing intersected with vertical drips of water left from the firemen's hoses, creating a perverse gingham pattern. In the heat of fire, nails pushed out of doorframes, pushed to the surface of plaster, prying their way out.

Wentworth knew that fire burned in a V, heating the highest parts of the room first, leaping through open doors toward the ceiling of the next room, licking up wallpaper, rolling back paint, a rash blooming before the path of the flames.

Entering a burned house was like entering a dream mind—some elements were missing entirely or moved to other locations, the rooms the same but clouded, slightly off. Everything was itself and not itself—like walking through the mind into the shadow parts—the bed the firemen had hauled away from a window now posed in the middle of the room. Fire desires and consumes; it is filled with impatient wanting, the roar of needing more. Wentworth had seen how fire pressed its back against a closed door and moved past it, pushing through every crack.

Outside, trees bent away from the structure, the leaves and branches blackened. The exterior paint dissolved into gobs of crusted tar—the spots where the water in the wood cells boiled and escaped, causing the paint to crater like a peeled sunburn.

Wentworth expected all of this, and he entered the house carrying a yellow No. 2 pencil, stopping at each door molding, each wall and wainscoting, lightly removing a dot of soot with the pencil's eraser.

Three days after she had run out of the burning house, my mother was back with a flashlight, following Wentworth and his precise, aquatic movements through the gloom, the bright pencil held out before him like a feeler, a neon lure. The flashlight beam passed over rubble, dark shapes, as he tried to determine, from a professional standpoint, whether the house could be saved. The fire had burned the entire west kitchen wing—eating away through the ceiling to the eaves above, stopping at the slate roof. Water had flooded the lower rooms and the basement garage, leaving wires and plaster hanging from the ceiling in coughed-out chunks. The appliances were disgorged, melted. We had lost everything that had been in those rooms—the kitchen, porch, hallways, and bathroom—pots, toys, clothing, a closet-full of wrapped Christmas presents, a player piano, bookshelves.

In what remained of the screened-in porch, they found the bodies of the two kittens, curled around each other in a makeshift bed of towels; the dog and the mother cat had found their way out.

But the fire had not spread to the rest of the house, thanks in part to two firemen who had spent the night monitoring it, wandering through rooms up and down the stairs thinking, *So many beds—whom have we missed?*

During the first few days after the fire, neighbors and members of the local church had come to help sift through the wreckage; they had carried ash out in wheelbarrows, then dug through it, lifting out a door hinge or a nail, a spoon or a cup.

Now Wentworth stopped and bent down near the corner of the fireplace in the living room, touched the eraser to a molding.

"Ya, we can do that," he said, and then, standing, ran the eraser along the mantel. "Ya, that'll come down."

My mother's flashlight beam fixed on Wentworth like a leash, glancing off his shoulder or to the wall or the floor or the window casing where he was tapping the pencil, erasing. Wentworth, after all the silence and wandering, turned to her suddenly and said that his crew could start the next week.

While we were safe with relatives, my mother and father spent their days in the cold shell of the house, their nights in Scituate Harbor, at seafood restaurants, or in the aqua-blue room at the Clipper Ship, with is faint smell of chlorine and mothballs, sanitary soap. And during this time, my mother tells me as if it were an addendum, she cried constantly. Not necessarily sobbing, although sometimes it was that, but more of a constant stream of tears, like a slow-leaking faucet. It was her fault, she feared—although the workmen all claimed it was then mistake—bad wiring or construction, a faulty appliance. But she knew otherwise. How to explain those rags? She had almost killed her entire family.

"It's not your fault," my father said again and again. Still, her tears made streaks down her sooty face; her nose was red and raw, her face striped.

An elderly neighbor who wintered in Florida was on his way to Logan Airport when he heard about the fire on a local radio station. He made a call from the terminal, telling us we could stay in his house until he returned in May.

His house was a large Victorian filled with long hallways and bathrooms with worn tile. There was a mudroom off the kitchen, and every day my mother would spend mornings in the Red House carting out our burned and smoke-stained belongings, boxing them, and bringing them to a pile in the Victorian mudroom. In the afternoon and evening, sometimes late at night, I would find her standing by the two stainless-steel sinks in the kitchen, up to her elbows in rubber gloves, washing smoked objects.

There is a photograph from that time of my father sitting in the living room of that house holding me on his lap. I am squirming in the photo, perhaps tired, perhaps bored, trying to wrench free of his grasp; I appear as a blonde blur in a mustard-colored turtleneck. My father stares straight ahead at the camera, and his face is one of direct surrender—the kind of look that only comes from extreme exhaustion, or the mental clarity that occurs after surviving severe trauma. It was evening when the photo was taken; a lamp had been clicked on in the background, next to a radiator and the corner of a table piled with books. My father's brown hair is styled in a long bob with bangs brushed across his forehead, and sideburns. He wears a pink-and-brown-striped cotton dress-shirt open at the neck. The photo captured the tension between us—I am a whirl of motion, waving a small stuffed bear that I had sewn from a kit of acrylic fur, foam rubber, and glass eyes; my father is extremely still, his eyes boring a hole through the camera lens and beyond to the eyes of the photographer, who is my mother. He is saying something with his eyes—he is saying that he feels defeated but is trying not to look defeated at the moment because of her, because of the children. *We could have all died,* his eyes are saying.

My mother had left her post in underwater salvage to come out and take a few pictures. They had six kids and a burned historic home between them. At Christmas, there had been few presents—Patrick had received a hockey game with metal players moved by levers and rods; Jess had received a wooden pony with yellow wheels that made a clicking gallop sound when she pulled it across the room by a string; I had received the Sew Your Own Bear kit. In photos, the smell of smoke seemed to permeate us, even in this temporary house. It had seeped into our hair and teeth, into stuffed animals, mattresses, and pillows, so that it seemed our bodies carried the musky odor of our burned belongings—it hung over us like a glower, a depression, a bad mood. The burned house was a ship that went down with all its passengers, my father thought, but somehow no one had drowned. It was a miracle he didn't quite understand.

The year of the fire, I was enrolled in a private kindergarten called Steeple School, in the same classroom as Suzy. The school was housed in a white, steepled Congregational church, a product of the continual church-mitosis that had been happening in Marshfield since the seventeenth century. The church had long since been without a parish, but ran a thriving kindergarten and nursery school, boasting a large staff, good resources, new playground equipment. Our activities involved a lot of pipe cleaners and Styrofoam balls, milkweed-pod parrots and construction paper, or felt animals stuck onto the wall behind bars of a "zoo."

In the classroom I spent little time with Suzy, fixing my

attention instead on my newly acquired best friend, Maryanne McGuire. On Halloween, Maryanne had dressed as a witch and approached me in her pointed hat, with black smudge on her face, carrying a broom. "I don't have a best friend yet," she said, "do you?"

I was dressed as a bride, in a truncated, hemmed-in version of one of my mother's cotillion dresses.

"No," I said. "Not yet."

Maryanne was a precocious reader, outgoing and funny. Her favorite book was titled *Ann Likes Red*, which included lines like "Ann likes red. Red, red, red. A blue dress Ann? I like red, said Ann. Red! Red! Red!" One might assume that the book concludes with Ann getting her monochromatic comeuppance and seeing the benefit of other colors of the rainbow. But I'm not sure whether this happened, and even if it did, we never focused on this message. We ran up and down the scrappy dirt hill behind school yelling "red, red, red." These lines became Maryanne's mantra, her code of living. It seemed that Maryanne (who also had red hair) wore, more often than not, the color red. Maryanne was cast in the school play, *The Little Red Hen*, playing, of course, the Red Hen. When asked her name, she would say "Mary-ANNE," emphasizing the Ann at the end.

At our borrowed house, my mother continued to line up the blackened items on a dingy towel spread on the left side of the sink. If the object to be washed was a toy, she would hold it up in the air without turning from her position at the sink and say, "Yes or no?" Whoever belonged to the toy would then decide its fate—if we said no, she would throw it in the dump pile, in the far corner of the garage; if we said yes, she would try to wash it. She would dunk the toy in water and begin scrubbing, occasionally rinsing it in the second basin. Then, when it seemed she had cleaned it as best she could, she would place it in a dish drainer, take it out to a different corner of the garage, beyond the mudroom, and put the clean object in a plastic laundry basket.

As a part of her biology major in college, my mother had worked banding small brown bats. The mouths of the caves were very narrow, and my mother, the only woman in the group, was the only person with shoulders small enough to fit through the openings. The caves were halfway up a hill—a series of crevasses that dropped straight down through rock. Her professor gave her a banding gun, strapped her in a harness, and lowered her down by rope. Inside, the cave was narrow and the walls were thick with sleeping bats. Every wall was alive with them, their bodies shitting and crawling over each other in their sleep, elbowing, blind. She dangled in the middle of the cave, headlamp strapped over a knit ski mask. She barely had room to swivel, to bring her arms up to her sides. Her legs felt loose and weak in the harness; darkness fell below her into the sound of dripping water.

She told me how she grabbed the soft body of each bat and clamped it with the gun. She wore heavy leather gloves, so there was no chance of being bitten. The bats barely woke up, and when they did, they screeched and peed on her. After she let them go, they fell a bit, a dark flutter below her where they landed farther down the wall and clung. The biology professor and the other students were above her, in the circle of daylight. Down in the cave, she heard nothing but the rustle and shriek of bats, and the occasional echo of a voice from the surface, followed by a jerk, a lowering of the rope.

With the dim yellowish glow of her headlamp, she was trapped in a dark jar. When she described this experience years later, she used the same words as she did about those months entering and leaving the burned house. She lived inside the smell of soot, the same way that she had lived among the bodies of the bats, within the vertical hive of bodies.

*   *   *

The Red House, having survived the fire, was restored—better than before, some people said. Wentworth, ripping down the damaged ceiling and wall plaster, had found something remarkable: a ceiling panel that resembled leopard skin. The boards were painted with swirls of black over a wash of tan milk-paint. All over the house, in fact, on the first and second floors, Wentworth found hidden ceilings beneath the lower, ruined ones. When he ripped the wet plaster down, there they were, perfect beams. Richard Warren Hatch had found a pile of similarly painted boards in a trash heap during his restoration of the house in 1959. At the time, Hatch was not living in the Red House and thus could only oversee the restoration on weekends. He had salvaged what he could of the boards and fitted them into the ceiling of a bedroom upstairs, but he always felt that he had let this historical aspect of the house be destroyed by ignorant workmen.

*　*　*

The restoration discoveries brought Richard Warren Hatch into our lives again. When he sold my parents the house, he had made it clear that he would never return. But the spring after the fire, he wrote my father a letter:

> *Dear Ron,*
>
> *If you can stand a surprise—when your old red house is ready, Ruth and I will come and inspect it. No week-end, no night driving, but a morning or early afternoon visit. Just send us a proper signal.*
>
> *Yours, Dick*

And he did return. Our devotion and restoration brought him back, and, as if on cue, when he saw the painted beams he thought had been lost, he fell to his knees and wept.

"He's no small man," my mother said. "Down on his knees in the living room weeping."

Hatch wrote my parents again immediately following the visit, the letter dated only "the day after."

Dear Pat and Ron,

I know that I have never been quite able to express my feelings about the Red House, I suppose because they were a combination that escapes definition. You see, it was not only the love of the house itself with its setting, its long history of family ownership, its every physical inch, so to speak, but something more than that . . . the fact that always there was love inside the house, love not made evident by overt signs simply but recognized by intuition and the heart, and that has been a resource on which I have drawn all my life.

A combination, as I say, quite beyond words, but which perhaps explains why, when I had to leave the house I felt that I could never go back—

Anyway I have to write to tell you both that Ruth and I came away yesterday feeling above all that there is the same combination in your house—your home—something transcending the skill and work and perfection of what you have done with the physical house. And so you both have done something immeasurable for my spirit.

"It doesn't look like our house," Kim said when she returned for a visit that summer, "it looks like a museum." She was referring to the new blankness of the low-ceilinged rooms, the walls stripped of wallpaper, the sixties neon gone from the bedrooms upstairs, as if the house had traveled back in time. Though householders of my parents' generation might have tried to keep some historical feel, they also might have put up a contemporary painting or two—a Georgia O'Keeffe print, a Pollock—or at least reserved a wall for pictures of their own children and parents, other relatives. I had seen such a wall of family photos extending the length of the second-floor hallway in Maryanne McGuire's house. The photos documented every year of Maryanne's childhood: her red hair growing longer, then banged, then ponytailed; a sister, then a baby brother joined her. There was no such hallway in our house; in fact, there were no hallways, just a series of rooms, branching off each other like rabbit dens. There were eight kids in the family, but still my parents hung no family photos—no baby pictures, no wedding photos, no grandparents sitting in funny old cars, or in boats, or leaning on cannons or monuments. Nothing. Perhaps they thought it was all too modern.

After the fire, my parents carefully rehung candleholders, secured a brass bed-warmer on the wall near the fireplace, scattered the mantels with hurricane lamps. Silvery daguerreotypes were propped on parlor moldings, Richard Warren Hatch's grandparents and other former inhabitants of the house—a reminder of the house's true lineage. The walls held a ledger from a Hatch Bible, a needlepoint sampler, and a series of wooden butter-molds secured with tiny hooks. The discovered beams remained exposed, and the floor too, the wide boards sanded and stained, strewn with faded hooked rugs. Rooms contained hard, straight-backed chairs and a clock reel used for counting and winding flax, a Victorian rocking horse missing its hair and saddle.

The refrained Hatch wills sat on the dining-room table for about a week after we moved back in. They stared at me every time I walked by—six documents framed in double-sided glass so that both front and back could be read. They were enclosed in thin wood bands, with picture-framing wire, and eye hooks screwed to the top. The paper behind the glass seemed fragile, the handwriting and ink tentative. In the shifting light of the window, I saw the reflection of my face moving over the field of writing and the crud that seemed to crawl up each document, a stain from smoke or water, a stain I knew was because of the fire, because of us.

Meanwhile, our old smoke-stained and burned belongings, those prefire items that were not salvageable—furniture, carpets, doors, and appliances—had been tossed in a huge pile in the woods along the road to the North River and buried. Another dump was eventually established for smaller smoke-stained objects that could not be cleaned—lamps, clothing, ruined board games, toys. This became known as the Toy Dump, the charnel ground of items from our childhood that did not survive. Grass, a few baby oak trees, and scrub pines eventually grew over the mound that had been buried beneath a pile of dirt by a backhoe, yet, after particularly heavy rains, the matted hair of a stuffed creature would be left exposed, the wheel of a melted truck. We pretended that the charred refrigerator, the plastic chair, the stained dolls or sled or stuffed rabbit had gone away, but we had buried it all so close to us, in our backyard, in the woods behind our house, and for years the earth kept churning things up. ❖

AN EXCERPT FROM *THE HOUSE ON DREAM STREET*

Dana Sachs

I LOVED BEING IN VIETNAM AS MUCH AS I EVER HAD, BUT MY relationship with the country wasn't delicate in the way it had once been. I wasn't worried that if I spent the day with another foreigner I'd somehow lose touch with the real Vietnam. Now, I no longer thought of my friends in terms of who was a foreigner and who was Vietnamese, and I didn't worry about coming across as the Ugly American. My nationality no longer defined my identity here. If I did something stupid, it wasn't because I was American. It was because I was stupid. And I found myself for the first time getting into arguments.

One night, I went with two new friends, Van and Duc, to see the French film *Indochine*. Van and Duc were talented painters I'd met through Steve. Their work would have fetched high prices had they chosen to pursue the increasingly hot market in Vietnamese art. But rather than schmoozing with potential patrons, they spent most of their time hanging out in Duc's studio, a stilt house on the edge of the West Lake, where they painted, drank whiskey, and pontificated about the state of the world.

The screening of the film, which was playing at the Eighth of August Cinema in the center of town, was a big event for Hanoi.

Indochine, a film about the Vietnamese revolt against French colonialism, was one of the first Western films to arrive as the country slowly opened its door to the outside world. Everyone wanted to see it, and not just the star-struck Hanoians who had managed to capture a glimpse of the star, Catherine Deneuve, while she was filming on location. Outside the theater, ticket scalpers proved they knew a thing about capitalism by rushing back and forth across the sidewalks and jumping in front of passing motorists in a frenzied effort to secure their sales. Inside the theater, nearly every seat was filled and the audience had to strain to see through a fog of cigarette smoke and to hear through the grinding crunch of sunflower seeds. But unlike the bemused, rather bored reactions I'd witnessed at the Tower of the Screaming Virgins a few months earlier, the audience at Indochine was clearly captivated. It represented most Hanoians' first chance to see a Western film projected on the big screen, and people's reactions to the production quality must have been similar to the way American audiences responded in 1939, when Dorothy stepped out of her black and white cabin and walked into Technicolor Oz. "Dep. Dep," I heard people whisper all around me: *Beautiful.*

After the film ended, the three of us went to get something to eat. It was nearly eleven already, past bedtime for most of Hanoi, and my favorite noodle shop had long ago pulled its metal doors shut for the night. A few establishments were still open, serving noodle soup and rice porridge to tipsy men trying to sober up on their way home. We sat down at a table on the sidewalk in the middle of the block, right next to a sewage drain that ran along the side of the road. The proprietor, a mustached man wearing a Tiger Beer T-shirt, was sitting on a stool next to his charcoal cooker.

"What do you want to eat?" he grumbled.

Duc and Van ordered fish porridge. I asked for a Bay Up— Vietnamese for Seven-Up.

Both of my friends were still feeling dazzled by the movie.

They were used to the grainy black and white or washed-out color that characterized Vietnamese cinema. In contrast, the French film's luscious palette and perfectly defined contrasts of light and dark left them breathless. They didn't like the movie, though.

"The French!" Van said, with a dismissive wave of his hand. "They don't know anything about the war. It's worse than that movie, I'll tell you." Van, who was my age, was a thin, often grouchy man whose delight in the world only became evident in the soft, romantic quality of his paintings. In contrast, Duc, who was nearly forty, was lumbering and cheerful, with a soft voice and a shag of bushy hair.

Van lit a cigarette. During the movie, he'd smoked his way through half a dozen 555s. "Westerners will see that film and think they understand Vietnam," he said. "It's like me saying, because I've seen a few videos, that life is easy in America, that it's just Walt Disney over there."

Duc and I laughed. The proprietor came over and plopped the rice porridge and Bay Up down in the center of the table. Van hardly noticed the food. Duc immediately took his bowl and spoon and began stirring sprigs of fresh dill into the thick mass of porridge.

I pulled open my drink and took a sip of the warm soda. "It's true," I said. I knew that Van and Duc had both seen Hollywood war movies on video. "The only thing most Americans know about the Vietnam War is what they've seen in *Apocalypse Now* or *Platoon*."

Instead of laughing, Van looked irritated, as if he found America's myopia more disturbing than Vietnam's. "Americans don't know anything about war," he told me. "You haven't had a war in your country in over a hundred years. You're lucky! But, still, whenever a single American dies in battle, you're furious. You lost 58,000 Americans in Vietnam. We lost two million Vietnamese. You bombed us. We never bombed you. But still, it was the United States, not Vietnam, who held a grudge."

In another situation, I would probably have agreed with Van. After all, at that time, the U.S. was still maintaining its vituperative trade embargo against Vietnam, keeping the struggling nation from fully recovering from the double economic disasters of the war and several decades of Communism. But the antagonism in Van's voice made me defensive. Not bothering to hide my sarcasm, I answered, "Oh, right. The Vietnamese would never, ever hold a grudge."

We looked at each other for a long moment, each of us trying to decide how far to let this conversation go. Finally, Van pulled back a little. "It's just sad, that's all," he said, his tone only slightly less caustic. "All over the world, people know about American hamburgers, American blue jeans, American cars. These are good things. They help to build a strong country. We Vietnamese beat the Americans and what are we famous for? War! In this century alone we've fought the French, Japanese, Americans, Cambodians, and Chinese. If we didn't have to fight all those wars, maybe we'd be rich now. We'd be the ones visiting Walt Disneyland and making blue jeans."

Van pulled his bowl of porridge closer, as if to signal that he'd had enough of this conversation. After only a couple of spoonfuls, though, he looked up again. This time he had a grin on his face and I could see that he'd thought of a way to move the conversation toward friendlier ground. He leaned forward and poked Duc in the arm. "Remember the Gulf War?" he asked.

Duc laughed. "Yeah," he said. He kept eating his porridge.

Van turned to me. "We Vietnamese appreciated the Gulf War. For once, there was this huge international conflict going on and we didn't have to fight in it. We just sat around like everybody else in the world, watching it on TV."

Loud voices behind us made us turn around. The proprietor, back on his stool by the charcoal cookers, was yelling at a newspaper boy, one of the hundreds of often-homeless children who spent their days walking the city streets, selling papers, cheap magazines, and horoscopes. The "boy" was at least twenty, with a slightly deranged look on his face. He wasn't arguing as much as whining, but the angry proprietor suddenly jumped up and boxed his ear. The newspaper boy raised his hand to his head and howled.

"I'm bleeding," he screamed.

The proprietor sat back down, pulled out a rag, and began to wipe the table in front of him.

"My ear! I'm bleeding," the newspaper boy screamed again. I had a momentary worry that he would pull out a gun and shoot us all, but this was not America. He cried for a few more seconds, then turned and wandered off down the street, holding his hand to his ear.

Street fights took place so regularly here that spectators watched them like fireworks, focusing for the instant of the flare and then losing interest as soon as it faded. I had more trouble forgetting such incidents. An American could hardly complain about the violence in Vietnam—after all, violent crime was relatively rare here—but the easy acceptance of petty brutality always bothered me. I watched the newspaper boy, who was peering into the rear-view mirror of a parked motorbike, checking for signs of blood.

"Let's go," I said.

As we got up to leave, Duc pulled a pack of chewing gum out of his pocket and handed sticks to me and Van. Van tore the wrapper off his gum and tossed the paper onto the asphalt of the road.

"What's wrong with you?" I snapped. "How can you pollute your country?"

Van turned and looked at me. "Americans," he said calmly. "You think you can tell us how to keep our country clean after you dropped napalm and Agent Orange on us?"

I was so angry and humiliated that I couldn't look at him. But I no longer felt the guilt I'd always experienced when I thought about the war in Vietnam, as if, just by being an American, I was responsible for what my country had done. I regretted the war more than I ever had, having seen how it affected this city, and the lives of the people I'd come to know. But over the past 18 months, my sense of this place had changed dramatically. I'd once thought of Vietnam with the same stereotypes that one would use to describe a battered woman: miserable, victimized, helpless. Now, I would have used an entirely different set of adjectives: tough, resilient, passionate. As much as Vietnam had suffered, it didn't need my guilt. It might need my help—normalizing relations was a good start—but what Van had said was true. The only thing Vietnam was famous for were the wars. I'd come to see the place as more complex than that. If I could go for weeks at a time in Hanoi without even remembering the wars, perhaps Americans could forget something new with Vietnam, and move beyond the past.

So I didn't break down when Van mentioned the napalm, and I didn't apologize either. And that was a good thing, too, because when I looked over at him, I saw that he was grinning, waiting to see how I'd react. I looked at him for a moment. "I don't know," I said. "Napalm or a Wrigley's wrapper. It's not an easy call."

In what might have been the clearest sign that the war was truly over, a Vietnamese and an American discovered that it wasn't that hard, actually, to joke about it. ❖

POETRY
PROCESS

IN THE BEGINNING

Lavonne Adams

I F YOU WANT TO WRITE A SUCCESSFUL POEM, FOLLOW THESE
steps: make sure your alarm buzzes you awake at exactly
5:47 A.M.; brush your teeth with toothpaste that has not
been tested on animals, since poets are expected to be a sensitive
bunch; brew a hefty cup of coffee or uncap your favorite caffeine-
laden soft drink; wrap yourself in that threadbare blue flannel
bathrobe (clothing underneath is optional); settle in front of a
computer screen guarded by some randomly chosen totem such
as "Stretch," the Beanie Baby ostrich with feet like miniature
catcher's mitts, or the bronze baby shoes your mother pressed
into your hands when you first left home. Before turning on
the computer, crack each knuckle on your left hand. Avoid the
temptation to write that first draft with pen and paper, to feel
each word being shaped beneath your hand since today's muse
is hip and won't waste time inspiring a poet who seems stuck in
the Romantic era. Besides, carpal tunnel syndrome is the modern
equivalent of starving in the garret—prerequisite suffering for any
serious poet—so don't try to cut corners.

I am, of course, just kidding, though there is some truth in
establishing routine in your writing habits since the creative part
of your mind works like a pump that has to be primed. There is,

however, no foolproof formula for starting a poem, let alone carrying the process through to its conclusion.

When we talk of "getting started," what we're often referring to is that phenomenon known as inspiration, as elusive as the fairy dust that enabled Peter Pan to fly. When Nobel Prize novelist Patrick White suggested that "inspiration descends only in flashes, to clothe circumstances; it is not stored up in a barrel, like salt herrings, to be doled out," he wasn't implying that only a select few are fortunate enough to receive these flashes of inspiration, or that we should sit around chewing on our lower lips, hoping for some divine message to cut through our foggy brains. If we do, chances are we may be waiting for a long, long time. Instead, inspiration is exhibited in the unique and interesting connections in subject matter that our subconscious or conscious minds make while we work on a poem. Thus inspiration, which occurs as a direct result of the writing process, is evidenced by our leaps into compelling language, metaphor, and imagery.

Ultimately, what you're really trying to discover is how you write, and the only thing that's going to work is what works for you. This philosophy implies a lot of experimentation. With this in mind, the majority of introductory-level writing textbooks offer "triggers," exercises that provide a starting point for the poem which, when successful, work like jumper cables on a dormant battery. These exercises often steer you toward recollecting important incidents in your life, or to interesting objects, to a bit of compelling history you've stumbled across in your studies, or perhaps to a musical selection that you find particularly moving. Whatever topic you choose needs to be one that interests you enough to examine it more thoroughly through your writing.

Many poets have catalogued the advantages to thinking a poem through before committing the first line to paper. For example, in *The Art and Craft of Poetry,* Michael Bugeja suggests making a list of events in our lives that lead to "epiphanies," which he defines as "moments of truth in which your mind seems at one with the universe." He explains that these are the moments that occur at key turning points in our lives, and that enable us to come to some important understanding about ourselves or about the world around us. Perfect subjects for poetry. He then suggests that we describe the event with that epiphany in mind (which will ultimately act as the theme of the poem). This process is an effective means of side-stepping the "So what?" poem, a poem that seems unable to rise above the level of a well-executed description, a poem with body but no soul.

On the other hand, many poets find that this type of advance planning undermines their desire to write the poem. For them, the joy of creation is found in working intuitively in the beginning, and then in luxuriating in the mystery of the poem as it unfolds (though if you choose this approach to writing, thoughtful revision becomes even more critical). Once again, there is no right or wrong . . . just different approaches to explore.

Since I'm a very visual person, I find it useful to begin with objects or scenes that I feel compelled to describe. As I write, I ask myself why I'm attracted to the object, why is it important to me? For instance, the poem "Sand Dollar" began with a description of a palm-sized sand dollar that I keep on my desk. But this description alone didn't provide me with any keen insight, hadn't made me view the world in any startling or unique manner, hadn't unearthed any sort of epiphany. I suppose I could have opened up the poem by describing how often I've meandered the length of the beach, searching for an intact sand dollar. I could then reveal that a friend, during his first visit to Bald Head Island, North Carolina, took five steps, leaned over, picked up this perfect specimen and handed it to me. Imagine my chagrin! Not a bad story, but not one that I felt particularly compelled to tell. Yet my desire to write about this sand dollar had not abated. What, I asked myself, should I do?

When a poem seems boring, as our lives unfortunately often are, award-winning poet Philip Levine suggests that we make something up. He illustrates with his own poem, "Listen Carefully" (from *The Simple Truth*), which describes a time when he shared a bed with his older sister. This poem has been a bane to critics around the country, who question whether Levine is hinting at some type of incestuous relationship, a suggestion that Levine finds quite amusing. He doesn't have a sister.

Following his advice, I utilized questioning techniques that I had learned in fiction-writing classes. "Who is holding that shell?" I asked, then waited for my mind to provide an answer. I envisioned a young girl who was gathering shells and placing them in a bread bag, like one I had seen a woman carrying on the beach the day before. While I don't really know this particular child, I relied on my own experience as an adolescent with divorced parents for the emotional "truth" that I wanted this poem to convey.

Talking about the initial stages of writing a poem without touching on form seems like heresy, since form is such a crucial aspect of poetry. But at what point should you begin to shape your poem? If you decide to compose in a set form, such as a sonnet or sestina, form and meaning are integrally linked, and cannot be separated in even an early draft. Writing in free verse, however, allows you the opportunity to get ideas down on paper—to focus on content, language, and imagery—without worrying about the ultimate shape the poem will take. Once the poem has gelled, you can choose line and stanza breaks that will enhance the piece during subsequent revisions.

What I have hoped to provide you with are not exactly guidelines, but suggestions that should lead to even more questions. Wallace Stevens stated that "poetry is a search for the inexplicable." If you accept this premise as true, why would you expect the process of writing a poem to be anything less mysterious? ❖

A View of the Creative Process

Mark Cox

I SEE THE CREATIVE PROCESS AS AN INFINITE SPECTRUM OF activities between two theoretical poles: subjective chaos and objective order. Then, for simplicity's sake, I divide this infinite spectrum into three stages: Vision; Re-Vision; and Revision.

VISION: Do what you want with little regard to communication or audience. Work intuitively and naturally, getting as much on paper as possible—getting what's in your head outside where you can see it—finding out what you're really feeling and thinking about. During this stage you may write thirty lines before one element (image, word, sound, pattern, line) emerges from the boil and makes itself heard. The point is to tap into the unconscious workings of the mind, to surprise yourself (I write very quickly, paying no attention to spelling, punctuation, or even line breaks). As this stage progresses, you may begin to notice a few connections (similar images, etc.), but you need not force anything to happen. The writer is a little arrogant in this stage, not because we think we know more about the world than anyone else, but because we trust ourselves—and the process—implicitly. In the same way that we have to trust our evolution as writers, we have to trust the evolution of the poem.

Re-Vision: At this point, selection begins, a kind of choosing that's partially conscious but mainly intuitive. During this stage, one trusts oneself and yet begins to ask questions about the "photo" that's evolving within the developing fluid. We might consciously choose an element, (for example, a word like "sand") and then return to a less conscious state to cluster around that word (for example, desert, beach, clam, oyster, pearls, sheik's pearl ring, camel, Iraq). Then perhaps we'll surface toward the conscious again and try to see how this could be merged with what we've done previously. The lines might start to break here. The stanza form might begin to materialize. We'll start looking at the poem as an object. There's more ambivalence about this part of the process, as if we're now questioning the things we had trusted earlier, but are still open to suggestions from all angles.

Revision: At this point, the hard questions begin. Am I making myself clear? Do I want to be perfectly clear? Is this subject important to anyone but me? Have I done this as well as I can? Am I indulging only those aspects of poetry that I'm best at right now? Have I learned anything new? How can I use this poem to understand myself and my world? What would the poem be like if I did it differently than this, exactly opposite to this? Would couplets work better? Does it sound too cheesy? Am I challenging my own ideas and temperament? What happens if I break a line here instead of there? Isn't there a better word that can be used without ruining the sound of the passage?

During this stage we might retype the poem many different ways. Or we might purposely strip the poem of everything that we think is strong about it. During this stage the poem is outside of us—an object—and we try to ignore the intense, personal investment we have in it. If, during Re-Vision, we were daydreaming with a Rubik's cube in our hand, now we're a mechanic bent over an engine. We have a checklist. We know that we are biased about our own work and do our best to strip that prejudice away for a while. We know that we have to be able to split up and rearrange the individual poem, in order to make that poem truly whole.

The questions might (and usually do) mean that we'll have to return to steps one and two with further thoughts on the matter. It is not a linear process, by any means. Once you've tapped into it, submitted to it, all the steps begin to alternate and mix and bleed into one another very rapidly. In fact, good revision is trying to draw a shape from the flux while enjoying both form and shapelessness, by honoring the process that requires both unconscious and conscious participation simultaneously.

Thus, it is the writing that I love and/or am disappointed in, not only the poem. It's my work that I care as much about as it is the poem at hand. And that means I have to both cherish and challenge the poem at hand while maintaining, in fact, in order to maintain, my trust in the larger body of work. ❖

A REVISION SEQUENCE FOR STUDY

I. 10/13/94

Once the animal is gone, you can hear the sea. And so the husks
of abandonned fasrmsteads barely stand, buckling at the knee,
their porches unable to support even a dog's weight, the wind a
dull, prolonged whistle in their rusted cantilevered downspouts,
the surrounding weeds a kind of silvered green flame against
the foundation, the window panes whole, unglaezed, having
slid whole from their glazing, having pooped whole in the swell
of heat and cold frpm their glazing. No graffitti here, the only
refuse a sardine tin turned ashtrayand a pair of tube socksand one
orange crush bottle, its bottom lined withdead wasps

II. 10/14/94

There is my grandmother's tortured, humped spine in the
landscape of the flinthills. I remember the mottled, milky
glimpse at the top of her nightgown neck of, and above us
outside, the sky a coarse smmoth grey, the bottom of a stone,
as fa as you can see.. And as far as you can see is about as far
as you can live. This land, it owns you, it has a reason for not
having forgiven you—it hasn't even considered you. Nomad or
sttler, you are but one more in a the millenia's worth. If I were to
otop now, here on the shoulder, and strip off my clothes, there
would be no one to laugh at me. And If i were to keep going,
keep taking off, layer after layer of flesh and bone until I stood
before the setting sunas the singular spine, I would be no more
than the dream my parents once had. One submits to land like
this and is eaten by it and dies grateful for the opportuniyty. But
now the car stands empty, its doors open, the motor out of uel
for dayyears now. For awhile the radio played to no one, and the
starlight made magical its beaten interior. The owner, he's afoot

Once the animal is gone, you can hear the sea. And so the husks
of abandonned fasrmsteads barely stand, buckling at the knee,
their porches unable to support even a dog's weight, the wind a
dull, prolonged whistle in their rusted cantilevered downspouts,
the surrounding weeds a kind of silvered green flame against
the foundation, the window panes whole, unglaezed, having
slid whole from their glazing, having pooped whole in the swell
of heat and cold frpm their glazing. No graffitti here, the only
refuse a sardine tin turned ashtrayand a pair of tube socksand one
orange crush bottle, its bottom lined withdead wasps

III. 10/15/94

There it is, my grandmother's tortured, humped spine in the horizon of the flinthills. One can only pretend to own land like this. then submit to it, be eaten by it and die grateful for the opportunity. I remember the mottled, milky glimpse at the top of her nightgown neck of, and above us outside, the sky a coarse smmoth grey, the bottom of a stone, as fa as you can see.. And as far as you can see is about as far as you can live. This land, it owns you, it has a reason for not having forgiven you—it hasn't even considered you. Nomad or sttler, you are but one more in a the millenia's worth.

If I were to stop now, here on the shoulder, beside the weeds like worn whiskbrooms, if I were to stop, strip off my clothes, and keep going, keep taking off, layer after layer of flesh and bone until I stood before the setting sun as no more than the dream my parents once had. But now the car stands empty, its doors open, the motor out of uel for dayyears now. For awhile the radio played to no one, and the starlight made magical its beaten interior. The owner, he's afoot

Once the animal is gone, you can hear the sea. And so the husks of abandonned fasrmsteads barely stand, buckling at the knee, their porches unable to support even a dog's weight, the wind a dull, prolonged whistle in their rusted cantilevered downspouts, the surrounding weeds a kind of silvered green flame against the foundation, the window panes whole, unglaezed, having slid whole from their glazing, having pooped whole in the swell of heat and cold frpm their glazing. No graffitti here, the only refuse a sardine tin turned ashtrayand a pair of tube socksand one orange crush bottle, its bottom lined withdead wasps

IV. 12/30/94

INHERITANCE

For awhile the radio played to no one, and the starlight made
magical its beaten interior. But the motor's had no fuel
for years, now. The old car stands empty, its driver's door open,
its owner, afoot.

Once the animal is gone, you can hear the sea. And so the husks
of abandoned farmsteads barely stand, buckling at the knee,
their porches unable to support even a hound's weight, a dull,
prolonged whistle in their rusted cantilevered downspouts. The
surrounding weeds are a version of silvered green flame against the
foundation. The window panes have popped whole in the swell of
heat and cold from their glazing. No graffiti here, just one orange
crush bottle, its bottom lined with dead wasps,

just your grandmother's tortured, humped spine in the horizon of
the flinthills, the mottled, milky glimpse above her nightgown's
neck, and above you, the sky a coarse smooth grey, the bottom of
a stone, as far as you could see. As far as you can see being about
as far as you can live.

If you were to stop now, like Weldon Kees, here on the shoulder,
beside the weeds like worn whiskbrooms, were you to stop, strip
off your clothes, and keep divesting yourself of even flesh and
bone, could you stand before that gangboss sun as the dream your
parents once had?

This land, it has good reason for not having forgiven you—it
hasn't noticed your presence yet.

V. 12/31/94

INHERITANCE

For awhile the radio played to no one,
and the starlight made magical its beaten interior.
But the motor's had no fuel
for years, now. The old car stands empty,
its driver's door open,
its owner, afoot.

Once the animal is gone, you can hear the sea.
And so the husks of abandoned farmsteads barely stand,
buckling at the knee, their porches unable to support
even a hound's weight, a dull, prolonged whistle
in their rusted cantilevered downspouts.
The surrounding weeds are a version of silvered green flame,
the window panes popped whole in the swell of heat and cold
from their glazing. No graffiti here, just one
orange Crush bottle, its bottom lined with dead wasps,

just your grandmother's tortured, humped spine
in the horizon of the flinthills,
the mottled, milky glimpse above her nightgown's neck,
and above you, the sky a coarse smooth grey,
the bottom of a stone, as far as you could see.
As far as you can see being
about as far as you can live.

If you were to stop now, like Kees, here on the shoulder,
beside the weeds like worn whiskbrooms,
were you to stop, strip off your clothes,
divest yourself of even flesh and bone,
could you stand before this magisterial sun
as the dream your parents once had?

The cattle comb themselves against the barbed wire.

The corn silks dry and twist against the wind.

This land, it has good reason for not having forgiven you—it hasn't noticed your presence yet.

VI. 1/2/95

FLINTHILLS

For awhile the radio played to livestock,
and the starlight made magical
its beaten interior;
but the motor's had no fuel
for years, now. The old car stands empty,
its driver door open, its owner, afoot.

Once the animal is gone, you can hear the sea.
And so the husks of abandoned farmsteads
buckle at the knee, their porches unfit
for a hound's weight, a dull, rusty whistle
in their cantilevered downspouts.

No gingham, here—just window glass
popped whole from the swell of heat and cold.
No cooling pie—just one Orange Crush bottle
lined with dead wasps,
just your grandmother's tortured, humped spine
in the horizon of the flinthills,

the mottled, milky glimpse above her nightgown's neck,
and above you, the sky a coarse smooth grey,
the bottom of a stone, as far as you could see.
As far as you can see being
about as far as you can live.

If you were to stop now, like Kees, here on the shoulder,
beside the weeds like worn whiskbrooms,
were you to stop, strip off your clothes,
divest yourself of even flesh and bone,
could you stand before this magisterial sun
as the dream your folk once had?

The silvered undersides of surrounding weeds
flame against the foundation.
The cattle of distant owners
comb themselves against the barbed wire.

This land has reason for not forgiving you—it hasn't noticed your
presence yet.

VII. 1/3/95

FLINTHILLS

For awhile the radio played to livestock,
and the starlight made magical
its beaten interior;
but the motor's had no fuel
for years, now. The old car stands empty,
its driver door open, its owner, afoot.

Once the animal is gone, you can hear the sea.
And so the husks of abandoned farmsteads
buckle at the knee, their porches unfit
for a hound's weight, a dull, rusty whistle
in their cantilevered downspouts.

No gingham, here, no cooling pie—
just window glass popped whole
from the swell of heat and cold,
an Orange Crush bottle lined with dead wasps,
and your grandmother's tortured, humped spine
in the horizon of the flinthills,

the mottled, milky glimpse above her nightgown's neck,
and above that, the bottom of a stone,
as far as you could see.
As far as you can see being
about as far as you can live.

If you were to stop now, like Kees, here on the shoulder,
beside the weeds like worn whiskbrooms,
were you to stop, strip off your clothes,
divest yourself of even flesh and bone,
could you stand before this magisterial sun
as the dream your folk once had?

The silvered undersides of surrounding weeds
flame against the foundation.
The cattle of distant owners
comb themselves against the barbed wire.

This land has reason for not forgiving you—
it hasn't noticed your presence yet.

VIII. 1/4/95

Flint Hills

For awhile the radio played to livestock,
and the starlight made magical
its beaten interior;
but the driver door's been open for years, now,
the old car stands empty,
its owner, afoot.

Once the animal is gone, you can hear the sea.
And so the husks of abandoned farmsteads
buckle at the knee, their porches unfit
for a hound's weight, a dull, rusty whistle
in their cantilevered downspouts.

No gingham, here, no cooling pies—
just window glass popped whole
from the swell of heat and cold,
Orange Crush bottles lined with dead wasps,
and your grandmother's humped spine
in the tortured horizon,

the mottled, milky glimpse above her nightgown's neck,
and above that, the bottom of a stone,
as far as you could see.
As far as you can see being
about as far as you can live.

If you were to stop now, like Kees, here on the shoulder,
beside the weeds like worn whiskbrooms,
were you to stop, strip off your clothes,
divest yourself of even flesh and bone,
could you stand before this magisterial sun
as the dream your folk once had?

The silvered undersides of weeds
surround and flare. The cattle
of distant owners comb themselves
against the barbed wire.

This land has reason for not forgiving you—it hasn't noticed
your presence yet.

IX. 2/95

FLINT HILLS

For awhile the radio played to livestock,
and the starlight made magical
its beaten interior;
but the driver door's been open for years, now,
the old car stands empty,
its owner, afoot.

Once the animal is gone, you can hear the sea.
And so the husks of abandoned farmsteads
buckle at the knee, their porches unfit
for a hound's weight, a dull, rusty whistle
in their cantilevered downspouts.

No gingham, here, no cooling pies—
just window glass popped whole
from the swell of heat and cold,
Orange Crush bottles lined with dead wasps,
and your grandmother's humped spine
in the tortured horizon,

the mottled, milky glimpse above her nightgown's neck,
and above that, the bottom of a stone,
as far as you could see.
As far as you can see being
about as far as you can live.

If you were to stop now, here on the shoulder,
beside the trees like worn whiskbrooms,
were you to stop, strip off your clothes,
divest yourself of even flesh and bone,
could you stand before this magisterial sun
as the dream your folk once had?

The silvered undersides of weeds surround
and flare. The cattle of distant owners
comb themselves against barbed wire.

This land has reason for not forgiving you—
it hasn't noticed your presence yet.

X. Final

Flint Hills

For a while the radio played to livestock,
and the starlight made magical
its beaten interior,
but the driver door's been open for years, now;
the old car stands empty,
its owner, afoot.

Once the animal is gone, you can hear the sea.
And so the shells of abandoned farmsteads
buckle at the knee, porches unfit
for a hound's weight, a rusty, dull whistle
in their cantilevered downspouts.

No gingham, here, no cooling pies—
just window glass popped whole
from the swell of heat and cold,
Orange Crush bottles lined with dead wasps,
and your grandmother's humped spine
in the tortured horizon,

the mottled, milky glimpse above her nightgown's neck,
and above that, the bottom of a stone,
as far as you could see.
As far as you can see being
about as far as you can live.

If you were to stop now, here on the shoulder,
beside the trees like worn whiskbrooms,
were you to stop, strip off your clothes,
divest yourself of even flesh and bone,
could you stand before this sentencing sun
as the hope your folk once had?

The silvered undersides of weeds surround
and flare. The cattle of distant owners
comb themselves against barbed wire.

This land has reason for not forgiving you—
it hasn't noticed your presence yet.

Approaches to Revision

Mark Cox

DaVinci, working on *The Last Supper*, enraged the person who'd hired him by sitting in front of a blank canvas for several days. We've all stared at a blank page, uncertain where to start. But there's a difference between the silence of meditation—knowing that you have the confidence and the ability, knowing that you are working toward something—and the silence that comes from paralysis, the inability to start. These silences have to be handled in different ways. The latter has to be handled by beginning, and letting the work begin to show you where it wants to go. Most of us are caught in between these extremes. We may be able to start easily and on cue, but we still run into one kind of blockage or another as we begin to shape, and to see the necessity of revising toward that shape. I'm hopeful that by outlining my understanding of the creative process in general, and by giving you some tools and conscious techniques for revision, you'll more easily bypass these roadblocks. And, in addition, find your way toward poems you might not have written otherwise.

Rules

Dogs don't have any trouble thinking conceptually—it's the little details they have a problem with. One morning, I opened the hood of my car to check the oil, and my dog jumped up into my engine compartment. He sat there very excited, waiting to take a ride. I had a hatchback in those days, and he was used to the back hatch opening in the same way that the hood had. He just sat down on my air cleaner and patiently waited for us to get started.

He was a zany, excitable dog, but I understood him. As I was thinking about this anecdote, I realized that what triggered my memory of it earlier in the day was being passed by a truck the same color as that old car. It also looked like every other truck I've ever been passed by on many highways. This made me think about what it's like to grow up having cars. And growing up in them—the excitement and energy of traveling to new places as a child. Naturally, this memory of my dog's emotions and behavior fits right in. No wonder I remembered it. Perhaps more important, the recognition of such triggers and catalysts is just as naturally followed by the potential to manipulate them for an audience—as I've just done.

Art is shaping as much as it is creating. Often, the inherent qualities of things already exist and it's in the shaping that we might possibly manage to create some new combination—some different synthesis or gestalt.

Getting into a car through a door instead of the hood is one of those rules we live by. But perhaps we tend to place too much emphasis on such rules. Later in the winter (Vermont), when my car was iced over, I had to crawl in through the hatchback, and I suddenly felt connected to the car in a completely different way. Maybe rules are less successful at telling us how to be, than they are at showing us how we are.

ART AND EXPERIENCE

It is understood that the poem will always be artifice; that is, that poem is always after the fact of the experience it recreates, reenacts, and conveys. It is also understood that certain rules must be collectively agreed to in order to communicate meaning. At the same time, however, much of poetry's energy comes from its desire to be more than artifice, to be experience itself.

When the brain is purposefully engaged in reading, it follows the characters/symbols of language, the lineation and argument of the text. Reading is a very conscious and personal cognitive act in this sense. However, when the brain is, in the act of reading, stimulated by the offerings of another mind, it must, by necessity, seek to simultaneously follow and understand the cognitive process of that other mind. And if, then, that other mind's (the poet's) process is different—perhaps intuitive, rather than logical—the reader may find him or herself participating in two vastly different processes at once. The manner in which the author performs the writing manipulates to what degree these two states interact.

Manipulate. Does the word sound negative? Yet this is exactly what artists do. We manipulate the medium—be it language or paint—in order to create an effect on the reader or audience. For example, think about the effects of concrete and abstract language. If I were to tell you that a flywheel revolves 240,000 times per hour, your mind will react differently than when I say, 4,000 revolutions per minute. Likewise, if I go on to say 66.6 revolutions per second. The abstraction of tremendous speed has its full impact only in a concrete example. In the last example, the numbers quoted have come down into a comprehensible range—sixty-six—but have simultaneously become more mind-boggling—per second. Of course, some people may not know what a flywheel is. So as a poet, revising creatively, one might start thinking about hamster cages or roulette wheels. One might start thinking of political revolution. One might write a poem about a fly on my steering wheel that tries to turn left whenever you want to turn right. We can play off it however we want, consciously and freely, following the language where it leads us, while also being conscious of that language's effect on our audience.

This means that poets must be flexible and willing to handle language in different ways, to approach language as if it is a new thing each day. I have to be willing to venture into what seems to be random, in order to discover new relationships between the parts of the order which I have imposed—which all my experience has imposed—on the poem at hand.

Some Questions

Here are some questions you might ask yourself about the poem at hand:

What would a painting of this poem look like? What would a symphony based on the poem sound like? What kind of atmosphere does it have? Is it cool or hot? Does it sing or talk or hum? Is it urban, suburban, or pastoral?

Who is speaking? A personal voice or an omniscient voice? And in what language: polysyllabic or monosyllabic; abstract or concrete; heightened or plain? Does the poem seem natural or artificial when related to life as you know it?

Does the poem ask questions or make pronouncements? Is the syntax convoluted or simple? Is it direct and explicit, or oblique and associational?

How is the poem shaped thematically? How many levels is it operating on? What is the central relationship? What is stressed —people, things, ideas?

Does any one sense dominate? Visual imagery? Sound and rhythm?

How does the poem exist in time? Is the experience framed or is the poem the continued surge of experience? Is the poem active and physical, or passive and meditative? How is the narrative structured—is it a story? A sequence of thought and observation?

SOME REVISION STRATEGIES

One must get to know one's own poem inside and out. In fact, one helpful way to revise poems is to free-write in prose, describing the poem's situation so that you know what's clear to you and what isn't and what might not be clear to the reader. Describe the speaker's/subject's room and house and life, and so on, in minute detail. What happened, where, why? Remember deeply. Invent and embellish freely. It will not necessarily be crucial to use any or all of this detail in the poem. But, if you write "the man was sitting in his chair in his bedroom," you should know, and be simultaneously discovering, everything about that bedroom and chair. Perhaps this is where writing's power—art's—comes from. This underlying knowledge and vision may be the source of the voice of the writing. For example, successful minimalist short-story writers may not give us a lot of description, but we sense that they know the situation and are choosing carefully what to leave out. In writing, all detail, if it's seen minutely and specifically in our heads, may be what acts as carrier for the abstractions of the particular emotional or intellectual moment. This means it will thus dictate—both consciously and unconsciously—the sound systems, rhythms, and narrative movement of the poem.

Another way to get a fresh look at your poems is to list six different potential titles, then look at the poem and notice how the poem would have to change according to the new focus on one element or another.

You might also try starting your second draft with the line you closed with in the first draft. Or try many different lines in starting and closing positions.

All of these are important ways of reminding ourselves that the poem is an object—that we must care as much about the act of writing as we do about the poem at hand. All of which means we have to both cherish and challenge the poem at hand while maintaining, in fact, in order to maintain our trust in the work.

It is also important to remember that there's no way to "ruin" the individual poem—you can always return to any earlier format whenever you wish.

This presentation, then, is designed to help the student poet see his or her work in new ways. You will find in the following pages a number of conscious methods for revision, each illustrated via changes in poem drafts.

General vs. specific: Discuss the differences in content, diction, figurative language, voice, and abstraction in the following examples. The illustrations on the following page were written by poet and professor Jonathan Holden for this purpose. ❖

Hell (A)

You will wake up
in the class you hated
most in high school.
Everything will be
the same
as it was,
the same disgusting
students doing
the same
things
they used to do.
Even your desk,
a typical high school
desk in a typical high school
room, will be the same.
It will be spring,
and as you sit
there, listening
to another dull
and meaningless
lecture,
you will be so
bored
and so horny
that you will kill
time
through idle sex fantasy
and daydreams
about sports,
wishing
you were out
of school.

HELL (B)

You will wake up
in your old seat
behind Peter Bowerbank
in 8th period Driver
Ed. Tommy Conger will
be there too, in back of
you, squelching his
Wrigley's, breathing
spearmint down your neck
And Lyle Smith.
Who had the loudest
artificial burp—
bulked against the side
board, honking
snores. Your desk
will be the same scarred
tablet, prehistoric,
with the purple fossils
in it—the blue rune
that said Eat the
Root, the one that read
Bird Bites. Chuck
Spine will have his comb
out to lubricate his hair,
It will be May.
and as you wait
in the lighted cave
of Room 101—wait to
evolve while Mr. McIntyre
repeats leave four
miles an hour—
you will think and
think of the little
wet click Mary Devore's
lips make as she smiles,

imagine the voltage
in her sweater, try
to think how
outdoors on the tight
green diamond
the throw from third
to first is easy—a lilt,
a flicker, bullseye,
and McIntyre will go
on, and the lukewarm
New Jersey haze,
like a light perfume, will
stretch south almost
to the bridge.

— JONATHAN HOLDEN

HELL (C)

You will wake up
in the classroom you hated most—
8th-period Driver Ed,
Tommy Prom-King belching
spearmint down your neck.
Nothing will have changed:
not the scarred, prehistoric tablet
they called a desk;
not the pimple poised for years
on Lyle Smith's fossilized nose.
It will be May,
and as you wait, evolving,
in the fluorescence soaked cave
of Room 101—
Mr. McIntyre droning,
Peter Blue-Balls groaning—
you will think
of the little wet click
Mary Devore's lips make
as she smiles, imagine
the voltage in her sweater,
consider how, outside,
on the tight green diamond
the throw from third to first
is easy—a lilt, a flicker, you're out—
and McIntyre will go on,
and the lukewarm New Jersey haze,
like a light perfume, will stretch south
almost to the bridge.

—ADAPTATION BY MARK COX

Discuss how this example synthesizes approaches from both
"Hell" (A) and "Hell" (B).

First Kiss: Portuguese Man O'War (Draft # 1)

I think the first thing I noticed was the thin blue line
snaking around my arm like a pulled copper wire
bracelet. Then maybe a glimpse of blue threading

through my hair, then an incredible heat on my thigh.
And the way your body warns you of danger, every hair
stood straight up. I remember turning to look behind me,

but only the Pacific, a surfer, the swell. Then, yes, the pain
and surprise, then my father pulling the thread off
my arm, my mother guiding me to the lifeguard station.

I was fifteen and crimson from the sun and the embarrassment
of my incongruous skinny legs and full hips, and I stood
shivering while the most beautiful man I'd ever seen

poured two gallons of chilled vinegar over my head.
It coursed behind my ears, into the hollow of my neck,
dripped down my back. Close your eyes, he said.

Jesus, didn't you see them on the beach?
I didn't wonder at the time, but now I know he could
see my nipples through the aquarium print one-piece.

You see, it should have been him. Not something twenty
meters long and as light as my hair on the buoyant
salt water. It should have been his hands, not a blue

thread curling around my skin like a lover, teasing,
barely scratching the surface of who I was becoming,
a fingernail against the back of my neck,

a thin tracing of a vein on the inside of my arm,
a tongue against the inside of my elbow,
sand against my lips.

—Jennifer Hancock

First Kiss: Portuguese Man O'War

I think the first thing I noticed was the thin blue line
snaking around my arm like a pulled copper wire
bracelet. Then maybe a glimpse of blue threading

through my hair, then an incredible heat on my thigh.
And the way your body warns you of danger, every hair
stood straight up. I remember turning to look behind me,

but only the Pacific, a surfer, the swell. Then, yes, the pain
and surprise, then my father pulling the thread off
my arm, my mother guiding me to the lifeguard station.

I was fifteen and crimson from the sun and the embarrassment
of my incongruous skinny legs and full hips, and I stood
shivering while the most beautiful man I'd ever seen

poured two gallons of chilled vinegar over my head.
It coursed behind my ears, into the hollow of my neck,
dripped down my back. Close your eyes, he said.

Jesus, didn't you see them on the beach?
I didn't wonder at the time, but now I know he could
see my nipples through the aquarium print one-piece.

You see, it should have been him. Not something twenty
meters long and light as my hair on the buoyant
salt water. It should have been his hands, not a blue

thread curling around my skin like a lover, teasing,
barely scratching the surface of who I was becoming,
a fingernail against the back of my neck,

a thin tracing of a vein on the inside of my arm,
a tongue against the inside of my elbow,
sand against my lips.

Jennifer Hancock
Critique of Draft #1

First Kiss: Portuguese Man O'War (Draft # 2)

Twenty meters long and as light as my hair on the buoyant
salt water
then, the thin blue line like a bracelet
around my arm
an incredible heat on my thigh
I remember turning to look behind me
every hair standing straight up
but only the Pacific, a surfer, the swell
then, yes, the pain
and parents guiding me to the lifeguard station.
I was fifteen and crimson from the sun and the embarrassment
of my incongruous skinny legs and full hips
and I stood shivering while the most beautiful man
I'd ever seen poured two gallons of chilled vinegar
over my head. It coursed behind my ears
into the hollow of my neck
dripped down my back.
Close your eyes, he said.
Jesus, didn't you see them on the beach?
But now I know he could see my nipples through
the aquarium print one-piece.
You see, it should have been him.
It should have been his hands curling around
my skin like a lover, teasing, barely scratching
the surface of who I was becoming,
a fingernail against the back of my neck,
a thin tracing of a vein on the inside of my arm,
a tongue against the inside of my elbow,
sand against my lips.

FIRST KISS: PORTUGUESE MAN O'WAR (Draft # 3)

Twenty meters long and as light
as my hair on the buoyant salt water,
a thin blue line like a bracelet
around my arm, heat on my thigh.
I remember turning into the swell to look
behind me, every hair standing straight up,
but only the Pacific, a surfer, a gull.
Then as my toes found sand
the pain wrapped around me like a towel.

I was fifteen and crimson from the sun
and the embarrassment, the awkward imbalance
of hips and breasts. At the lifeguard station,
I shivered while a man with tawny eyes and gold
hair on his forearms poured gallons
of chilled vinegar over my head. It coursed
behind my ears, into the hollow of my neck,
eased down my back in a sheet.
Close your eyes, he said. Jesus, didn't you see
them on the beach? I shook my head, mute,
on the verge of understanding poison,
the neurotoxins of desire. But now I know
he saw my nipples through the aquarium
print one-piece.

You see, it should have
been him. It should have been his hands
curling around my skin like a lover, teasing,
barely scratching the surface of who I was
becoming, a fingernail against the back
of my neck, a thin tracing of a vein
on the inside of my arm, a tongue against
the inside of my elbow, sand against my lips.

First Kiss: Portuguese Man O'War

Twenty meters long and as light
as my hair on the buoyant salt water,
a thin blue line like a bracelet
around my arm, heat on my thigh.
I remember turning into the swell to look
behind me, every hair standing straight up,
but only the Pacific, a surfer, a gull.
Then as my toes found sand
the pain wrapped around me like a towel.
I was fifteen and crimson from the sun
and embarrassment, an awkward imbalance
of hips and breasts. At the lifeguard station,
I shivered while a man with tawny eyes and gold
hair on his forearms poured gallons
of chilled vinegar over my head. It washed
behind my ears in waves and pooled in the hollow
of my neck. *Close your eyes, he said.*
Jesus, didn't you see them on the beach?
I shook my head, mute, on the verge
of understanding poison, the neurotoxins
of desire. It should have been him; his hands
curling around my skin like a lover, teasing,
barely scratching the surface of the woman
I wanted to be. His fingernail against the back
of my neck, a thin tracing of the blue vein
on the inside of my arm, a tongue against
the inside of my elbow, sand against my lips.

—Jennifer Hancock
Third Coast, fall 1999

ON VOICE

Mark Cox

IN ORDER TO DEFINE "VOICE" WE MUST FIRST BE SURE we're all thinking of that term in the same way. When we talk about voice in fiction we are usually referring to the manner in which characters speak, the stylistic hallmarks that allow us to immediately picture or characterize an individual narrator or character's stance toward the world. We ask, *Who is speaking to whom about what?* then gauge whether the diction and sentence structure are appropriate for the speech or reflection with which we are being presented.

When we say of poets that he or she has a "strong voice" or has yet to "find" his or her voice, what we're really locating is a certain sense of, or lack of, authority. Now as in fiction, this authority is deeply related to style, but poets have been known to change radically in terms of their style and still display a strong, unique voice. This is because authority is related as much to vision as it is to style. No matter how conflicted the attitude or content in question, there is a multidimensional wholeness at the heart of authenticity, a relatively conscious synthesis of all the voices that make up the chorus of a person's being. We have intellectual selves, we have sexual and physical selves, we have emotional selves, we have spiritual selves; we carry with us each of the children we have been and each of the jobs we have labored at. And each "self" has its own language. When shaking the pastor's hand after church, we do not speak or carry ourselves as we would when slapping an old friend on the back at the neighborhood bar. Nor do we comport ourselves at job interviews in the same way we lean back with family at the kitchen tables of our lives. So, since each self truly has its own way of speaking, its own way of emphasizing things about the world, perhaps style and authenticity are not such separate issues after all.

Voice in our lives, in our vision as writers, has to do with how we synthesize the various voices of which we are made. Voice in our writing has to do with making fictions seem real and consistent in light of one's intentions. It has to do with appropriate diction, appropriate sentence structure and syntax, appropriate and well-modulated levels of emotion and intensity between different psychological states. If the poem employs a speaker who is forty years old and who is at times during the poem looking back on something that happened when he was seven, it would be natural at points in the poem to vary perspectives and levels of diction, to seemingly get so close to that memory that the language lapses, becomes more childlike. Likewise, a harried or confused narrator might think in fragments or a dramatic, heightened tone we would not accept as direct speech.

Nor are these issues purely personal ones for a writer. Our beloved English language is itself a hybrid mongrel aching with tension and ambivalence. Our Anglo-Saxon heritage is extremely physical, offering harsh sounds and direct cadences of one- and two-syllable words: "meat" and "root," for instance. It is from the Norman/Latinate influence that we've been given words like "sustenance" and "ethereal." Though one shouldn't overgeneralize, it is no accident that the more intellectual diction of science and abstract thought is traced to Latin, while the diction of immediate feeling and dramatic imagery is often rooted in Old English. Our language is as comfortable with imagery, with physicality, with being grounded in the concrete world, as it is comfortable with abstract thought and reflection. Add to this the differences in formality you can hear between American English and British English (the fierce desire of the American idiom to free itself), and you have a very volatile and energetic language. Most effective poets to one degree or another, consciously or unconsciously, use these tensions to their poems' advantage.

Revision, then, is not merely the act of shifting words around. These words and the ways in which they are arranged are the embodiment of how the author and her characters view the world. The sentence structure and syntax are actually reflections of how they exist within the flow of time. And as such, revision can lead us both into a sharpening focus of our visions and further and further into the unknown—into what we can't quite recognize about ourselves. Revision is the means by which we gradually gain perspective on the different facets of ourselves and by which we come to know all the many voices that must come together to create our one voice.

Another way to envision it: revision, the experimentation with language and style, is the smoke in the bank that shows us the alarm system's laser beams. It allows us to see what is beyond us, particularly our personal limitations and patterns. Once we can see patterns of style, we can understand that they are reflections of patterns in our way of being, reflections of involuntary frames of reference so deeply ingrained in us that we don't even remember them, let alone recognize them. Viewed in this way, experimentation and revision offers us nothing less than the ability to change ourselves, to live consciously.

To my mind, my body of work is really one long poem. I see it as the record of my being in time. Sometimes I will approach that very lyrically, trying to absorb the subverbal feelings of a moment in time; other times I find myself trying to narratively pin that moment to my detective's bulletin board to understand the moment's relationship to other moments. Both modes are important to me, parts of who I am. Ultimately, on my good days, I choose not to limit myself, to take risks, to love the writing process more than what gets written; to love revision even more than the early bursts of energy that trigger poems. On my good days, occasionally, a voice coalesces for me and I write it down. ❖

THE POWER OF THE LYRIC

Michael White

I T MAY SEEM STRANGE TO EVEN CONTEMPLATE THE power of something as personal as a lyric poem. In our culture, poetry has little, if any, commercial value. And frankly, being a poet tends to rank low on the list of possible careers your parents may have discussed with you. Yet among the language you have stored in your memory—even if you don't think of yourself as a poet or poetry fan—I bet there's plenty of verse. I'm not just talking about nursery rhymes, Dr. Seuss, or the dozens of Shakespeare lines most of us can recite or at least vaguely remember . . . if I mention Wordsworth's daffodils, Keats's nightingale, or Frost's birches, chances are you not only know what I'm talking about, but you may have some personal, emotional reaction to the mere suggestion of those poems. Poems have a way of sticking around, lasting sometimes longer than the people, the culture, even the language from which they came.

Such longevity becomes even more remarkable when one considers the artistic limitations poets accept. Think, for a moment, of the massive resources expended on making the average movie: how many people, how much incredibly advanced technology it took to create that enjoyable ninety-minute experience. Even compared to writers in other genres, the poet seems to operate at a great disadvantage. The playwright doesn't have to worry so much whether every phrase will hold a reader's interest; she can count on a skillful production to do much of the work. And the spell of a really good novel (which compels me often to stay up all night, reading hundreds of pages, to find out how it will turn out) is a result of the novelist's skillful blending of plot, character, dialogue, and many other literary devices not generally available to the poet.

But poets design their poems—in the way they imagine them, as a stream of sound and sensation in the reader's mind— to emphasize different artistic qualities. Key among these are imagery and rhythm, which of course are also featured in other kinds of writing, but not to the same extent. To write poetry as effectively as you can, it's important that you recognize these differences, and work at using imagery and rhythm not simply as enhancements to meaning, but as primary tools for creating it.

In fact, many poems consist of little more than artfully arranged imagery without commentary. Think of the haiku, for instance, truthfully one of the world's greatest literary traditions. Basho (1644–1694) is often considered the ancient master of the art. His poem about heat lightning, as translated by X. J. Kennedy, reads like a cryptic glimpse into the cosmos:

> Heat lightning streak—
> through darkness pierces
> the heron's shriek.

This is a subtle little poem. Readers looking for an easily identifiable message or idea won't find it. But those willing to imagine the world of the speaker, and the experience of waking in the middle of the night, perhaps, to an almost simultaneous occurrence of the flash of light and the eerie cry of the heron (are they connected to each other somehow?)—those readers may find it a memorable poem about those glimpses of the Beyond we are sometimes allowed, by accident or grace. The feeling I get from this is too primal, too mysterious to be summarized, nor would you want to try: it just *is,* like life itself.

To write poetry, you need to be able to trust the image. Basho didn't add extra commentary to explain how he wanted his reader to feel about the poem, thank God. You, also, should try to use images with the confidence that a good sharp image or two may be all you need to convey the feeling. If you try to use concrete (rather than abstract) language, you can usually say more in far fewer lines. When creative writing professors encourage students to use imagery in their poetry, we often speak in terms of the five senses: you can use visual, auditory, olfactory, tactile, and gustatory (taste) imagery in a poem. It's important in most poems to appeal to more than one sense, because that's the way we experience the world. It's unreasonable to expect a poem to use all five senses, but you still ought to try to explore a sensory range appropriate to the experience you're describing.

One very helpful exercise I like to give students to help them develop their capacity to think in images is the image notebook. For five days in a row, let's say, I ask my writers to carry a small notebook wherever they go: they are to jot down interesting images they encounter or remember, without commentary. The idea is to try to record pure description of people, places, events, and the like, which your eye happens to pick out, or which, for some reason, you happen to remember. You only have to write a page a day, and it can be as sloppy as you like. Try going to a restaurant one day, and find what for you is the most interesting table; do a "sketch" in language of the interaction. Or go anywhere: a park, a coffee shop, the beach, and try to rely on your powers of description to take something home that you saw, heard, felt, tasted, touched, and/or smelled. Use similes (it was like:) or metaphors, use colors and details, but most important, let the image stand on its own. You will be surprised at how many potential poems you'll stumble across if you simply observe in a disciplined way. Usually, at the end of the five days, I have the students turn one of their entries into a poem. Many of my students continue keeping their image notebooks month after month, and most of their poems come out of this habit.

The sound of the poem is also extremely important, whether they are written in open or closed form. Poems may have a strong narrative element, but it's a very different use of narrative. For instance, most of my poems tell some simple story of some sort or another. My poem "What I Wanted to Tell You" tells a story about frustration: the speaker wants to see someone, but can't, because he's caught in traffic, a train barges through the scene, and he simply has to deal with it. It doesn't make much of a story, really. You couldn't turn it into a novel or a movie. But it is these simple, mysterious moments that often hold the most promise for poets. I find that a very simple narrative line is often best for layering on images that evoke emotional complexity (in this case, the speaker is simultaneously frustrated and entranced). And it is the rhythm not only holding it together, but subtly leading you through the experience. In this case, there is a basic five-beat line—a loose iambic pentameter—which I try to control and indent in a way that to me suggests the power of a train passing through, a force against which we are pretty helpless. Many poems you read incorporate a similarly deliberate use of rhythm. To discover it, and to hear how it informs the meaning, you probably need to read the poem aloud, carefully, to yourself. Pay attention to the line breaks: do you feel you are meant to stop, take a breath, and reflect at the ends of lines, or do you think the poet wants you to keep moving forward? What makes you feel this way? Look for relationships between the lengths of sentences and the lengths of lines. The heart of a poem is always in its beat, its pace, its movement.

In other courses you may have taken, you may have focused on the meaning, the theme, or the symbols of a poem. In creative writing courses, we tend to focus more on the craft—how to create the meaning, rather than the meaning itself. The lyric voice, which has its roots in words meant to be sung, is one that engages us by appealing to our senses, and by taking a form that adds something important to the act of reading. These are the special provenance, of poetry; and they help it reach deeply into moments and aspects of our lives that other forms of writing can't touch. These qualities are the reason poetry lasts, for its own sake and for ours. ❖

A Note on Writing
Poetry in "Forms"

Michael White

WHAT "FORM" MEANS VARIES GREATLY FROM GENRE to genre, but in poetry, it usually refers collectively to the "received" traditions of English verse that centuries of poets have found most useful and expressive. These include not only the incredibly powerful systems of rhythm-generating metrics that evolved concurrently (mostly in the English Renaissance) with our language, but a whole universe of verse structures and fixed forms like the sonnet, blank verse, the villanelle, the sestina, the ballad, and so on. But form can also refer to other traditions such as the shaped or "concrete" poem (think of John Hollander's "Swan and Shadow"); early modernist experiments in typography (think of e. e. cummings); the many schools of free verse (think of the cadenced, biblically inspired long lines of Walt Whitman or Allen Ginsberg; or of the minimalist poems of William Carlos Williams) . . . Form, in short, can refer to almost any objectifiable model for shaping lines of poetry on the page.

Yet even this definition of form can be limiting for beginning writers. The "form" of a sonnet, for instance, is often defined as an external shape (i.e., fourteen lines of iambic pentameter conforming to one of several long-standing rhyme schemes)—which has little to do with the emotional or imaginative ground of the tradition. Trying to write poetry by means of the form/content dichotomy (fitting your ideas into a ready-made shell) is like a young musician trying to play the blues solely by copying its most common rhythms. A blues song—especially as played by a master like Coltrane—is alive, a way of thinking and responding to experience that cannot be reduced to mere numbers. Nor can any of the verse forms in English poetry be safely reduced to external description—not for the writer. Form is not a box! The form/content approach to writing poetry will most likely defeat your best efforts.

Think of form rather as performance, or occasion , , , think of it as theatre. Poetry, of all the arts, has always manifested itself orally: think of the current popularity of poetry slams, the coffee-house scene, the "spoken word." Now think of each of the poetic forms as a different mode of private/public performance, with a different emotional chemistry and purpose.

What do you do with yourself—with your feelings—in the early giddiness of love? Let's say you're a guy, and last night your sweetheart let you kiss her for the first time. Tonight you are on your way to pick her up for a special dinner date. If you have any sense at all—and it seems you might—you will be bringing her a dozen roses, right? The classic bouquet of roses is a convention that exists simultaneously on a public and a private plane. Your parents and grandparents participated in the same convention. Yet the feelings behind it, in your case, are your own.

The gift of roses will probably impress her (and part of the reason for giving it is that it will make you happy, too)—but if you want to impress her even more, try writing her a sonnet. The sonnet form (from *sonetto*, Italian for "little song") has its origins in romance: sonneteers once sung their sequences in court with a lyre for accompaniment. Its complex rhymes are simultaneously pleasurable, theatrical, and meaningful; and when a sonnet is written well, it is a delight to see how much of the poet's personality and emotional state can be expressed and heightened through the conventions of a public art. A sonnet—like a bouquet of roses—can be a lovely, extravagant, and effective gift.

This is not to imply that the sonnets are strictly for courtship . . . the sonnet is actually extraordinarily versatile, which may be why it is one of our greatest literary forms, and why contemporary poets such as Frank O'Hara have written sonnets compulsively. What I am saying here is simply that the human dimension of the poetic occasion needs to be emphasized. Each formal tradition represents a different kind of performance—with its own special aural capabilities and emotional tendencies—which may or may not bring the best out of you as a writer. If you want to write a meditative, nuanced narrative in the style of Robert Frost (but in your own voice, of course) it may be helpful to use the blank verse form (unrhymed iambic pentameter) as he so often did. If you want to write a poem of grief, rage, or loss like Dylan Thomas's "Do Not Go Gentle into That Good Night" or Elizabeth Bishop's "One Art," it may be wise to try to develop your own version of the villanelle—an eerily haunting form of song—as those poets did. It may not be very useful for a writer to be able to define the form intellectually . . . but it is invaluable to read deeply, to try to get an instinctive feel for what each form can do—its characteristic moves—and try to find your own balance between the public and the private. Try to absorb the tradition from the inside, not from the outside, and you'll find the concept of "form" not only less frustrating, but far more empowering, both as a reader and a writer.

Note: I don't think poets necessarily should start out with traditional forms. Typically, in my introductory workshops, I ask students to stick to free verse in the beginning, until they have gained some confidence, developed a clearer sense of their own voice, and are beginning to think (and trust) in images. But at some point in the apprenticeship process, I have found that working through a sequence of assignments in traditional forms will further a poet's development dramatically. The challenges of writing in form create breakthroughs. Many poets will discover abilities they didn't know they had . . . and even those who return to free verse for good will do so with a better ear for the sounds of the mother tongue. ❖

POETRY

SELECTIONS

Lavonne Adams

SAND DOLLAR

Your mother is now so far down
the beach that she looks lean and sallow

as a popsicle stick; your little brother
buzzes her heel.

It is August,
three months since your father packed

his battered brown suitcase
and drove twelve hours to Atlantic City,

feverish for the quick fix
of the roulette wheel;

you tell your friends he died
in a fiery crash.

You are fourteen;
you can take care of yourself. All around

you are fragments

of shells not good enough

for the rolled-down bread bag dangling
by your side; you only want things whole.

And then you find that perfect shell:
a sand dollar

that lies light
against your skin. The sound of the ocean

becomes like the hum of your mind—
there but not.

There's a part of you
that would like to snap

a crescent from the edge of this shell,
to revel in that crisp breaking.

You know what is inside: calcium
has spun stalactites in the cave where bits

of skeleton, like bone doves, rustle.
The shell once held life, moved

along drifts on the ocean's floor;
yet it is hard not to see

it as manmade—a splash
of plaster dried to graininess.

Imagine some artist
hunched over a workbench, needling
that pattern—like a fine sketch

in pen and ink—onto its back.

What are the words you would choose
to describe this work?

A flower blooming on a mound of sand?
Or an imprint of yourself, arms flung wide

as if floating
in your own peculiar freefall?

EVERYDAY STILL LIFE

This room is a study of white
on white: the vivid drape
of sheets bleached to the softness

of pulp; the white walls grayed
by gloves of shadow; in the corner
on a white wicker stand, a frieze

of fresh white chrysanthemums.
The perfect subject for a still life,
nothing here is truly inanimate.

The sheet's selvage is soughed by a breeze
as plaster draws away from itself, creating
delicate veins. After the climax

of bloom, the flowers relax
in their own sweet descent.
Beyond the window, live oak boughs

crenelate with moss. And on the brush
of lawn not yet lush enough to mow,
five dandelions halo to radiant white.

AT THE MUSEUM OF CHILDHOOD, EDINBURGH

Against one wall, a TV plays
a video of a dusky '50s Edinburgh
street where cotton dresses flutter
as a jump rope slaps its cadence:
    ". . . in came the doctor . . ."
Like a yard sale behind glass,
there's the first version of Candyland—
its gingerbread boy plumper,
its colors more subdued.
And there, a tin top that once spun
open to reveal a tiny farm
with tin cows and pigs.
    ". . . in came the nurse . . ."
Touted as the noisiest
museum in the world, today
its five galleries are
on the cusp of vacant.
    ". . . in came the lady with
    the alligator purse . . ."
But those who are here shuffle
from case to case, stand and stare
like a clownish chorus
of mute Pagliaccios, swallowing
the sound of their grief.

From *In the Shadow of the Mountain*

Across the throat of the Caribbean extends a chain of islands, which are really smouldering furnaces, with fires banked up, ever ready to break forth at some unexpected and inappropriate moment.

Anonymous geologist, 1902

St. Pierre, 1902

Like feather dusters, coconut palms
skim cobweb clouds above
steep winding streets where
bougainvilleas unfurl their pink lace.
Stevedores muscle the weight
of what must be lifted and carried
to the bay, a blue tongue rimming
the harbor. Below red-tiled roofs,
wooden shutters open into rooms
cooled by thick stone walls and
tamarind trees, lush with pods;
everywhere, mangoes blush like sunsets.
This scene is a postcard, an entreaty.
But remember, the mountain
is always over your shoulder,
wearing veils of clouds
that hide its real face.

i. The Usine Guerin Sugar Mill
First, a wave of centipedes
and speckled ants that can kill
a grown man. Trying to hold them back,
wokers moat the yard with oil, douse
the horses that writhe and buck,
ants gnawing their eyes. Inside

the mill, insects swarm the machinery,
dropping into vats, clogging vents.
Time becomes a syrup. Unlike the fear
that stoppered their veins for weeks, this is
a visible enemy that can be quashed,
flailed with sugarcane clutched in fists.

In a once-dry crater near the mountain's summit,
a lake steams with silica and sulphur.
Boiling water cascades from a newly risen cone
until the earth crumbles like a gun site.
Water tumbles down a ravine, thrums
over boulders, prying trees loose by the roots,
scalding everything that's green.
Gravity and momentum. Not thick
lava that hardens to obsidian—black
and glossy as a mirror—this mass of mud
churns the delta, consumes the mill until
all that's left is the smokestack,
like a guidepost pointing at the sky.

ii. Fer-de-Lances
Behind each eye, twin mounds
rise as if swollen with
their own venom.
Perhaps these snakes
were shocked awake
where they lay curled
like cochleas after a night
of searching for prey.
As the temperature
in the twenty rivers that course
the mountain's sides
began to rise, snakes
fled to Saint Pierre,
where they now strike

at the heat of a leg or
a child's soft pulse. Skin
turns back and blisters
as if charred; eyes
weep blood. By day's end,
two hundred animals and
fifty humans dead, while
heaped in the street, carcasses
of a hundred snakes
like tarnished brass
dull in afternoon light.

JOSEPHINE (II)

Grandmère calls the mountain an old man
who clears his throat and spits out ash
then falls back asleep. But his pipe has been lit
now for weeks.
                    Mistress Prentiss tells me
not to fear the mountain, but
her dresses and shoes are packed,
silver and linens in three large chests
to be hefted, one by one, onto the back of the gardener
who will carry them to the quay.
Ships fill the harbor like flies.
I'm like the linen left behind. If she leaves,

I'll walk the dirt road to Fort-de-France,
everything I need bundled and carried
on my head—my brush, an extra dress,
my mother's silver bracelet stamped with
fleurs-de-lis worn so thin they look like feathers.

Fernand Clerc

Hummingbirds, like strange fruit, drop into the streets
as my horse snorts sulphur fumes from his nose.
My inclination is to flee,

but with wealth comes a certain responsibility
to maintain control, to adhere to routine though
hummingbirds, like strange fruit, drop into the streets.

Scoffing at those who cower, the editor of *Les Colonies*
acts as if this is only a storm, the ash falling a mirage.
I am disinclined for him to see me flee.

And I laughed over sherry at shopgirls who, at the first rumble,
        streamed
from their stores, corsets and mismatched boots clutched to
breasts.
Still, hummingbirds, like strange fruit, drop into the streets.

Then, this morning, the barometer's needle swung wildly
as lightning ripped incessantly through Pelée's churning cloud.
My inclination is to flee,

but at what point is it acceptable to leave?
In every quarter of town, shutters are latched
and blackbirds, like decaying fruit, drop into the streets.
My inclination is to flee.

Landscape, May 8

At 100 miles per hour, Pelée's cloud
churns down the mountain, bares
trees of their leaves and branches, blackens

every trunk. Within moments, what was
flesh is not; iridescent dust
chars throats; superheated steam sears lungs.

In every gutter along the quay, rum burns blue.
What was commerce is now rubble;
with each breeze, ash lifts and resettles.

Even the statue of the Virgin,
thrown forty feet from her pedestal,
presses her face to the ground.

MID-AUGUST LANDSCAPE

More than a month
since the last eruption,

carts trundle the Rue Victor Hugo,
lapilli and ash pushed to the side

like snowdrifts. Birds
have not yet returned,

though here and there,
a new banana shoot,

a foot or two of cane
like green ribbons

in the distance. Along
the Place Bertin, bits

of skulls, like crescent moons,
glimmer. Those who scavenge

say they are not looters,
not grave robbers,

but inheritors of what was left
behind. One carries

a tray of clay pipes,
another a harp still strung.

THE MOST MARVELOUS MAN ON EARTH

The poster isn't true. My name
is Auguste Ciparis, not Ludger Sylbaris.
There was no lava; it was not night.
I wasn't anchored to a beam
beneath a window, unconscious
on a bed of straw. I wasn't
the only living object that survived
in the "Silent City of Death."
There was one other. The truth,
they said, won't sell tickets.
So each night, I wait for the crowd
that will fill the sideshow,
that will stare at The Human Skeleton,
The Leopard Girl, and finally at me.
They don't believe I survived St. Pierre,
assume a circus hoax until
I shed my shirt, show them
my melted back, like congealed wax.
Some women faint, others scream;
they avert their eyes as if the evidence
of my body is something indecent,
then look back again, as if
there is something to be learned
from the contours of my skin.
In my back pocket, I carry
a postcard of the island
folded in half, which I open
like a small book, like a prayer.
On it, each building is intact.
See the lighthouse in the corner?
I wanted to live

at its top, the world spread out
like a field in front of me.
A black and white imprint
of what was once alive,
even this card is a ghost.

Mark Cox

SUN TEA

Along the river, beyond the porch,
the shadows of individual leaves
conspire to create shade. Not one
moment can separate from the past
and yet the present exists!

Though higher consciousness
is just an awareness
of the limitations of consciousness,
though the past deepens leaf by leaf,
layer by layer, until one's childhood
cannot be told
from the childhoods of everyone.

Such bitterness in the brown stains on cement,
in the clinging of wet socks,
in the bristles of worn whisk brooms
littering the porch.
Birds know better what to make
of the past—their nests
give new shape to it. To them,
the sky is not a lid
lowering an inch each day,
their hearts are not half-eaten fruits,
they have no memory of winter.

As we do,
hearing these ice cubes crack and split
before dissolving in our glasses.

LIKE A SIMILE

Fell into bed like a tree
slept like boiling water
got up from bed like a camel
and showered like a tin roof.
Went downstairs like a Slinky
drove to work like a water skier
entered the trailer like a bad smell
where I changed clothes like a burn victim
drank my coffee like a mosquito
and waited like a bus stop.
A whistle blew.
Then I painted like I was in a knife fight for eight hours
drank like a burning building
drove home like a bank shot
unlocked the door like a jeweler
and entered the house like an argument next door.
The dog smiled like a chain saw.
The wife pretended to be asleep
I pretended to eat.
She lay on the bed like a mattress
I sat at the table like a chair.
Until I inched along the stair rail like a sprinkler
entered like smoke from a fire in the next room
and apologized like a toaster.
The covers did not open like I was an envelope
and she was a 24-hour teller
so I undressed like an apprentice matador
discovering bullshit on his shoes.

The Night Watchman's Son

Where they live,
the moon is the last swallow of milk
in a glass on a table,
the stars crumbs of pie crust,
and you can hear the man's keys
as he shifts in his chair.

Every night, the boy says, the man
adjusts the glasses on his nose,
tunes the radio beneath a courtesy light,
then drives off to work,
while all his children gather at the sill,
which makes their chins feel important,
to watch the white dust of his going
settle into the gravel.
Where they live
you have to turn off the lights inside
to see out.
It's like the smoke from a cup of coffee then,
from a blue Thermos on the table of a tiny brown house
where a dog has buried its face in its body.

I am afraid this often, he says,
filling his lawn with trees,
and sometimes when I draw, I don't
put the moon in at all,
I leave it out to scare myself more
and make the wind sound like a lady crying
and the garage door closing loud all by itself.

The night is this big, he's decided
as he bears down, it will take
lots of walking to make sure—that,
and yellow crayon
for the windows of their house.

SONATA

At ninety, the piano plays him.
He's like a man by the sea
the wind knows it must wear down,
sculpt to a profile,
then fill out again,
billowing his sleeves and trouser legs
into a younger musculature.
Over and again, the music greys
then reddens, the part
in its hair shifting left to center
until those few blades of sea grass
are all that's left to be
combed over the rocks,
and the thin fingers skitter,
leaving impressions in the keyboard
that waves wash level,
cleansing its audience of shell halves,
now glistening, now scoured dry.
And the house, the house just outside
this sonata's frame,
begs him to turn around
to pick his way back
along the stony runner,
his hands stopping his ears.
But, at ninety, the music plays the piano,
which plays the man, who finally, fearlessly,
plays himself, which is the landscape,
which is everything that ends.

Things My Grandfather Must Have Said

I want to die in the wintertime,
make the ground regret it,
make the backhoe sweat.

January. Blue Monday
after the holiday weekend.
I want it to be hard on everybody.
I want everyone to have a headache
and the traffic to be impossible.
Back it up for miles, Jesus.
I want steam under the hood, bad directions,
cousins lost, babies crying, and sleet
I want a wind so heavy their umbrellas howl.

And give me some birds, pigeons even,
anything circling for at least half an hour,
and plastic tulips and a preacher who stutters

"Uh" before every word of Psalm 22.
I want to remind them just how bad things are.
Spell my name wrong on the stone, import

earthworms fat as Aunt Edith's arms
and put them under the folding chairs.
And I want a glass coffin,

I want to be wearing the State of Missouri
string tie no one else liked. . . God,
I hope the straps break

and I fall in with a thud. I hope
the shovel slips out of my son's hands.
I want them to remember I don't feel anything.

I want the food served straight from my garden.
I want the head of the table set. I want
everyone to get a pennant that says,

"Gramps was the greatest,"
and a complete record of my mortgage payments
in every thank-you note.

And I want to keep receiving mail for thirteen years,
all the bills addressed to me,
old friends calling every other month

to wonder how I am.
Then I want an earthquake or rising water-table,
the painful exhumation of my remains.

I want to do it all again.

I want to die the day before something truly
important happens and have my grandson say:
What would he have thought of that?

I want you all to know how much I loved you.

Sarah Messer

Starting with that time

he shot a man in Mendota
for calling him pretty, *hey pretty, your hair's
like spun sunshine,* and then
the man fell down dead. Son of a
tin smith, he had inherited
those quick but delicate hands, and
always went for his revolver
as quick and absentmindedly as
an itch the same way he went
for those squirrel-boned
women even smaller than himself
with breasts like shallow teacups.

As an outlaw, he fell in love
with the wrong women—a seamstress
who sniffed glue, who sewed
her own sleeves to her arms
and flew off a bridge; a sad-faced
war nurse; a rich Northerner
who carried her father's
jawbone in her purse—
each one disappearing more
from herself, until he found
that he was mostly in love
with the shadow of a dress,
a wrist, or the outline of a mouth

pressed to the glass on the window
of the next train leaving town.

In the meantime, he killed:
any man who could ever be called
his friend. Ambushed the town
of Independence, killed 12
at Olathe, 20 at Shawnee, tied the scalps
of those he suspected most
to his horse's bridle, and rode
west. The mayor of Lawrence,
Kansas suffocated in a well beneath
his own house as the whole
town burned, the contents of every
train and wagon turned over.

In the end he came to me
because I was the timberline, way out
west, the last stand of trees.

Each night I told him about
the guns hidden in my house:
a .44 caliber in the chamber pot, a rifle
beneath the stairs, bird guns between
folded linen, revolvers hidden
in drawers, on shelves, the four boudoir
pistols plastered in walls, wrapped
in the hair of dolls.

He hid himself inside the sheen
of Smith and Wesson, the one breech
double-barreled Winchester,
my only Navy Colt. He hid because
I was the hideout, the inert
and sturdy home where he polished
his thoughts, the timber
of each trigger, the powder

in the coffee tin, the bullets
in the freezer.

In the end, I was
the safest place for him
to put his mouth.

SOME WOMEN MARRY HOUSES

I
My mother, blind from the swamp-gas,
the kudzu, almost married
a gas station—had five or six
kids in a cardboard box backyard;
almost drank motor oil in a Styrofoam cup; almost slept
with the drawer to the register open
under ghost Esso, flies licking
lip-corners, a wide-wale
corduroy grin; almost burned
our infant skin off, birthing on those
gas rags—
                              But this
did not happen. She married
a meat-shop owned by a prominent
butcher. He puts a neat bullet
in the temple of every yearling.
*It's painless, they don't even know
how they die.* Each evening she takes
buckets outside and washes
the red walls down.

II
Each day, my grandmother walked
a bridge of stretched cat intestines
under horse-hair power lines.

Her husband found her often inside
the belly of a violin. She was all
he ever wanted in a woman: exotic as
the parlor's Oriental, the throats
of his seven caged birds. He steamed

stripped wood and clamped it
to her body. He glued seams

and clefts above the sacral
joints he kneaded each night when
they made love, so she could sing
all those pretty high notes
from inside their polished home.

III
I live alone and love
the abandoned walls, the water-
damage, the shelf-paper
tongues lolling from cabinets, mid-morning
sunlight on telephone wires, the telephone,
the leafy, leaning second-story porch.

It's easy to love the house, so quiet
in the haze of morning windows—
it's easy to love the chimney, still warm
from last night's fire, and solid
at the center, something to put my hands upon
        when no one will enter me.

IN THE MARKET,

a transaction is made, and the snake
is lifted from the basket by the back
of its head, the body dangling
like a girl's braid. With a flash
of silver the head is scissored
into Tupperware and the skin
peeled down like a condom, like the arm
of a wet shirt, the slick inner
muscle exposed and thrown
to the counter like a party ribbon.

Now the animal is pure meat,
the long cords pulled apart
from the spine, a broken zipper.
The customer wants only
the liver, the size of a lover's earlobe,
said to improve brain function,
to replace lost memory.

Memory can become a medicine that,
clamped beneath the tongue, heals
all past and recent conflagrations.
But scars are the prisons skin builds
around injury, the angle of the roof
increasing as each blade is drawn in
and out. And memory is the room
where you wait in the dark.

You still had your key. You heard
my footstep on the landing, the tumblers
rolling in the lock. You sat like a priest
at the edge of the sofa, your clothes
the color of earth and organs, like an animal
caught at the roadside, you wanted
to catch me with a new lover,

my nylons already shed, limp in my
hand, returning at 3 a.m.

Above the market's temporary roofs,
the tin and blue plastic, it is raining.
Below them, the butcher has killed
five snakes. He works on the sixth,
his fingers plying the spinal cord,
his face jiggling. The customer stares
at the organs pinning down the paper
towel—gray ghost bodies, five tiny fists.

He looks like you: like there is
something lost to him, something
he doesn't even realize yet
that he has forgotten to say, something
that was stripped away by a larger
man's hands moving down a tiny spine,
in childhood, in the dark, his fingers
hooked into the softest places, into
the coiled knot of thighs and clamped
jaws snaking away beneath footsteps
in the hall, beneath the rotting house sill,
the roots and leaves and soiled market
basket, the locked back rooms.

The customer is asking for two
more, wanting to know how
this will work, this new world
where nothing is forgotten, even this
feeling that sometimes makes him strike
at nothing, that makes him glide
as if dreaming, sidewinding
in the night, his body triggered, one long
hearing instrument spread out upon
the earth, the path up from the garden—

and his hand stays perched
at the collar bone like yours was when
the shard of light, my shadow,
entered the house—your hand pale
against your shirt like a poised wing,
like the snake arched, waiting.

Malena Mörling

IF THERE IS ANOTHER WORLD

If there is another world,
I think you can take a cab there—
or ride your bicycle
down Junction Blvd.
past the Paris Suites Hotel
with the Eiffel Tower on the roof
and past the blooming Magnolia and on—
to the corner of 168th street.
And if you're inclined too,
you can turn left there
and yield to the blind
as the sign urges us—
especially since it is a state law.
Especially since there is a kind of moth
here on the earth
that feeds only on the tears of horses.
Sooner of later we will all cry
from inside our hearts.
Sooner of later even the concrete
will crumble and cry in silence
along with all the lost road signs.
Two days ago 300 televisions
washed up on a beach in Shiomachi, Japan,
after having fallen off a ship in a storm.
They looked like so many
over-sized horseshoe crabs

with their screens turned down to the sand.
And if you're inclined to, you can continue
in the weightless seesaw of the light
through a few more intersections
where people inside their cars
pass you by in space
and where you pass by them,
each car another thought—only heavier.

A STORY

The swallows have a story
they tell no one,
not even the rats,
the rats you once saw standing
on their hind legs
at the dump
late in the dark,
the car silent.
Not even the empty shopping cart
of the wind
as it wheels through the foliage—
Everyone has a story,
like a string of invisible Christmas lights
wound into the heart.
And every story has a story
that hides inside its own labyrinth.
The past has a story
as wide and as deep as the world.
Every word has a story
and every stone.

Wallpaper

On the one hand,
out the filthy window
   of the train
the world goes by,
   a three-dimensional
wallpaper.

Momentarily
in the woods,
   the thin carpet
of snow
   is cut to fit
perfectly around
   every tree.

And shortly there after,
   on the river,
large pieces of ice
   are drifting
in the sunlight
   like glistening
serving platters.

On the other hand,
there is of course,
   the invisible
wallpaper
   of the mind
always clinging
   to everything.

Even to the sorry,
   sideways houses
along the tracks.

And to the garbage
somebody puked
   all over a hill
that just went past.

On the one hand,
the wallpaper
   of the world
and the wallpaper
   of the mind
are separate
   layers of
what is seen
   and unseen.

On the other hand,
   they are one
and the same
   seamlessly
merging inside
   the skull.

Michael White

RE-ENTRY

Then it hit me. Fumbling for a smoke,
I sank down heavily onto a concrete bench

beside the circle drive. There was no view
except for the rows of glare-shot windshields, shimmer

of asphalt—bypasses and freeways—and
a venomous, blood-orange dusk above it all.

I took a deep drag. Thirty days had passed
since I'd checked in, and wandered through the ward

with tom implosions in each ear—as fireflies
flooded the trelliswork of synapses—

for three straight days, before I knew where I was.
It was the top floor of State Hospital,

our dayroom windows facing out across
the vast exhaustion of the Midwest, where

electrical dust-storms tinged the air, an aura
of migraine settling over the river hills . . .

Day after day, we'd gather there for Peer Group—
some in wheelchairs, some with our IV poles—

each trying to calm the tremors in his hands.
Whenever someone spoke, whenever someone

started to piece a narrative together
out of threads of smoke—the infused ache

of what the flesh remembers—I could feel
the tenor of fear in everything he said,

the word on the tip of his tongue on the tip of my tongue.
I'd listen and gaze out, listen and gaze out over

the fallow prairies, half-imagined hayfields
of my only landscape: buckled faultlines

leveling off in miles of bottomland,
where massive burr oaks loomed like cumulus

adrift upon a plain of dust. I'd stare
and stare—untethered, ravenous—at sheets

of lightning smoldering here and there beneath
a remote steel-blue cloudbank, as the room

filled with acetylene sun, the conduits of
my nerves burned clean . . . And this was the only cure

there was. One day I rose, and put on my street clothes,
nothing in my pockets. I remember

riding the elevator five flights down—
the sudden *whoosh* when its doors opened on

the ground floor . . . Struggling to compose myself,
I strode across the lobby with a wink

for the receptionist, but by the time
I stepped out into the sunlight, I was shaking.

The Levee

I am this dust on the river road, I'd think.
I am this dust on the tasseled fields—deep summer's
scent of brushfire threaded through this breeze—

and at that age, I could believe. My world
consisted of a sallow-looking downtown;
streets named after trees; the girls I worshipped

secretly; the cemeteries fringed
with spikes; the breaks in the river hills to the south
(great floodplain vistas fading away to the south),

where everything ends in a narrow fringe of swampoaks
and cottonwoods overlooming the river . . . Part of
me is always homing, scrambling down

the face of the levee, forcing my way through willows
and driftwood—flotsam of old tires and rusted oildrums—
down to the Corps of Engineers' embankment,

down to the seam where the elements touch, the dense
aortal dark of slaughterhouse and prairie
sweeping past me . . . There at the tip of the wing dike,

kneeling and sinking back, I'd finger the sand grains
—fragments of mussel shells—and let the sun-scaled
body of current carry me away . . .

Sometimes, I'd close my eyes, and in the cries
of crows—the howls of semis two miles off—
in the barely audible, hoarse note of a tractor

raising dust in the fields across the river,
I could hear the year click shut. One evening,
smoldering down to the nub, I thought I could feel

an odd, irregular throbbing in my jawbone—
skull—the balls of my feet . . . The others were back
in the trees: I crouched alone on a spit of sand,

the pulse of an engine pounding all around me,
out of the pores of the limestone cliffsides. Something
was coming towards me, something was churning its way

upriver towards me, thrumming louder and louder
until I could see the train of barges shackled
together—laboring into sight—until

I could see the tow: its funnel pouring gouts
of black exhaust, its pilot house ablaze
with fumes and glare, its six-foot bow wave breaking

along both banks . . . I was amazed, transfixed
by its deliberate and delicate
corrections—centering in its marks—as slowly,

it drew abreast, and I could see the man
inside of it, the one responsible
for all those tons of steel and displaced river.

I remember the eerie, flickering pall
cast up from the instrument panel onto his face,
and I remember the moment he turned towards me,

and sounded his airhorn three long blasts for me
as if in recognition . . . *River rat,*
I thought, and waved. And then he was gone. And after

that agitation passed—long after the gnats
all started up again—I ran as hard
as I could through the flood-washed cottonwoods—
over the levee—

back to the road, and my friends . . . In our back yard
today, camellias are having their second spring;
our concrete birdbath fills with the slough of blossom . . .

Suddenly, it's over. Suddenly,
the tendons of clematis flower and fade out
over our garage roof—its metaphor,

its metamorphosis, is over and done with . . .
What I want is what I had: the landscape
beneath the landscape; hawks and cliffheads; hum

of bridges; summer's sumac, gold and cobalt
clarities which deepened as the river
gradually dwindled . . . What I want is what

I was—that self lost utterly in vagrant
days that sank in flames as I spent them there—
my element silt, my posture prayer, my god

appearing sometimes in the guise of gnats
or hawks, or hundreds of incidents that bloomed
alone like bloodlit clouds across the dark

opacities of surface . . . Once, a man
appeared like that, *a man appeared like that,*
and as he passed—as waves of unimaginable

clamor shuddered through that place which still
absorbs me so completely—suddenly,
he glanced at me, and claimed me for his own.

WHAT I WANTED TO TELL YOU
for Rebecca Lee

couldn't wait, and I kept taking the steps
    to your beach house three at a time in my mind, but
the truth is, I was caught in traffic back
    in Forest Hills. Before I knew what hit me—

what the slowdown and clanging hysteria meant—the tandem
    diesels lumbered past, all decibels
and oilsmoke, and then maybe a hundred coalcars
    and flatcars slid through the fogged dusk. I admit

I loved the spectacle, the patience of joggers
    and leashed dogs—even the starlings swirling up
from the blossomy lungs of the live oaks—and I wanted
    to step out, rush into that magnitude

the way my mind does sometimes, going for broke,
    not letting go . . . But I stayed firmly put
instead, and slipping into neutral, read
    the boxcars' open secrets: *Big Blue, Norfolk*

& Western scrolling through the neighborhood—
    where mansions shuddered in their berths, where April
sulked and lost its grip, where in the wrack
    of body heat, the agony of steel

on steel, I spoke to you like this.

THE
WORKSHOP

Making the Workshop Work for You

Tim Bass

I REMEMBER HANDING MY FICTION WORKSHOP CLASSMATES A short story I'd written. I had spent hours working on it—writing, editing, waiting for my s-l-o-w printer, racing to the copy shop, hustling to get to class.

That was the easy part.

As the story left my hands and each of my classmates took a copy, I felt powerless, self-conscious, and a little tight in my stomach. *They* had my story now. They would take it home and read it and come back in a few days and discuss it in front of each other, in front of my professor, in front of the whole world.

Will they rip it to shreds? I wondered. Or will they see it as the literary masterpiece that I know it is? What will they say about my story? What will they say about me?

Furniture and Nerves: What Is the Writing Workshop?

When most people hear the word "workshop," they think of a place for building coffee tables or upholstering sofas. People who know these crafts often seek help from others—they trade suggestions and pitch in to shape the wood or cut the fabric.

Creative writing workshops function much the same way. Writers show up with a story, a poem, or an essay, and they seek advice from others who have similar interests and talents. Together, they examine and critique the writing, and then they discuss ways to build it, strengthen it, refine it. Instead of belt sanders and circular saws, they use ideas.

The format is simple: You hand out a piece of writing to your classmates, they read it and mark it up, and everybody gets together and talks about what you're doing well and what you need to work on some more.

This often makes people nervous. Many writers ask themselves the same questions I asked: What will the readers say about my story? Will they rip it to shreds? Some writers feel that the workshop sets them up for target practice. They fear the inevitable "negative" comment that shoots through the writing and pierces their souls.

So here's my first sliver of advice about workshopping: Go easy on the drama. It's a classroom, not a firing range. The writer's workshop provides a phenomenal opportunity—a bunch of writers have agreed to invest their time, energy, and talent to help you improve your work. Stop worrying and be thankful.

The workshop has two goals:

1. To give your work a constructive critique that points out strengths and weaknesses to help you revise.

2. To allow everyone at the table to learn something about their own writing, regardless of whose work is under discussion.

As a writer and a reader, you have everything to gain in a workshop.

First Things First: Before the Workshop

For you, the writer, the workshop starts before the workshop. If you prepare, you will give yourself the best chance of getting what you need most from your classmates and your professor.

Preparation is simple: think, plan, and write—early. Fight off procrastination and get busy. Give your readers a piece of writing that you're proud of—a piece that is fit for their time, attention, and energy.

Unfortunately, too many writers show up for workshops with half-baked work—flat images, tired language, illogical plots, one-dimensional characters, empty dialogue, colorless scenes. These flaws do not happen because the work comes from a bad writer. Rather, they appear because the writer believed in one (or more) of the lies that writers tell themselves when they are unorganized, undisciplined, or unmotivated to do their best work.

Here are just a few of those lies:

I do my best writing under pressure. No. People do their fastest writing under pressure, and it shows. We've all read (and written) those quickie pieces: Two friends are driving through some unknown land late at night, and an old man is in the back seat—he's either dying or drunk or just asleep, but it's not clear. And that's it. The friends are just driving the car and smoking cigarettes and making wisecracks, and the old man is just lying in the back seat saying nothing. All three are going nowhere—just like the story. The whole situation is a pointless mess. It holds together no better than spilled water.

Writers write best when they give themselves time—time to think through the project, time to plan it, to decide what the point is, time to write on it, then write more, then more, then let it cool off, then read it and revise it and write more. Before the workshop.

A good piece of writing is less like conceiving and more like giving birth. It takes time. And labor.

By the way, the aimless story about the two friends and the old man—I wrote that. In a hurry, at the last minute. I'm still embarrassed.

I can't think of anything to write. In the effort to write creatively, many people often cut short or overlook the most creative aspect of the work: thinking. Too many people take to their keyboards without considering some essential questions: What is this piece about? What is the point of my essay? What form should this poem take—villanelle? Sestina? Free verse? What is the best point of view for telling this story? How can I say something that hasn't been said a million times before?

It isn't possible to have a full answer to every question before striking the first key. But writers owe it to themselves—and to their readers—to think about the big questions in advance, to know what's at stake before ever sitting down to write.

I don't know anybody who can't think. But I know people who don't think. When writers say they can't think of anything to write, they should think some more. Your creative writing professors are not here to tell you what to think. We'll give you an assignment, a few examples, some advice. But the thinking is up to you.

I write only when I'm inspired. This exhausted line makes me think of someone lighting a stick of incense and sitting cross-legged to wait for the heavens to open and beam down brilliant ideas and endless energy.

Too bad it doesn't work that way.

Don't get me wrong—I'm all for inspiration. But as writers, we cannot afford the luxury of waiting for a divine force to give us what we need for our poems and stories. That's our job, and we must work at it. We have to think our projects through, then face the intimidating blank screen and write, write, write.

We should write every day. We should write when we feel like writing, and write when we don't feel like it. We have to protect our writing time from getting sucked away by work, classes, playtime, and everything else that crowds our day.

I've heard it said that writing is ten-percent inspiration and ninety-percent perspiration. Maybe that doesn't sound like fun, but it's true. Writers who work at their craft end up with good poems, stories, and essays. And they don't get muscle cramps from sitting on the floor with their heels yanked up to their thighs, waiting for inspiration.

It's OK if the writing is weak. The workshop is for rough drafts, anyway. Wrong. Writers who run a first, rough draft into a workshop will get little help. The readers will point out all the obvious problems that the writer should have fixed before printing the piece. The writer will think, *I already know about all that stuff. Why don't they tell me something new?* Answer: Because the writer didn't give them a decent draft to work with, and they're too nice to say it out loud.

Never bring a rough draft into a workshop. Bring in your best effort, not your first effort. Then your readers can help you make a strong piece stronger.

Handing Out without Passing Out

Usually, the workshop timetable goes this way:

1. You hand out your poem or story to your classmates and professor one class meeting before your workshop.

2. Everybody takes the piece home to read it, mark it up, and write comments.

3. At the next class meeting, the group discusses your piece, then hands you back the marked copies and written comments.

As you can see, everything depends on your handing out the work on time. That sounds simple, but some students can't get the hang of it. Too often, people show up late to hand out their work. Or they're stressed out. Or they're late and stressed out. Sometimes, they don't show up at all.

These steps can help you get quality writing to class on time, and without a meltdown:

Avoid procrastination. Think your story through, write early, and give yourself time to revise and polish. Don't cheat yourself and your readers by bringing in a rough draft that you knocked out at the last minute. Your readers will recognize it. They won't be able to offer you much advice, other than to say, "Next time, write earlier."

Save your work, save your sanity. Click the Save button early and often. Back up your work on a diskette.

Yes, spelling and grammar matter. Don't let mistakes undermine your creative ideas. Make sure your work is free of all mechanical errors. If you need help with spelling, grammar, or punctuation, get a writer's handbook; they're inexpensive, and they never go out of date. Also, UNCW's Writing Center offers free help to students who need to work on the mechanics of writing. Computer programs that check spelling are useful; programs that check grammar are not. Ultimately, your work is your responsibility, so take care of it.

Make your work easy to read. Pay attention to form. Put your name on your creative work. Title it. Number the pages. Staple the pages. Use a standard typeface and size, like Times New Roman, 12 point.

Print early. Don't let printer problems ruin your work, or your day. People who print at the last minute are begging for trouble, and they usually get it.

Get copies early. Have one copy made for everyone in the class.

Don't taint the water. Often, writers hand out their creative work and announce to the class, "This piece is terrible. I had a lot of deadlines in my other classes, and I ran out of time to write." This is often a thinly disguised plea: "Read this with low expectations, and be nice to me." Bad idea. Don't try to spin the workshop in your favor. Let your readers form their own opinions.

Listen and Learn: The Writer in the Workshop

The writer's role during the workshop is simple: Listen to the discussion and absorb the critique.

To get the workshop moving, some professors will ask you to read a few lines from your poem or a few paragraphs from your story. Some professors will do the reading themselves. Others will ask one of your classmates to "shepherd" the story into the workshop by reading a selection or summarizing the piece of writing. Still other professors will start the discussion without reading from the work at all.

After that, though, most workshops follow the same pattern: The class discusses the writing, and you stay silent. The class's job is to critique the writing; your job is to listen, take notes, and look for ways to revise.

You might feel exposed by this process—after all, your creative effort lies on the table, and you don't know what others will say. It's natural to feel vulnerable and anxious, nervous, on display. But remember: The purpose of the writing workshop is to help—help you revise, and help the other writers in the room improve their own work. So relax. Your professor and your classmates aren't criticizing you; they're offering you their ideas.

When the discussion ends, your professor might invite you to comment on what you've heard in the workshop. This gives you a chance to explain your goals and choices in writing the story, poem, or essay. You may also ask questions to clarify your understanding of the class critique. Never criticize your classmates for their comments. And never make excuses for weaknesses in your work ("I ran out of time," "I had three midterms this week," "I don't care what you think, because the scene really did happen this way").

FLIP SIDE: THE ROLE OF THE WORKSHOP READER

As the reader, you will do most of your work *outside* of class. The writer will hand out the piece during one class for a workshop discussion during the next. Between those times, you have to prepare.

Read the work, and mark it. Receiving a piece of writing for a workshop means receiving both a reading and a writing assignment. Read the piece closely, and mark it up. Underline places where the writing shines—vivid description, a unique turn of phrase, a ripe image, a smart line of dialogue. Also underline sections where the writing needs work—a weak character, an illogical plot shift, a flat line, a poorly developed stanza, a spot where the writer tells instead of shows. Write notes in the margins. If you get lost, say so. If you believe the writer is playing games with you, say so. If something doesn't make sense, say so. Flag the errors in spelling, grammar, and punctuation.

Assess the work. After reading and marking, write a one-page letter to the author. Explain your reaction to the piece of writing, and offer *specific evidence* about why you feel this way. Don't write an empty overview—"I liked this poem a lot. There are places where I was sort of confused, but overall, great job." Provide details. Be direct and honest. You have the writer's undivided attention, so make it count. Treat your classmates as you want them to treat you—by giving them thorough, thoughtful feedback.

About the letters: I require my classes to type the comments and give one copy to the writer and one copy to me. Your professor might handle this differently. Ask for directions.

Now that you've prepared in advance, you're ready for the workshop. You'll go in with something to say—to the writer and to the whole class.

Strike a balance. During the workshop, point out strengths and weaknesses of the work. Focus on giving a fair, honest assessment so the writer can revise and make the work stronger, clearer, more vivid—a better piece to read. This does not mean pummeling the work for the entire class time; it also does not mean spending the hour showering compliments on the writing and the writer. Likewise, you have no obligation to balance the discussion precisely—fifteen minutes of "positives" followed by fifteen minutes of "negatives." Just give the piece a thorough critique. Provide constructive criticism.

Keep it courteous. Snide remarks and cheap shots don't belong in any workshop. The author is a classmate whose work deserves respect. Often, people write about deeply personal topics—sexuality, violent pasts, destructive relationships, the death of someone near to them. Writers take brave risks in opening their lives to everyone's view, and in the workshop those feelings of exposure lie near the surface. Regard your classmates and their work with care. Treat them as you want to be treated.

Avoid warm-and-fuzzies. It's possible to overdo the kindness in a workshop. Don't fawn over the writing. Don't "take up for my friend." Don't try to offset every "negative" comment with a "positive" one. Just stay honest and think of something useful to say.

Silence isn't golden. Writers need to hear from *everybody* in the workshop, not just the extroverts. No one has the right to sit back and stay quiet. Speak up. Let others learn from your opinions. This might not be easy at first, but it gets better with time and practice.

Sign it and return it. *At the end of the workshop, give everything* back to the writer so he or she can use it for revision. Sign your name on your typed comments **and** on the marked copy of the writer's work. Make sure the writer knows who's saying what.

The Role of the Workshop Professor

Like your classmates, your professor is a reader. The professor will read and mark your work, then provide a written evaluation. In class, the professor will direct the workshop discussion and try to use your writing to teach everyone in the room something about their own craft.

Your professor might assign a grade to the workshop writing—perhaps a tentative grade that could change depending on your revision. In many cases, though, the professor will not assign any grade until after you do thorough revision. If you have doubts about the grading process, ask your professor to clarify.

The Writer after the Workshop

Your readers will give you a lot of paper at the end of the workshop—their marked copies of your piece, plus their written comments (usually typed on a separate page, and signed). Gather everything and take it home, then read it all. As you read, write down the suggestions that you find most useful.

Your job at this point is not to follow through on each suggestion. That's impossible. Plus, it would create a terrible revision—a collage of fragments.

Rather, your responsibility is to pull out the comments that you find most useful, and then create a plan for revision. Don't simply start rewriting. Make a plan. Think differently about your work. Open yourself to the vast possibilities for the piece. Then get busy writing.

Some writers do not want to comb through the workshop comments so soon after class. They prefer to set the stack of papers aside and let the experience cool off before starting the revision. That's fine—as long as the writer *does* work through the workshop material soon. Failing to do so wastes everyone's time and effort and does nothing to improve the work.

Longer Does Not Equal Stronger

Some writers believe that revision means they should write a longer poem, story, or essay. They assume that more length means better work.

Not necessarily.

Yes, revising a piece of writing often does require putting many more words on the page—to set a scene, for example, or to round out a character or draw a sharper image. But just as often, revising means making a piece shorter—cutting, editing, slicing away the fat, moving sections around, and deleting what does not belong.

I have revised stories that grew from an original twelve pages to a finished sixteen or twenty. Likewise, I once wrote a preface that ran about eight pages—and then listened in horror when a professor said it was overwritten and asked me to cut it drastically. I didn't want to hack away at the piece—after all, this was my work, and I thought the eight pages were pretty good. But I combed through the preface in search of the core of the story. I deleted every nonessential word. When I finished, the preface had shrunk to three pages—less than half the original length. The result: The story moved faster and got to the point quicker. It was a better read.

Revision requires seeing our writing differently and doing what needs to be done to improve it. Often, this means writing more. Sometimes, it means writing less. And always, it means working harder.

FINALLY, A CLOSING NOTE

I didn't set out to sound so preachy in this essay, but I managed to do it anyway. I know you will do what you want with everything I've said here. That's your choice.

I hope you will head into your writing workshops well-prepared and excited, and take from them a load of ideas and motivation for becoming a better writer and reader.

Now, get busy writing. ❖

What to do with Workshop Feedback: A Guide for the Bewildered

Robert Anthony Siegel

S o. You are walking out of class, having just workshopped your story (or poem, or essay, or cross-genre experiment), and you can barely see the hallway you walk through because you are so lit up with the excitement of hearing your work talked about by readers. Suddenly, the piece you wrote seems real in a way you could not have imagined before: not a private entertainment (like computer solitaire) but a public act, an attempt to communicate. You have *written* something, and it means something.

The problem is *what*. Because during the discussion of your piece certain things were said that seemed to indicate points of confusion. A scene or a line was not quite clear; somebody thought your protagonist committed suicide when he was only taking a nap; somebody else called the piece a love story, when it is really about the *impossibility* of love in a virtual age. Besides, many opinions were stated and numerous suggestions made, along the lines of *I really like the girl. Why isn't there more of her? And the ending doesn't work for me. I think you should cut it.* While somebody else said *I love the ending. But you need to get rid of the girl.* And then there was a lot of yelling.

To make matters worse, you now carry in your arms a stack of copies of that same story (or poem, etc.), bearing the written comments of those same classmates, and you can already see, leafing through them as you walk, that the written comments are *different.* The reader who said in class that she liked the ending has written in the margin—with a thick black felt-tip, underscored three times—CUT. And the reader who said you should put in more of the girl has systematically drawn a line through each of her scenes. What made them change their minds? Can you trust their opinions? Should you take their advice?

The short answer is no. But the long answer is much more interesting, so here it is: workshop critiques, though often framed as ideas or suggestions about revision, are in fact neither of those things. They are reactions. They are emotional, personal, situational, and therefore highly changeable. That reader who wanted to see more of the girl, for example, though he cut all her scenes, may be in the process of breaking up with his own real-life girlfriend, or he may be doggedly, stubbornly resisting falling in love with somebody. Who knows? He may not even know. The mind is pulled out of shape by the heart in ways it cannot understand. The point is that a group of intelligent and thoughtful readers will almost certainly produce an array of very different and sometimes contradictory responses to the same piece of writing. A consensus may emerge in the classroom discussion, but that consensus may be based on the interplay of personalities or the onset of sheer exhaustion, rather than on real insight into the future development of your piece.

Does this mean that workshop comments are worthless? On the contrary, once you accept them as highly personal reactions—imperfect things of the moment—they become very valuable indeed. Maybe you had been wondering about the girl yourself. You weren't sure what the problem was, but you knew that something wasn't completely right with her. You had tossed around some ideas—put her in a wheelchair, make her clairvoyant—but nothing seemed to do the trick, and then you chewed the end of your pencil for a while. Dinnertime rolled around, and all the good shows were on, and finally you forgot all about it.

I would suggest that your classmates' conflicting suggestions—to give us more of the girl or lose the girl—are valuable because they confirm your sense that something needs to be done with her; in particular, that her role within the story is still unclear. But when it comes down to the specifics of how to address this problem, I think you will be better off seeking your own solution. That solution may incorporate ideas generated in the workshop, or it may not. The key point is that it is *your* solution and reflects your understanding of what the piece is to become, not somebody else's (no matter how articulate or confident or persuasive that person may be).

I have focused on the example of the girl because I believe it shows the careful, temperate, above all disengaged way in which workshop suggestions must be understood. But I don't want you to become so skeptical about workshop feedback that you can't take advantage of it. Let me therefore switch to another, less ambivalent example. Of course, I mean the nap that was misinterpreted as suicide.

Now, looking through your stack of manuscripts, you are probably asking yourself how anyone could be stupid enough to misread the best nap in the history of literature as an act of suicide. You may even be wondering how fifteen seemingly intelligent readers could make the same bizarre mistake at the same time. Later that night, however, while trying to go to sleep, it may occur to you that this can't simply be coincidence, that somehow the *napness* of the scene isn't quite as clear as you had thought it was. Of course, you will resist this thought. *There's nothing wrong with that nap, it's just very subtle.* But the seed of doubt has been sown, and in the days that follow, your uncertainties about the nap will start to recur, will grow in frequency, will finally coalesce into a great, mind-shaking insight: *Hey, if my readers don't get it, I'm not communicating with them.*

This reminder that the reader-writer relationship is based on the act of communication may well be the single greatest service a workshop can perform. Your readers are not privy to your intentions; they only know what you have written. Their comments on your manuscript reveal just what they have understood, given the words you have put down on the page. For this reason, they can alert you to any slippage between what you meant to say, and what you are actually saying. They can also help point out where the confusion is creeping in. (To get rid of the suicide problem, for example, you may want to begin by cutting the line comparing his necktie to "a life-choking hangman's rope.")

Let me sum up for you. Workshop feedback can be scary. It can overwhelm you with brilliant, foolproof suggestions for making your manuscript better, and there is a danger that you may feel intimidated into taking these suggestions before you have figured out what you yourself want to do with the piece. Workshop feedback can also be confusing, because some of those brilliant, foolproof suggestions will probably be contradictory. Your feelings of intimidation and confusion will lessen, however, when you realize that your classmates' critiques are nothing more than personal *reactions,* and that they are affected by many circumstances you can't know about, including mood at the time of reading or quality of lunch before reading, among other things. Once you understand this point, their comments become really useful, because they allow you to see what you are actually saying on the page, rather than what you assume you are saying.

But perhaps the most important thing that workshop feedback can give you is that feeling of being read. It changes the act of writing from a solitary act, an attempt to speak, to a communal act—an attempt to *communicate.* That change in emotional context will help power your growth as a writer. ❖

Editing and the Creative Writer

Barbara Brannon

T HAT LITTLE VERB *EDIT* IS A SLIPPERY ONE FOR US poets and writers.

Like its cousins *type* and *print* and *copy,* here in the digital millennium it's taken on a multivalent array of meanings —even switch-hitting as different parts of speech—to the point that writers aren't sure anymore what the concept of "editing" entails.

Some writers think it's easiest just to ignore what goes on behind the editorial curtain. Do your best writing, submit your finished manuscript, and the publishing wizards will wave their magic wands and everything comes out perfect and ready-for-prime-time. At the other extreme, the control freaks want to make certain not a single comma gets changed, not a space gets shifted, from the way they wrote it. After all, we're creative writers—not reporters or scholars or secretaries. Our writing is *art,* and who's to question that? Who knows better than we do how our work ought to appear in print?

Oops, there's one of those slippery words again. *Print.* Are we talking about the ink-on-paper pages of a book or journal? The virtual world of the Web? A piece of limited-edition framed art? An original lithograph? Or that action we take when we send the file to the LaserJet?

You get the point.

The business of editing lies out there in that foggy, fuzzy, unfamiliar space beyond the manuscript. To clear the fog a bit, it helps to break the process down into discrete steps—yours, and the editor's.

First, the things you will do *before* submitting the work for an editor's consideration.

1. *Write.* This is the creator's near-exclusive territory. In most cases you'll need to complete your manuscript—story, poem, essay, an entire book—before sending it to prospective publishers. That means *all* of the planning, drafting, outlining, researching, typing. You'll eventually be called upon to supply the book's acknowledgments, preface (as opposed to a foreword, which is generally contributed by someone else), dedication, epigraph, illustration captions, and the like, as well.

(One exception is the nonfiction book on a particular topic—a how-to book or cookbook, for example. You might succeed in persuading an editor to sign a project like this before you've even finished it.)

It might be worth realizing, if you don't already, that at this point—in fact from the very beginning of your first draft—you own the work you've written. Your copyright belongs to you from the moment of creation, and you don't have to register it to make it so. (If this seems like a minor point, consider that until as recently as 1977 an American writer could lose his copyright for failure to observe certain conditions of registration.) The legally recognized right of a writer to exercise exclusive control over her work—to decide when and how it may be published, sold, displayed, or copied—is a great privilege and a valuable intellectual and economic asset in our society.

You need not worry that you're risking your copyright when you submit your work to respectable editors; their modifications won't affect your ownership. Your text and even your title are very likely to change along the way. Editing is by nature collaborative and social, dependent on the give-and-take of multiple viewpoints—so you shouldn't be surprised when you're asked to rewrite any portion of your work or to accept suggested changes.

A healthy resiliency, and the ability to step outside your own work and look at it as other readers might, will help you take best advantage of the editorial process. But that's still a ways off. Let's go back to the writer's tasks.

2. *Revise.* This, too, is the writer's personal responsibility—the often wrenching and intimidating task of revisiting, revisioning, rethinking, and rewriting that yields an improved version of your text. Though the terms *revise* and *edit* are often used interchangeably, revising more accurately refers to something you do to your own work, while editing is what someone else does to it. If you have followed the oft-repeated advice to "kill your inner editor" and free your writing in early drafts, you'll need to resurrect an "inner reviser" now and put everything on the table for reconsideration.

3. *Workshop.* Hey, wait a minute—that's a noun. Although the craft term *workshop* entered literary parlance in the first half of the twentieth century, when universities started adopting it for their fine-arts studios, its role as a verb is a recent phenomenon.

You won't find *to workshop* in the *OED*. But it usefully describes what happens when you submit a working version of your manuscript, or part of it, to a likeminded group of writers for their response and advice. It's the central activity of an apprenticeship in creative writing. And we don't have a better word for it, so the noun just has to do double duty.

Workshopping gives you the advantage of feedback before you send your work out to a thumbs-up-or-thumbs-down editor. Dedicated, unbiased readers can spark entirely new ideas or help you spot weaknesses. Under their scrutiny you and your work grow stronger.

4. *Vet.* No, this one isn't a noun. But it's an important task that can save you a great deal of anguish down the road.

The aim of vetting is to *get it right.* If your writing involves special subject-area information, ask an expert in the area to read and review it to identify errors of fact. Does your novel take place in nineteenth-century Paris? Have a historian look it over. Does your story involve contemporary politics, law, medicine, or military maneuvers? Ask a professional who knows the turf and the lingo to go over it carefully. Are there living relatives of your characters who might raise a fuss if you didn't get the details right? Discuss things with them first to defuse possible objections. If you suspect that something in your work may cross the legal boundaries of libel, obscenity, privacy, or someone else's copyright, you'd be wise to vet it for those reasons—a responsible editor surely will.

5. *Check* your final draft. Print it out and look over the pages: make sure it's the right version of your file, that it reflects all the changes you meant to make, that it's properly headed (with title and page number on every page), and that no pages are missing. Copy it—hard copy and disk file (you've been backing up all along, right?)—and keep the "insurance copies" in a different location. Name and organize your drafts in an orderly fashion; your editor is eventually going to want a word processing file that matches the manuscript printout you submitted.

At this point you're officially handing your baby over to the guardians who will nurture it to maturity. They'll have their responsibilities—and you'll have yours.

So, what will the editor do after receiving your work?

6. *Read.* Publishing houses look at thousands of manuscripts each year or each month, and they employ first-pass readers to winnow down the stack to a few that suit their needs and standards. If yours is among them—and eventually singled out—an acquisitions editor will work with you on your publishing agreement, your deadlines, and suggestions for revision. You'll be

offered a contract, which you should read carefully and consider wisely. Every contract is subject to negotiation: educate yourself and obtain trustworthy advice before you sign. You'll be expected to provide a revised, completed manuscript "acceptable in form and content" to the publisher by a deadline spelled out in the contract.

7. *Review.* Your editor, or editors, will go over your mansucript to ensure that it's free of legal problems or factual errors. Although typically only nonfiction is formally vetted or fact-checked by outside experts, publishers have good reason to verify that any book that will appear over its imprint is free of outright mistakes, libel, invasions of privacy, infringement of copyright, and similiar problems. You may be required to modify some passages, provide source information, or obtain releases or permissions. Obtaining and paying for for permissions and artwork are generally the author's responsibilities.

8. *Edit.* If your acquisitions editor or project editor does any work on your manuscript, it will generally involve suggestions regarding structure or organization, cuts or additions, or other substantive matters. But this sort of attention to developmental or line editing is increasingly rare. Count yourself lucky if you have an editor who's invested in your writing at this level.

The project editor will add front matter and other structural elements of the book. The publisher supplies the ISBN number and Library of Congress cataloging information. In due time, the publisher also works with you on matters relating to the promotion and marketing of your book.

9. *Clean up.* It's generally the editor's job to clean up the computer formatting to prepare for electronic copyediting and page layout.

10. *Copyedit.* Copyediting involves matters of mechanics (capitalization, hyphenation, italic/roman/boldface styling, treatment of numbers, and the like), as well as spelling and grammar. The copyeditor will make these changes on your word processing file

or (less often these days) a hard copy of your manuscript.

Copyediting is the process of applying consistency to a text so that the author's meaning shines through most clearly—like polishing a lens so that no distracting flaws or dust remain to impede the view. Copyeditors strive for consistency on three levels: with the established conventions of language and culture (usually standard American English); with the established conventions of the publishing house (usually based on the *Chicago Manual of Style*); and with the work's own internal purpose, discipline, and vocabulary.

When you've finished reviewing the copyedited manuscript and returned it to the editor, the editor (in most cases) will incorporate your final corrections into the computer file and turn it over to a designer for typesetting and page layout.

The author's responsibilities go hand-in-hand with the editor's right up to the moment the book goes to the printer—and beyond. These are the things you will do along with the editor:

11. *Approve.* At each stage of work on the book, you'll have a chance to review and okay the edits, and to revise further if needed—all on a rigid schedule of deadlines. Missing a deadline for returning a copyedited manuscript or set of proofs may throw the entire publication schedule off.

Most editors are trained professionals with many years of experience. They're right more often than not. But not every editor is adept at dealing with every author's unique material—and editors do make mistakes. If you detect something that doesn't sound right, discuss it with your editor, and if you find something improperly changed, the term to know is "stet"—*let it stand*. It is your manuscript, after all. You should be able to trust that your editor is widely read, detail-oriented, and sensitive to the subtleties of your voice and particular style.

12. *Proofread.* Don't confuse this step with editing: proofreading involves checking typeset page layouts that, except for

mistakes that have been overlooked in copyediting or have crept in along the way, are ready to be printed. The arrival of page proofs is *not* the time for revising—F. Scott Fitzgerald's legendary rewriting of *The Great Gatsby* in printer's galleys notwithstanding. You should familiarize yourself with, and use, standard proofreader's marks for clearest communication. As with earlier corrections, the editor will take responsibility for entering changes in the page layout file.

For a nonfiction book with an index, this is the time to create the index as well. It's often the author's responsibility to produce the index or to pay an indexer to prepare it; your contract should indicate if this is the case.

13. *Enjoy the finished product.* As you look back over the weeks and months it's taken to reach this point, congratulate yourself. You've navigated a complex, collaborative process, and *your* words, *your* sentences have been scrutinized and shaped and dressed up for public display. Your readers will expect no less. ❖

Contributors

Lavonne Adams's chapbook, *In the Shadow of the Mountain* (North Carolina Writers' Network, 2004), won the Randall Jarell/ HarperPrints Chapbook Competition. Her earlier chapbook, *Everyday Still Life* (North Carolina Writers' Network, 1999), was awarded the Persephone Poetry Book Publication Award. She is a lecturer and the BFA coordinator in UNCW's Department of Creative Writing.

Tim Bass, a former newspaper reporter, is a lecturer in the Department of Creative Writing.

Karen E. Bender is the author of the novel *Like Normal People* (Houghton Mifflin 2000). Her fiction has appeared in magazines including *The New Yorker*, *Granta*, *Ploughshares*, and *Zoetrope* and has appeared in *Best American Short Stories*, *Best American Mystery Stories,* and the Pushcart Prize anthologies. She teaches creative writing part-time at UNCW.

Barbara Brannon directs the Publishing Laboratory and teaches courses in book publishing, editing, and design. Her research interests and publications include poetry, travel writing, and the history of the book.

Wendy Brenner, associate professor, is the author of two collections of stories, *Phone Calls from the Dead* (Algonquin, 2001) and *Large Animals in Everyday Life* (Norton, 1997), which won the 1997 Flannery O'Connor Award. Her stories and essays have appeared in *Seventeen*, *Allure*, *Travel & Leisure*, and many other magazines.

STANLEY COLBERT, former distinguished visiting professor, previously served as CEO of HarperCollins Canada and literary agent for writers such as Jack Kerouac and Robertson Davies. At UNCW, he was instrumental in founding the Publishing Laboratory as a student-run micropress.

MARK COX, professor, is the author of three books of poetry, including *Natural Causes* and *Thirty-Seven Years from the Stone.*

CLYDE EDGERTON, professor, has published eight novels and many stories and articles. His most recent novel, *Lunch at the Picadilly*, was published by Algonquin Books of Chapel Hill in 2003, and his first nonfiction book, *Solo: My Adventures in the Air*, was published in 2005 by Algonquin.

PHILIP FURIA, professor and chair of the Department of Creative Writing, is the author of five volumes of biography and other nonfiction, including *Irving Berlin: A Life in Song* and *Skylark: The Life and Times of Johnny Mercer.*

PHILIP GERARD, professor, has published six volumes, including novels, texts, and historical nonfiction. His most recent release is *Secret Soldiers: How a Troupe of American Artists, Designers, and Sonic Wizards Won World War II's Battle of Deception against the Germans* (Dutton/Plume, 2003).

DAVID GESSNER, assistant professor, has published four books: *A Wild, Rank Place; Under the Devil's Thumb; Return of the Osprey; Sick of Nature;* and, most recently, *The Prophet of Dry Hill.*

VIRGINIA HOLMAN is the author of *Rescuing Patty Hearst* (Simon & Schuster, 2003), a memoir of growing up with her mother's untreated schizophrenia. She has received a Pushcart Prize, a North Carolina Arts Council Fellowship, and a Rosalynn Carter Fellowship in Mental Health Journalism. She has taught writing at UNCW and UNC Chapel Hill, and has served as writer-in-residence at Duke University Medical Center.

Rebecca Lee is an associate professor whose short stories and essays have appeared in *Atlantic Monthly* and *Zoetrope*. She has received the Rona Jaffe Award and the National Magazine Award for Fiction. Her novel *The City Is a Rising Tide* was published by Simon & Schuster in 2006.

Sarah Messer, associate professor, has received awards and fellowships from the National Endowment for the Arts, the Fine Arts Work Center in Provincetown, and the North Carlina Arts Council. Her book of poetry, *Bandit Letters* (Kalamazoo, Mich.: New Issues in Poetry and Prose) was published in 2001. Her memoir, *Red House: Being a Mostly Accurate Account of New England's Oldest Continuously Lived-in House*, was published by Viking and was a Barnes & Noble "Discover Great New Writers" pick for fall 2004.

Malena Mörling is assistant professor in poetry. She is the recipient of several awards and fellowships, including the Academy of American Poets Prize, the Rona Jaffe Foundation Writer's Award, and the Lotos Club Foundation Prize. She is the author of *For the Living & the Dead: Tomas Tranströmer, Selected Translations* (Ecco Press, 1995) and *Ocean Avenue* (New Issues Press, 1999). Her collection *Astoria* was published by University of Pittsburgh Press in 2006.

Dana Sachs serves as a part-time faculty member at UNCW. Her magazine and newspaper articles have been widely published, and her memoir, *The House on Dream Street: Memoir of an American Woman in Vietnam*, was published in 2000 by Algonquin Books of Chapel Hill.

Robert Anthony Siegel is an assistant professor of creative writing. Random House published his novel *All the Money in the World* in 1997. His short fiction has appeared in *Story, Post Road,* and elsewhere; his novel *All Will Be Revealed* is forthcoming from MacAdam/Cage in 2007.

MICHAEL WHITE is an associate professor of creative writing. His work has appeared in magazines and anthologies such as the *Paris Review*, the *New Republic*, and the *Best American Poetry* annual. He received the Colorado Prize for poetry for his second book, *Palma Cathedral*, as well as a National Endowment for the Arts fellowship and several fellowships from the North Carolina Arts Council.

TERRY TEMPEST WILLIAMS, a former distinguished visiting professor at UNCW, has published several works of nonfiction, including Refuge. She is the recipient of the National Wildlife Federation's Conservation Award for Special Achievement.

ACKNOWLEDGMENTS

The Publishing Laboratory gratefully acknowledges permission from the following contributors and their publishers to reprint selections in this volume.

Adams, Lavonne. Poems appear in *In the Shadow of the Mountain* (North Carolina Writers' Network, 2004) and *Everyday Still Life* (Persephone Press/North Carolina Writers' Network, 1999). "At the Museum of Childhood, Edinburgh" originally appeared in *The Comstock Review*.

Bass, Tim. "A Refrigerator, Odd and Wonderful" is reprinted by permission of *Small Spiral Notebook*, © 2004 by Tim Bass..

Bender, Karen E. "The Fourth Prussian Dynasty: An Era of Romance and Royalty," from *Like Normal People* (Houghton Mifflin, 2000), first appeared in *The New Yorker* (1999).

Barrett, Mary Ellin. *Irving Berlin: A Daughter's Memoir* (New York: Simon & Schuster, 1994).

Brenner, Wendy. "I Am the Bear," from *Large Animals In Everyday Life* (Athens: University of Georgia Press, 1996, and New York: W. W. Norton, 1997). Story first appeared in *Mississippi Review*, vol. 23, no.1/2 (1994).

Colbert, Stanley. "My Mother, 90210" first appeared in *Creative Screenwriting* (1997).

Cox, Mark. "Things My Grandfather Must Have Said," "Nostalgia," and "On Voice," © Mark Cox. All other poems are from *Thirty-Seven Years from the Stone* (Pittsburgh: University of Pittsburgh Press, 1998).

Edgerton, Clyde. "Lunch at the Picadilly" first appeared in *Carolina Quarterly* (winter 1998). "Advice on Writing Fiction" originally appeared in slightly different form in *A Companion to Southern Literature*, ed. Lucinda MacKethan and Joe Flora (Baton Rouge: Louisiana State University Press, 1999).

Furia, Philip. "Blue Skies," from *Irving Berlin: A Life in Song*. (New York: Schirmer Books, 1998).

Holman, Virginia. "Their First Patient" was originally published in *DoubleTake* (winter 2000), and later in *Reading Critically Writing Well: A Reader and Guide*, ed. Rise B. Axelrod, Charles R. Cooper, and Alison M. Warriner (Bedford/St.Martin's, 7th ed., 2005).

Mörling, Malena. "If There Is Another World" first appeared in *Five Points* 9:2/95 (fall 2005). "A Story" first appeared in *Thirty-something American Thirty-something Poets*, ed. Gerry LaFemina and Daniel Crocker (DuBois: Mammoth Books, 2005).

"Wallpaper" first appeared in *Hunger Mountain* (fall 2005). All three poems appear in *Astoria* (Pittsburgh: Univ. of Pittsburgh Press, 2006).

   Sachs, Dana. Excerpt from *The House on Dream Street: Memoir of an American Woman in Vietnam* (Chapel Hill, N.C.: Algonquin Books, 2000).

   White, Michael. "The Levee" and "Re-Entry" first appeared in *The Paris Review*.

* * *

The editors gratefully acknowledge the assistance, effort, and patience of the following UNCW faculty and students during the production of this book: Mel Boyajian, Barbara Brannon, Lisa Cicarrello, Stanley Colbert, Kate Cumiskey, Philip Gerard, Elizabeth King Humphrey, Linda Jacobus, Judi Kolenda, Patricia Moyer, Lesley Parker, Rebecca Petruck, Andrea Quarracino, Angela Rizzo, Robert Siegel, Lorrie Smith, Neil Smith, Hoang-Anh Tran, Matt Tullis, Audrey Weis, and Heather Wilson. A special thanks goes to Ranjan Adiga, Mallory Tarses, Kate Walsh, Judi Kolenda, and Bryan Sandala, each of whom participated in the copyediting and proofreading of the fourth edition of *Show & Tell* in spring 2004, and to James Dempsey and Kerry Molessa, who oversaw production of the fifth edition in 2006. This edition of *Show & Tell: Writers on Writing* was composed in the Adobe Garamond Pro typeface in Adobe InDesign CS on the Macintosh G4 computer.